T0168357

John Bascom
and the Origins of the Wisconsin Idea

Banners celebrating one hundred years of the Wisconsin Idea adorn the exterior of Bascom Hall at the University of Wisconsin—Madison, August 5, 2011. (Photo by Bryce Ritchter / UW—Madison. © 2016 Board of Regents of the University of Wisconsin System)

John Bascom
and the Origins
of the Wisconsin Idea

J. David Hoeveler

The University of Wisconsin Press

Publication of this volume has been made possible, in part,
through support from the Anonymous Fund
of the College of Letters and Science at the University of Wisconsin–Madison.

The University of Wisconsin Press
1930 Monroe Street, 3rd Floor
Madison, Wisconsin 53711-2059
uwpress.wisc.edu

3 Henrietta Street, Covent Garden
London WC2E 8LU, United Kingdom
eurospanbookstore.com

Copyright © 2016
The Board of Regents of the University of Wisconsin System
All rights reserved. Except in the case of brief quotations embedded in critical articles and reviews,
no part of this publication may be reproduced, stored in a retrieval system, transmitted in any
format or by any means — digital, electronic, mechanical, photocopying, recording, or otherwise —
or conveyed via the Internet or a website without written permission of the University of Wisconsin
Press. Rights inquiries should be directed to rights@uwpress.wisc.edu.

Printed in the United States of America

This book may be available in a digital edition.

Library of Congress Cataloging-in-Publication Data
Names: Hoeveler, J. David, 1943– author.
Title: John Bascom and the origins of the Wisconsin Idea / J. David Hoeveler.
Description: Madison, Wisconsin: The University of Wisconsin Press, [2016] | ©2016
| Includes bibliographical references and index.
Identifiers: LCCN 2015038423 | ISBN 9780299307806 (cloth: alk. paper)
Subjects: LCSH: Bascom, John, 1827-1911. | University of Wisconsin — Presidents — Biography.
| University of Wisconsin — History. | Progressivism (United States politics)
| College presidents — Wisconsin — Biography.
| Community and college — Wisconsin — History. | Social gospel — Wisconsin.
| Wisconsin — Politics and government — 1848-1950.
Classification: LCC LA2317.B2 H64 2016 | DDC 378.0092 — dc23
LC record available at http://lccn.loc.gov/2015038423

ISBN 9780299307844 (pbk.: alk. paper)

For
Nora Diane

The present may be thought to be no time and place for prophets, and yet we seem to see the kingdom of heaven coming along these very lines of union between scientific research and religious insight; man and God, nature and the supernatural, working together for a perfect individual and social life, redeeming the present and by it marching victoriously into the future.

John Bascom, "The New Theology,"
baccalaureate sermon delivered at the University of Wisconsin, 1884

Contents

Illustrations

Acknowledgments

I wish to express my sincere appreciation to the people who have assisted my work on this project. They represent these institutions: the University of Wisconsin–Milwaukee Library; the Genoa (New York) Historical Society; the Cayuga County Historical Society; the Williams College Archives; the University of Wisconsin Archives; the Wisconsin Historical Society; the University of Wisconsin Press. I owe much to the two outside readers who gave careful attention to the manuscript and much valuable advice for improving it. As always, it is a pleasure to acknowledge the love and support of my wife and companion-in-scholarship, Diane Long Hoeveler.

The dedication of this book honors our first grandchild, Nora Diane Hoeveler, born in September 2015.

Milwaukee, Wisconsin

January 2016

John Bascom
and the Origins of the Wisconsin Idea

Introduction

The state of Wisconsin in the Progressive Era gained national attention. That period of American history generally references the years from about 1901 to 1918. At all levels of government new initiatives occurred. Urban reformers attacked city "machines" and imposed civil service requirements for public employment. They provided for public regulations of utilities and took new measures to improve the health and safety of the citizenry. State legislatures wrote new laws for protecting the environment. They intervened in business and labor issues. In quest of a better democracy they wrote constitutional provisions for the initiative, the referendum, and the recall; several states extended the suffrage to women. Three presidents of the Progressive Era—Theodore Roosevelt, William Howard Taft, and Woodrow Wilson—turned their attention to what the American public judged the most crucial issue for national reform: the power of trusts and corporations. Congressional action added that subject to the list of reform priorities.

Wisconsin acted energetically in many of these areas. It took the lead in several of them. Its prominence in progressive reforms brought visitors to the state to observe the pioneering efforts that made Wisconsin appear as a locus of innovative legislation. Political leaders from around the country also wanted to learn from the new departures undertaken by Governors Robert M. La Follette and Francis McGovern. But Wisconsin was winning recognition in another way, too—by the role of its university, located a short walk from the capitol building in Madison. Soon the term the "Wisconsin Idea" was gaining currency. This connection above all intrigued observers. University president Charles Richard Van Hise made himself an ambassador to the Wisconsin public to explain the value to the state that would come from the research of the university's faculty. Here he made a starkly utilitarian appeal. New knowledge coming from the laboratories and field studies of academic scientists had direct applicability

3

to agriculture and industry all over the state, he assured. Studies in plant fertilizers or in plant hybrids, for example, enhance the productivity of Wisconsin farms. Hence derived one of the epithets associated with the Wisconsin Idea: "the boundaries of the University are the boundaries of the State." Hence also the moniker the "service university."

The Wisconsin Idea also has a political reference. It describes the role of university experts who assisted state legislators in making laws in an overall effort better to serve the public. Charles McCarthy ran the Legislative Reference Library, created by the state legislature in 1901. It made available a wealth of information for this purpose, much of it the academic research of university experts, but it also saw a wide use by the general populace. McCarthy also coined the label "Wisconsin Idea" in 1912. His book of that title elaborated in much detail the legislative history of Wisconsin progressivism. The state gained national attention as the "laboratory of democracy" for its prominence in path-breaking progressive reforms.

The Wisconsin Idea had yet another standard: academic freedom and the open pursuit of new knowledge. The board of regents in 1894 issued what became a nationally famous pronunciation defending the "fearless" pursuit of truth as an essential purpose of the university. That ideal had a visible public defender in President Van Hise. All of these directions and ideals underscored the wide recognition gained by the University of Wisconsin. In 1908 President Charles William Eliot of Harvard called it the most important state university in the United States. That same year the influential journalist Lincoln Steffens told Van Hise: "When you stop to look beyond your own state you must find no little personal satisfaction in the thought that you are leading not only your neighbors but the whole round world."

This study goes to the deeper roots of the Wisconsin Idea. It examines the Wisconsin Idea as just that, an intellectual entity. It locates its conceptual beginnings in the life and thought of the man who inspired it and who lived to see its realization in the intellectual careers of his successors at the university and in the state government. John Bascom served as university president from 1874 to 1887. He was a rare kind of individual, a deep thinker—metaphysician, theologian, moral philosopher, enthusiast of science—who brought this cerebral life into the political and social issues of his day. He championed temperance; he wrote and spoke for coeducation and women's suffrage; he took up the cause of workers' rights, including unionization and the strike. No other president of any large American university had such a record.

John Bascom wrote prodigiously. This study does not endeavor to review all aspects of his thinking. It approaches his abundant works selectively, with the intention to learn how Bascom first conceptualized the Wisconsin Idea. But that purpose follows no narrow trajectory. It will take the history back to Bascom's early philosophical life and his encounter with several intellectual currents, most importantly German philosophical idealism. The great "Copernican revolution" wrought by Immanuel Kant in Germany had significant extensions to the United States, especially to the American transcendentalists—Ralph Waldo Emerson, Theodore Parker, Margaret Fuller, and others. Bascom had admiration for all of them. His own path took him to Auburn Theological Seminary because Laurens Perseus Hickok, America's most prominent post-Kantian philosopher, had located there.

Bascom also rooted his thinking in liberal Protestant theology. Christian principles and Christian ethics underscore all his thinking, and they supplied Bascom his reformist program in the categories mentioned. Bascom from his youth had recoiled from the harsh tenets of Calvinism; he could see them in the father he never knew and in the emotional travail of the mother who embraced them. At Andover Theological Seminary, Bascom came under the influence of two major principals of Protestant Liberalism—Moses Stuart and Edwards Amasa Park. From there Bascom entered into the manifold disputations that marked a great era in American religious thought. It flourished in the religious periodicals that Bascom read and to which he contributed. This literature represented the best in American scholarship in these decades before the emergence of the modern American university. Bascom also offered his ideas, especially his reformist politics, in more popular outlets, like the *Independent*, a weekly magazine of news and opinion.

A third intellectual influence entered into Bascom's thinking: evolution. He loved science. He held in awe the natural world around him, and he marveled at the applications of science in the age's wonderful creations, down to the ingenious inventions so visible in the industrial age in which he lived. Bascom joined the expanding group of religious liberals in the late nineteenth century who wanted to integrate science into theology. Evolution provided them their best opportunity. For Bascom, evolution signified the reality of change. All things are in flux. Bascom believed that this truth has special importance for religion. It discredited religious orthodoxy, rigid creedal formulations, and all efforts to make religion a matter of inflexible dogma or scriptural literalism. To that end Bascom also called for the open-ended pursuit of truth, whether in religion or in social thought. He wanted the quest for new truths above all to mark the spirit of the university. His ideals anticipate the famous reference to the "fearless sifting and winnowing" of ideas made by the UW Board of Regents in the 1894 statement.

John Bascom made a creative synthesis of these intellectual systems and from them forged the beginning of the Wisconsin Idea. The story that follows takes this history deeply into the lively contest of ideas in the nineteenth century. Herein lies Bascom's special achievement, in moving from an immersion in these heady subjects out into institutional leadership at a major state university. And this intellectual effort extended beyond the published word. It entered Bascom's classrooms and his informal meetings with students, from which enthusiasts like Robert La Follette and Charles Van Hise gave it significant extensions.

1

Preparations

John Bascom had a classic New England genealogy, with a French twist. Both the Bascoms on his father's side and the Woodbridges on his mother's had long roots in England and ancestral arrivals to Massachusetts Bay Colony in the first decade of its New World founding. They shared with a whole generation of English Puritans memories of struggle against the established Church of England, the despised King Charles I, and his ecclesiastical enforcer Archbishop William Laud. The Bascom ancestry, however, goes back to France and the bloody history of Protestantism in that Catholic country. "Bascombs," "Bascombes," and "Bascons" came, it seems, mostly from the southwest Basque region of France, where the Calvinist Huguenots had gained a large presence and influence in the top levels of the social hierarchy.[1]

These Calvinists, of course, reinforced that strand of the Protestant Reformation that came from John Calvin's magisterial work of theology, *Institutes of the Christian Religion* (1536). It had some defining principles: original sin and human depravity, predestination, arbitrary grace, the vicarious atonement. Calvinist loyalists included Swiss, German, and Dutch Reformed adherents, English and American Puritans, and Bascom's Huguenots. Calvinism yielded several creedal formulations, most important for the English and Americans the Westminster Confession of 1646.

In America the Calvinist identity of the Bascoms persisted, embraced by several generations of ministers in the Congregational churches of New England.

---

1. Rev. M. M. Henkle, *The Life of Henry Bidleman Bascom, D.D., LL.D.* (Louisville: Morton and Griswold, 1854), 12; "Bascom Family" website http://todmar.net /ancestry/bascom.htm; "Bascom Family Genealogy" http://www.renderplus.com /hartgen/htm/bascom.

One of them Bascom referred to as "a minister of the old Puritan type," but he
could have so labeled any in that long ministerial line. It extended down to
Bascom's father, the senior John Bascom. He came from Connecticut, attended
Williams College, and prepared for his ministry at Andover Theological Semi-
nary. His missionary work took him far afield.[2] On an assignment in northern
Pennsylvania he met Laura Woodbridge. Her family had prominence in New
England history. The line included one of the founders of Yale College in 1701
and others with active service in the French and Indian War and the American
Revolution.[3] After their marriage Laura and John relocated to western New
York, first at Lansingville and then Genoa, in the Finger Lakes region. Three
daughters came from this union: Harriet in 1816, Mary in 1818, and Cornelia
in 1822 (William, born in 1820, died a few months old). And then came their
only surviving son, baby John, on May 1, 1827. The family joy, however, was
short lived. For some time Rev. John Bascom had been experiencing declining
health. He died in March 1828.[4] Son John, ten months old when his father
died, had, of course, no recollection of him.

The Genoa that young John Bascom knew he did not remember fondly.
Laura Bascom and the four children lived in a small farmhouse and had twenty
acres that yielded little. They faced chronic deprivation. Nor could the boy find
much compensation in the environs. "That portion of the State," he recalled
later, "though not uninteresting, makes no very strong appeal to the imagination of a child." Already much of the land lay ravaged by human hands, and
unspoiled nature no longer captured the eye. Happily for the boy he could
romp among the ravines and the creeks around Cayuga Lake where a "real
beauty and unexpected romance" relieved the prevailing monotony of the flat
terrain beyond. He also enjoyed the nearby Salmon Creek, a little stream that
flowed through the trees a mile from his home. The Bascom house stood on the
old stage route that connected Ithaca at the bottom of the larger lake and
Auburn at the top of Owasco Lake. The family lived nine years in Genoa after
the father's death and then moved a short distance south to Ludlowville, and
closer to Cayuga Lake.[5]

2. On the senior Bascom's missionary work, see *Connecticut Evangelical Magazine and
Religious Intelligencer*, January 1815, 25–27; *Panoplist and Missionary Magazine*, February
1814, 90.

3. *The Woodbridge Record, Being an Account of the Descendants of Rev. John Woodbridge of
Newbury, Mass.* . . . (New Haven, CT: privately printed, 1883), 5–6.

4. *Cayuga Republican*, March 12, 1828.

5. John Bascom, *Things Learned by Living* (New York: G. P. Putnam's Sons, 1913),

Western New York of the early and mid-nineteenth century has attracted the interest of historians for a number of reasons. The area was booming in population growth. Completion of the Erie Canal two years before Bascom's birth set up a chain of commerce and new and expanding towns to accommodate it, from New York City out to Buffalo, by way of Albany. These shifts also reinforced a demographic trend already underway—the influx of New Englanders, the "Yankees," into New York State. They brought a measure of democratic politics into a conservative state, and they brought an agenda of moral reform whose imperial outreach could grate on the more worldly sensibilities of the native white "Yorkers." The trends reinforced each other, and the western regions of the Empire State saw an outburst of Protestant revivalism, so marked by the campfires of these intense religious meetings that the region earned the label the "burned-over district." Its primal force, Charles Grandison Finney, urged new birth in Christ, gave large roles to female believers, and preached antislavery. Temperance societies flourished in the midst of religious renewal; and all these factors laid the grounds for a volatile mix of religion and politics.[6]

In Ludlowville young John Bascom saw marks of the new political culture of his region. This little town began Bascom's political education. Next to the family lived Benjamin Joy, an energetic and morally charged small farmer and hardware store owner. New York State, and the Yankee regions of the western section especially, reverberated with reform movements. Both counties of the Bascoms' residences contributed. Young Bascom could see Joy's barn from his own backyard and knew him from his large presence at the Presbyterian church in Ludlowville, where Joy led the choir. He embraced orthodoxy, holding as strictly to the Calvinist Westminster Confession as he did unwaveringly to his reform causes. This large man, with "big black eyes and thin, lantern-jawed visage," as a resident later recalled him, preached temperance and abolition of slavery everywhere he went. The "fanatic" Joy provoked violent resistance on both these issues. If, as often happened, an offended listener threw a whiskey

---

1–3. This book, published two years after Bascom's death, constitutes mostly a series of reflections about life and recollections of individuals important in Bascom's life. It is only roughly an autobiography.

6. L. Ray Gunn, "Part IV: Antebellum Society and Politics [1825–1860]," in *The Empire State: A History of New York*, ed. Milton M. Klein (Ithaca, NY: Cornell University Press, 2001), 369; Dixon Ryan Fox, *Yankees and Yorkers* (New York: New York University Press, 1940), 201; Bruce Bliven Jr., *New York: A Bicentennial History* (New York: W. W. Norton, 1981), 113–14.

bottle at him, he rejoiced that there was one less such vessel available to ruin human lives. In the towns around central and western New York "Uncle Ben Joy" stood with Gerrit Smith as legendary abolitionists. Bascom and other boys in the area, so impressed as they were with Joy, joined in his efforts. They often went with him to neighboring villages "to capture an audience for his own more strenuous speech." Never through the rest of his life did John Bascom slacken in his commitment to temperance nor in his opposition to slavery so long as it endured in the United States.[7]

Other influences emerged in Bascom's early years. He grew up in a family of females. The widowed mother tried mightily to sustain the family. All members labored hard to make the small farm productive. Bascom remembered milking cows with his mother and handling other workaday tasks. But the family faced near poverty. Laura Bascom tried to sustain herself through religious faith. Bascom remembered from the family library a collection of books, especially ones by Jonathan Edwards, heavily reflective of his father's Calvinism. Laura, her son recalled, devotedly read such English divines as Thomas Scott, Philip Doddridge, and Thomas Baxter. But this severe religiosity, Bascom believed, made his mother morose, set her in morbid thoughts, and rendered her emotionally distant from him. No true love of mother and son could flourish, he lamented. Here began John Bascom's long recoil from Calvinism, one that would soon have clear intellectual markings.[8]

Bascom grew up in an area where modern feminism had its beginnings. Only forty miles northwest of his home lay Seneca Falls, the site of a meeting in 1848 that produced the famous "Declaration of Sentiments" on behalf of American women's rights. To the east was Oneida County, locus of an important study by historian Mary P. Ryan. Here, she found, a special combination of evangelical Protestantism and middle-class mores created the representative phenomenon other scholars have labeled the "Cult of True Womanhood."

7. Theo L. Cuyler, "A Veteran Worker, and the Lessons of His Life," *Independent*, March 4, 1869, 1; idem, "Early Temperance Reformers," *New York Evangelist*, October 1, 1885, 1; Gunn, "Antebellum," 335; Bascom, *Things Learned*, 41–42; Rev. Theodore L. Cuyler, "Pen-Jottings of Early Temperance Reformers," in *One Hundred Years of Temperance: A Memorial Volume of the Centennial Temperance Conference* (New York: National Temperance Society and Publishing House, 1885), 142.

8. John Bascom, "Books That Have Helped Me," *Forum* 3 (May 1887), 271–72; idem, *Things Learned*, 8–9, 15; idem, "Jonathan Edwards," *Collections of the Berkshire Historical and Scientific Society* (1894), 20. Only in John Bunyan's *Pilgrim's Progress*, which he read over and over, did Bascom find any surcease from a dreary religion. Bascom, *Things Learned*, 6.

This culture norm of white American femininity gave religious and moral symbolism to domesticity. It sustained the dual gender patterns so starkly visible in the nineteenth century, but also gave women their access into the various moral reform programs of the day.[9] John Bascom never imbibed these norms in any personal way, never prescribed to pietistic notions of True Womanhood. The mother he knew and the harsh life he and his sisters experienced kept them at a considerable distance. His feminism came from other sources.

Some of it was close at hand. All three of Bascom's sisters attended the Troy Female Academy in their state. It had an arrangement by which young women of poor circumstances could enroll free and then teach school to repay their tuition. This exceptional institution set itself against the general model of education for young women in America, the "finishing school," and further distanced that traditional gender norm from John Bascom in his early life. Troy had the remarkable leadership of Emma Willard. She had a basic goal— to provide for her students the same superior education that the best colleges of the day gave to men. She attached no radical social changes to that ideal, adhering as she did to "separate spheres" for the sexes and avoiding challenges to the patriarchal family. But at Troy young women could study what young men could study at Yale or Dartmouth, a broad program ranging from the sciences to the traditional mental and moral philosophy courses. Troy graduates, Anne Firor Scott writes, exhibited "a certain kind of seriousness of purpose beyond the domestic and religious spheres, and a degree of personal aspiration which precluded that tendency to 'show and frivolity' the proponents of women's higher education always deplored."[10] Harriet, Mary, and Cornelia Bascom all embodied the Troy personality. Within the culture of domesticity that Bascom could see around the burned-over district of his youth, he had three counterexamples from his own family. But the sisters did something even more important for their younger brother. They pooled their financial resources so he could attend the school of their father, Williams College.

At Williams College, which John Bascom entered in 1845, he would have four years of "almost unalloyed pleasure." Arthur Latham Perry, who first knew Bascom when they were students at Williams and then for many years as academic colleagues, offered this description of Bascom at Williams: "He entered

---

9. Mary P. Ryan, *Cradle of the Middle Class: The Family in Oneida County, New York, 1790–1865* (Cambridge: Cambridge University Press, 1981).

10. Anne Firor Scott, "The Ever Widening Circle: The Diffusion of Feminist Values from the Troy Female Seminary, 1822–1872," *History of Education Quarterly* 19 (1979), 3, 5, 7, 9, 12.

college eighteen years old, six feet tall, as straight as an arrow, with sandy hair and complexion, a pronounced Roman nose springing from between eyes always bright though usually quiet, the whole countenance and bearing, whether on the wicket-field or in the recitation-room, indicating a restful self-possession and an easy mastery over all that belonged to him." Then, Bascom the student: "The first positive and profound impression made upon his classmates in recitation was the entire ease with which he handled his Euclid, then used as a college text-book. Whether it were proposition or problem, it was all child's play to him. . . . He strode over these [mathematical] fields, while his classmates toiled and tugged. . . . He was looked on as a genius, which indeed he was. This facility was not an acquisition, it was a congenital bestowment or inheritance. He himself always thought and spoke of it as one and the same gift with his intuitional insight in philosophy."[11]

The Williams intellectual experience marked a transition toward that philosophy for Bascom. And Williams, too, was in transition. It had earlier come under strong Calvinist influences, especially the energetic outreach of the "New Divinity" movement, whose leaders sought to restore the proper influence of Jonathan Edwards. However, the college now had as its president the legendary Mark Hopkins. His family had long roots in New England, and, like Bascom, Hopkins as a boy found great pleasure in reading Bunyan's *Pilgrim's Progress*. Although he grew up in the western region of Massachusetts, New Divinity territory, Hopkins played an important part in leading Williams away from Calvinism and into a liberal religious position, a "pure Christianity" denoted by its moral content.[12] Here he had a special influence on Bascom. Hopkins had little patience for dogmatics and less for the Calvinist clerisy that perpetuated narrow Christian creeds.[13]

In thus modifying Williams, Hopkins utilized his own classroom teaching and later wrote his own moral philosophy textbook. Both practices had long use in the Protestant colleges of the United States. Thus, as president, Hopkins presented in the moral and mental philosophy courses he taught to the seniors

11. Arthur Latham Perry, *Williamstown and Williams College: A History* (published by the author, 1904), 803–4.

12. David W. Kling, "The New Divinity and Williams College, 1793–1836," *Religion and American Culture* 6 (Summer 1996), 213.

13. See, for example, Mark Hopkins, "Influence of the Gospel in Liberalizing the Mind," *American Biblical Repository* 10 (October 1837), 419–24; D. H. Meyer, *The Instructed Conscience: The Shaping of the American National Ethic* (Philadelphia: University of Pennsylvania Press, 1972), 16.

at Williams a version of Scottish "Common Sense" Realism. It had made its appearance in the colonial colleges, first at the College of Philadelphia (Penn), under Francis Alison, and at the College of New Jersey (Princeton), under John Witherspoon, in the years before the American Revolution. Scottish Realism had served the purposes of defending the philosophical supports of Christianity from the skepticism of David Hume and the radical epistemology of George Berkeley, and even from the late disciples of Jonathan Edwards. Increasingly, among the colleges founded in the decades after the Revolution, the Scottish system established a near academic hegemony. And among American Protestant thinkers generally it had an eclectic adaptation, by Calvinists—liberal and orthodox—Lutherans, Unitarians, Methodists, and others. "No other single philosophical movement," writes E. Brooks Holifield, "has ever exerted as much influence on theology in America as Scottish Realism exerted on the antebellum theologians."[14] John Bascom remembered: "I started with a rigid puritanic nurture, and with a New England training in Scottish philosophy." The "New England" signified Mark Hopkins.[15]

So what advantages might the Scottish philosophy have had for Bascom at this stage? This philosophy came principally from Thomas Reid, professor at Aberdeen and Glasgow Universities, and in more popular and widely used forms from Dugald Stewart of Edinburgh. Francis Hutcheson of Glasgow initiated the Scottish input in moral philosophy. Reid had modified the empiricism of John Locke, who postulated that all knowledge begins in sensory experience. Philosophy had unraveled from there, as Immanuel Kant learned as well, moving into the immaterialism of George Berkeley and David Hume, or so Reid believed. Berkeley and Hume insisted that we can know only perceptions, and, more threateningly, Hume added that such notions as that of a substantial mind escape any secure rooting in epistemology. Reid responded by challenging Hume with his powerful statement of philosophical realism. He affirmed a direct and true report of the external world by the senses—we cannot know perceptions alone; they attach always to particular existents. We do not have simply in

---

14. E. Brooks Holifield, *Theology in America: Christian Thought from the Age of the Puritans to the Civil War* (New Haven, CT: Yale University Press, 2003), 175; Sydney E. Ahlstrom, "The Scottish Philosophy and American Theology," *Church History* 24 (September 1955), 257–72.

15. Bascom, "Books That Have Helped Me," 263. Perry remembered that Hopkins taught a version of the Scottish philosophy. *Williamstown*, 804. For a rich history of the early Scottish philosophical influence in America, see Douglas Sloan, *The Scottish Enlightenment and the American College Ideal* (New York: Teachers College Press, 1971).

our minds mere perceptions that suggest, or at best mirror, external objects, he said; we know the object by a direct mental act.[16] In this and others ways Reid and the Scots—James Beattie, Thomas Brown, Stewart—endeavored to undo the skepticism they attributed to Hume's epistemology.

But the Scottish thinkers fought against materialism, too. Hume had taken philosophy in that direction, many of his interpreters argue. Hume explained our alleged assured convictions by reference to passions and sentiments, the imagination, and other genetic habits, so that scholars like Norman Kemp Smith ground Hume in a naturalistic framework. Hume had also resolved to impose a strict empiricism on his new "science" of the human mind. He ascribed little role for the dictates of "reason" or for any innate ideas or a priori proposi- tions. And he scorned the fanciful flights of the "metaphysicians."[17] Of course, Reid and others had more to fear from the naturalism coming out of France, as did the defenders of the Christian faith in America. Thus, observers have long noted how the Scottish philosophy, in combating these threats, became the intel- lectual props for religion, immensely suitable for the curriculums of America's Protestant colleges. And it served Bascom the collegian well, at least for the time being.

The Scots defended against skepticism and materialism by describing a clear dualism of matter and spirit. Consider the opening paragraph of Thomas Reid's seminal book of 1785, *Essays on the Intellectual Powers of Man*. Human knowledge, Reid writes, has two locations; one relates to body, one to mind, or, to "things material and things intellectual." Herein the dualism: "The whole system of bodies in the universe . . . may be called the Material World; the whole system of minds, from the infinite Creator, to the meanest creature endowed with thought, may be called the Intellectual World."[18] Reid, all his life closely tied to the Church of Scotland, strongly fought materialism. A devotee of Newton, he described the mechanical laws of nature as the means by which God chooses to govern the physical world, that is, by secondary causes. "The *physical laws of nature*," Reid stated, "are the rules according to which the Deity commonly acts in his natural government of the world." But those strictures do not pertain in the intellectual, or spiritual realm, the realm of moral truth and

16. Meyer, *Instructed Conscience*, 38–42.

17. David Fate Norton, *David Hume: Common-Sense Moralist, Sceptical Metaphysician* (Princeton, NJ: Princeton University Press, 1982), 4–7; John Biro, "Hume's New Science of the Mind," in *The Cambridge Companion to Hume*, 2nd ed., ed. David Fate Norton and Jacqueline Taylor (Cambridge: Cambridge University Press, 2009), 40–49.

18. Thomas Reid, *Essays on the Intellectual Powers of Man* (1785; Cambridge, MA: MIT Press, 1969), xxxiii–xxxiv.

the will. Elsewhere Reid wrote: "It is to be observed, that the voluntary actions of man can in no case be called natural phenomena, or be considered as regulated by the physical laws of Nature." Certainly such ideas helped Bascom in his recoil from his Calvinist inheritance.[19]

Finally, the Williams experience had a special redeeming source for Bascom. It came from Mark Hopkins's brother Albert, himself a formidable figure in the college's history. He had graduated from Williams in 1826 and later became its professor of natural philosophy (science) and mathematics, holding this post until his death in 1872. Bascom considered Albert Hopkins "the centre of the religious life of Williams College."[20] He valued him for several reasons. Bascom saw in him a liberal spirit and a religiosity removed from doctrinal preoccupations. This science teacher brought to his subject a spiritual sensitivity, a vision of the world that Bascom considered a vision of the supernatural. Hopkins played a catalytic role in encouraging, however unintentionally, Bascom's break from the faith of the ancestral past. Albert Hopkins helped him gain a lively sense of the world as the dynamic interplay of spiritual and material realities. For Albert Hopkins, "the supernatural is ever lapsing into the natural," a conviction that enabled Hopkins, Bascom recalled, to welcome ideas about pre-Darwinian evolution ("development") as they gained attention during Bascom's undergraduate years at Williams. As a benevolent individual who projected Christian love, Hopkins gained the gratitude of this student.[21]

Bascom finished his Williams years in a restless state. What to do now? His family had expected all along that he would enter the ministry. Now uncertain of commitment to Christian orthodoxy, however, he put off that decision. He taught school for a year and then gave law a try. He studied and practiced in Rochester for eight months. The cerebral side of the legal life attracted him; the actualities of practice did not. So Bascom took on a crash course to teach himself Hebrew and set his sights on theological studies. He would attend the Auburn Theological Seminary, located about twenty miles from his old home

19. Terence Cuneo and René van Woudenberg, introduction to *The Cambridge Companion to Thomas Reid* (Cambridge: Cambridge University Press, 2004), 3, 15 (first quotation), 17 (second quotation).

20. John Bascom, "Professor Albert Hopkins," *Bibliotheca Sacra and Theological Eclectic* 32 (1875), 350; Frederick Rudolph, *Mark Hopkins and the Log: Williams College, 1836–1872* (New Haven, CT: Yale University Press, 1956), 94–95.

21. Bascom, "Professor Albert Hopkins," 351–54, 360–61, 353 (quotation). Perry says that, at Williams, Bascom "fell at once under the personal religious influence of Professor Albert Hopkins, participating in his daily prayer-meetings." *Williamstown*, 804.

in Ludlowville. Ostensibly this decision had the advantage of bringing him close to his family, but another reason was even more compelling.[22]

John Bascom said of the seminary at Auburn that "I was drawn thither by the presence of Dr. Laurens Hickok."[23] The sentence introduces one of the brilliant philosophical minds of nineteenth-century America, not well remembered today but a major figure in his time. As for Auburn Theological Seminary, it represented the work of western Presbyterians to accommodate the rising population of their denomination and to supply ministers for the new churches. But it also signaled the efforts of "New School" Presbyterians to gain more influence in American Presbyterianism in an emerging rivalry with the "Old School." That group had its institutional location in Princeton Theological Seminary, the fortress of Calvinist orthodoxy, where Charles Hodge long reigned. New Schoolers had a usually favoring posture toward religious revivals, an active "political" agenda that included antislavery, and a more moderate, or liberal Calvinist theology. Only fifteen years after Auburn's founding in 1822, the Presbyterian Schism of 1837 split the denomination. Hickok had done much work on behalf of the New School and later, in 1856, became moderator of that branch. He had introduced his magisterial book *Rational Psychology* in 1849, shortly before Bascom's decision to attend Auburn.[24]

Hickok profoundly influenced Bascom's thinking, as will be noted. Late in his life he wrote of Hickok: "Of all the men I have known Laurens P. Hickok was best fitted to command high and uniform respect." The student long appreciated in his teacher his open mind and the habit of inquiry he inspired in his instruction. "Doubt and uncertainty were as much in order as belief," Bascom said of his mentor, "and the mind was trained to take possession with cautious conviction of its own captures." Bascom recalled the experience with Hickok at Auburn as "the most delightful and exhilarating of any that I have ever known. I felt the safety of a strong man guiding my thoughts in new and bold research." Bascom would later have a few disagreements with Hickok, but the two remained lifelong friends, always in close communication.[25] Nevertheless, after one year

22. Bascom, *Things Learned*, 46–47, 51–52.

23. Bascom, *Things Learned*, 53.

24. *History of Cayuga County, New York* . . . (Auburn: n.p., 1908), 174–78; George Marsden, *The Evangelical Mind and the New School Presbyterian Experience: A Case Study of Thought and Theology in Nineteenth-Century America* (New Haven, CT: Yale University Press, 1970), 43–45, 152–54.

25. John Bascom, "Laurens Perseus Hickok," *American Journal of Psychology* 19 (July 1, 1908), 359; idem, *Things Learned*, 120–22.

Young John Bascom, 1854. (Wisconsin Historical Society, WHi-121040)

at Auburn, Bascom made a decision: he would not complete his seminary studies there.

Why did Bascom decide to leave Auburn? Several possibilities present themselves. First, and most likely, he left because Laurens Hickok left. Hickok accepted an invitation to be vice president of his alma mater, Union College. Second, Bascom's vision was failing him and further intense study might cause full deterioration of his eyes. Third, he had received from his own alma mater an offer to return as a tutor at Williams College. This invitation he accepted, though it led to two inglorious and unfulfilling years. Fourth, while at Auburn he married Abbie Burt, a flourishing schoolteacher and the daughter of Rev. Sylvester Burt of Great Barrington, Massachusetts, a Williams graduate. Tragedy struck, however, and Abbie Bascom died just two years thereafter, in 1854. All of these incidents drove Bascom to a decision. He would resume his theological studies, and, however much doubts were growing within him, he would prepare for a career in the ministry.[26]

So he next enrolled in Andover Theological Seminary. That institution had opened in 1808 as the Calvinists' reaction to the Unitarian takeover of Harvard. But, however orthodox in its early years, Andover was opening up to new ideas and beginning the long trajectory that would make this seminary, by the 1880s, the country's foremost *liberal* Protestant seminary. Within New England Calvinism moderating influences had already been at work. Timothy Dwight, Lyman Beecher, and Nathaniel William Taylor took the lead. Taylor at Yale Divinity School effected a theological shift that grew to a far reach. It made important qualifications in the Calvinist orthodoxy, especially in attributing to the human will a capacity to resist sin. Soon gaining the reference the "New Haven theology," this liberal strain provoked the Princetonians and other guardians of orthodoxy.[27]

At Andover, Moses Stuart led the shift toward moderate Calvinism. He had arrived there in 1810 to fill the chair of sacred literature and began a career that lasted until his retirement in 1848. Stuart made careful efforts to accommodate new directions in biblical and historical scholarship coming from Germany in his effort to fortify Christian theology on a modernist basis. He had died in 1852, just two years before Bascom arrived at Andover. Bascom certainly agreed with Stuart on one matter: The religious scholar, Stuart believed, must employ all useful new knowledge, in all fields of learning, to advance

26. Bascom, *Things Learned*, 54–55.

27. Bruce Kuklick, *Churchmen and Philosophers: From Jonathan Edwards to John Dewey* (New Haven, CT: Yale University Press, 1985), 94–111.

the understanding of God's word. The Bible remains the sole means of truth and salvation, but we advance progressively in grasping its full meaning, he insisted.[28]

The theological turn at Andover continued through Edwards Amasa Park. Bascom knew Park as his professor at the seminary and remembered him for his "subtle, analytic mind" and "acute intellect." He attributed to Park a theological system "so liberal and so well sustained" that it merited recognition and appreciation. "His powers were brilliant."[29] Park had become professor of sacred rhetoric at Andover in 1836 and professor of theology in 1847. He had recently taken on Charles Hodge of Princeton in a significant dispute about the authority of scripture. Park and the New Englanders wanted a more selective and discriminating reading of the sacred texts. Park was giving them compelling reasons for such a reading. For theology, as for science, he wrote, "we *must* speculate." We have to conjecture, discriminate, and intuit, ultimately drawing conclusions that rest on reason and common sense. In ways similar to Bascom later, Park pleaded for "the inquiring mind" in all investigations of religious truth. In many ways Park, in the long run, may have had almost as much influence on Bascom as did Hickok.[30]

Bascom did not complete his seminary studies at Andover. An opportunity again intervened. From Williams College he received another invitation from President Hopkins, extended to his brilliant former student, this time to join the college faculty. Hopkins wanted him to teach rhetoric. Bascom had no love for that subject, but the invitation did force a decision on him: He would now select the classroom over the pulpit. So back to Williams he went in 1855. And here the liberalizing intellectual influences that propelled Bascom's thinking continued. At Williams the young professor confronted three new challenges: German philosophical idealism, French and English positivism, and Spencerian and Darwinian evolution. By the end of his career at Williams, and just shortly before he moved to Wisconsin, Bascom had also begun to give his religious and philosophical ideas a social application. He was outlining an agenda of economic and political reform. At Wisconsin he expanded the project.

28. Jerry Wayne Brown, *The Rise of Biblical Criticism in America, 1820–1870* (Middletown, CT: Wesleyan University Press, 1969), 57–58, 96–97, 99, 108.

29. Bascom, *Things Learned*, 123–24.

30. Park's essay challenging Hodge, titled "The Theology of the Intellect and of the Feelings," first appeared in *Bibliotheca Sacra* 7 (July 1850), 533–69. Kuklick, *Churchmen and Philosophers*, 205–6; Daniel Day Williams, *The Andover Liberals: A Study in American Theology* (New York: King's Crown Press, 1941), 19; Holifield, *Theology in America*, 343–44.

One can pick up this story in 1866. In that year Bascom contributed two philosophical essays, one to *Bibliotheca Sacra* and another to the *American Presbyterian and Theological Review*. His subject was intuitions. Bascom was entering into a long, ongoing philosophical discussion. For indeed, Europeans and Americans alike were still wrestling with the contested legacy of Immanuel Kant. Bascom's essays placed him on the side of idealism in philosophy, though in a qualified way. He had first sensed the appeal of it when he was studying at Williams where he read the American transcendentalists, especially Ralph Waldo Emerson and Theodore Parker. Then he fell more fully under idealism's sway through his relationship with Laurens Hickok at Auburn Theological Seminary. Of course, all his encounters took him back to Kant and the Kantian extensions into German idealism.

The term "idealism" in philosophy references the belief that reality is mental; that is, what we know of the world, the "reality" that we describe, comes to us as a construction of our minds, and that thoughts or ideas constitute our "reality." All that we know, then, is consciousness, or the data of consciousness. Mental entities, not physical items, are the only realities. Now this belief appears even among those, like John Locke, whom we call empiricists; Locke tells us that we know the world as formed by the sense data received by the mind and organized in meaningful ways by mental processes. Furthermore, certain qualities of things, like the blue color of a ball, can claim certainty only in subjectivity. The critical issue emerges when we ask, how reliable are these reports of the senses; are they true representations of what exists "out there"?

From Locke, British philosophy took a rapid rush into subjective idealism. The Anglo-Irish philosopher George Berkeley insisted that we know only sense data and not the external objects they allegedly represent. His strong and extreme form of idealism, which had a parallel expression in Jonathan Edwards, maintains that nothing exists without a perceiving intelligence. In theological rendering, we have the condition that only the active mind of the omniscient deity sustains the existence of the universe. In David Hume, however, the reality and agency of mind collapse altogether. As noted, Hume insisted that what we call mind is, in fact, only an assemblage of perceptions, or "impressions." We have an awareness only of perceptions, and thus we cannot posit or sustain any validity for a mental subject that underlies these perceptions. With Hume, too, such fundamental ideas as cause and effect, an a priori maxim long judged necessary for understanding the world, fall to the more uncertain status of mere habits of thought derived from repeated experience. Causality had only subjective status for Hume and only convenience as opposed to necessity as an idea.

The Scottish philosophy represented one response to skepticism. Kant and German idealism represented two others. Kant, like Reid, awoke from his "dogmatic slumber" in reading Hume. His *Critique of Pure Reason* appeared in 1781 and his *Critique of Practical Reason* in 1788. All of the American transcendentalists would know Kant's ideas about intuitional Reason, even if they derived them from indirect sources, like the British Samuel Taylor Coleridge and Thomas Carlyle. Kant began by acknowledging, and conceding to the empiricists, that all knowledge begins in experience. Locke, of course, had so insisted, discrediting notions of a priori truths. But experience does not suffice for knowledge, Kant answered. He explained that the Understanding employs the several "forms of intuition" to create the structure of knowledge, the only structure we have available for us. By means of the forms of intuition, however, the mind, Kant assured, organizes sensations; that process furnishes our knowledge of the experienced world. More precisely, by making space, time, and causality (three of the twelve forms, the "categories") the organizing principles of mind Kant demonstrated the fact of an active human intellect. We structure the world through a priori synthetic judgments; we cannot otherwise constitute our experience. But Kant's critical (or transcendental) idealism did not allow our knowledge to move with any certainty beyond the base on which he rooted it—sense data plus the forms of intuition. For the reality furnished by the forms of intuition did not necessarily correspond, for Kant, to ultimate reality. They can deal only with sense data, the nuts and bolts of phenomena.[31]

Despite the constraints that Kant placed on knowing anything beyond our senses as arranged and presented to us by the forms of intuition, his followers wished not to live under such restrictions. Kant had insisted that we can know all the sensory attributes of an object, but not the object "in itself," the *"Ding an sich."* So he created his own dualism, that of phenomenon and noumenon, leaving open the *possibility* of a realm of existence beyond sense data. Pure Reason, the term Kant used to describe theoretical or speculative thinking, cannot leap beyond objects of experience, our temporal, and spatial, and causal grasp of the external world, to a possible anterior or transcendent reality, he said. But Kant, in *The Critique of Practical Reason*, gave reasonable assurance of this realm's reality, a realm of moral truth, of God, and of freedom (that is, a realm where causality may not apply, a realm of indeterminism) and one exempt from the logical antinomy of First Cause. Kant did even more. Summarizing a key conclusion Kant bequeathed to his successors, Frederick Beiser writes: "Kant maintained a universal naturalism, so that everything that occurs in nature must be subject to universal laws; yet this does not entail materialism

---

31. Henry E. Allison, *Kant's Transcendental Idealism: An Interpretation and Defense*, rev. and enl. ed. (New Haven, CT: Yale University Press, 2004), 99–116.

since he limited nature to the realm of appearances, denying that the laws of nature are applicable to things in themselves. Kant therefore undermined the central contentions of materialism: that *everything that exists* must be in nature."[32]

As he was finishing his student years at Williams, Bascom found himself in a state of intellectual restlessness. He did believe that the Scottish thinkers had rendered useful service. Certainly they undercut the dangerous speculations of Hume and others, and the Scots did their own good work in certifying spiritual reality. But he also believed that the Scots did not effectively break from the empiricism they were overcoming. Bascom found Reid's case for direct perception unconvincing and the dictates of "common sense" dogmatically posited. Reid, Bascom believed, failed to provide the critical access to "the region of noumena" because he had cemented mental perception to empirical objects and held them in static union. Bascom wanted sensory experience to open up to a higher, supersensuous reality. "The Scottish philosophy," Bascom asserted, "makes a determined effort to break away from the meshes of empiricism, but carries much of the net with it."[33]

But the Germans' idealism spoke compellingly to him. Intuition, he had come to believe, could unite the fragments of experience into larger realities; it could embrace the universe. Bascom faulted Mark Hopkins for holding the German thinkers at bay, using his Scottish system to fend off the bolder speculations of Kant, Fichte, Schelling, and Hegel, the powerful German idealists. The Williams student looked for a more interactive dualism, of matter and spirit, than the Scots could provide. He found theirs too stark, too compartmentalized, and leaving reality bifurcated. Now Hickok gave him a new lead and then Bascom went his own way.

Hickok published another book, *Empirical Psychology*, in 1855, and Bascom reviewed it in the widely read *North American Review*. Designed as a college textbook, Hickok's offering sought to give a larger place to Kantian thinking in the nation's classrooms. Bascom wished to assist in that effort, especially in making the ontological case for freedom, in Kantian fashion. He thought Hickok's discussion of the will the best section of the new book, and he gave it a major emphasis in his review. "In no department of knowledge is a true conception more important, or more difficult to be reached," he said.[34] Hickok, like the

32. Frederick Beiser, "The Enlightenment and Idealism," in *The Cambridge Companion to German Idealism*, ed. Karl Ameriks (Cambridge: Cambridge University Press, 2000), 24–25.

33. John Bascom, *An Historical Interpretation of Philosophy* (New York: G. P. Putnam's Sons, 1893), 292–94, 297, 298 (quotation).

34. [John Bascom], "Empirical Psychology, or The Human Mind as Given in

New School Presbyterians in general, defended freedom of the will against rival theories of determinism, especially the orthodox Calvinists', and carefully linked this principle to his idealist system. Reason signifies spiritual reality, he explained, a realm exempt from the constraints of the sensual world of ordinary experience, the location of the Understanding. In short, a free will, acting in a manner uncaused by and exempt from the power of any antecedent influence, can make sense only under the validity of the Reason.[35] And nothing, for Hickok and Bascom, too, more crucially linked the primal traits of human beings, as distinguished from brute existence, to the nature of God, or uncaused being. Nothing more affirms the spiritual nature of human beings.[36]

In the review, Bascom bubbled over in enthusiasm for Hickok's defense. It represented to the Williams teacher not only a plenary doctrine of human freedom but also of indeterminism as ontologically grounded. Bascom saw clearly that Hickok's duality of spirit and nature empowered this doctrine of freedom and that fact explains why for now Bascom would stand with Hickok. All other forms of determinism, Bascom now insisted, can win consent only under the normative causality that governs physical nature, or by the purely logical processes of the Understanding. Determinism corresponds only to the material world, "only in the stream of nature," the realm of sense data, wherein the Understanding operates. Here Hickok's Reason proved invaluable to Bascom. "A free will," he continued, ". . . is something supernatural—above and beyond the flow of nature." Bascom generally followed Hickok's argumentation but gave it a more vigorous expression. His position stands out from Hickok's by the passion of the younger Bascom's writing on this particular subject. His urgent plea cites the dire conclusions that come if we relinquish the case for free will. Bascom wrote:

> The moment that we deny freedom to ourselves on the ground of any impossibility in the conception, that moment we deny it to God, and heaven and earth at once sink into the unmeasured, uncontrolled stream of causation. There is no more any supernatural. In destroying himself,

---

Consciousness," *North American Review* 84 (April 1857), 373. Bascom identifies himself as the author in *Things Learned*, 212.

35. Capital "R" Reason signifies the Kantian "practical reason," or intuitive insight, as distinct from "reason" as a logical faculty. Hickok and Bascom did not always use the capitalization. I will use "Reason" where the writer clearly intends the word to mean intuitive insight.

36. Laurens P. Hickok, *Empirical Psychology, or The Human Mind as Given in Consciousness* (New York: Ivison & Phinney, 1859), 236–75.

man wrecks the whole universe. It remains no longer the offspring and the
theatre of self-guiding action; but a deluge of physical causes, rushing
down through the infinity of the past, sweeps over and swallows up all its
outposts and battlements. Freedom lost and consistency maintained, there
will remain above the flood not a single mountain-top on which the temple
or city of our God might rest.[37]

One can hardly doubt that something personal inspired Bascom here. Surely
Hickok had delivered him, if deliverance were still needed, from the Calvinism
that weighed so heavily on him in his family history and early life.

In his first essay on intuitions Bascom began stating the key issue. "There has
been a steady and increasing tendency in modern philosophy to recognize
ideas in our mental furniture not arising from experience, but necessary to it.
These, whether known as convictions of common sense, as regulative, or as
intuitive ideas, must always play an exceedingly important part in mental and
moral philosophy. Their acceptance or rejection at once defines the radical
tendencies of any system of mental science, and enables us easily to predict its
leading conclusions."[38] Bascom, of course understood that both the Scottish
systems and the German argued for a transcendent or supernatural reality,
accessible to us by the means referenced. Both ways of thinking opposed skepticism and materialism. Bascom thus believed that religious faith had much at
stake in the philosophical discussions of intuitions. Intuitions, or Reason, he
insisted, open up to us the vast reach of the human intellect, our higher spiritual faculties, and with them the invisible realm of nonmaterial existence, the
supernatural. "Because our reasoning faculties cannot transcend themselves,
or those necessary conditions that give them foothold," Bascom wrote, "God
gives us wherewith to reach himself, a higher intuitive organ."[39] Intuitions,
then, become "the chief organs of faith." But faith is not abstract, Bascom
avowed. It does not leap above or beyond experience. "All our thinking,"
Bascom believed, "involves a constant interplay of facts and ideas." Intuitions
guide our thinking so that we see experience whole and reach its unifying

37. [Bascom], "Empirical Psychology," 367–68, 374, 376 (quotation).
38. Bascom, "Intuitive Ideas and Their Relation to Knowledge," *Bibliotheca Sacra* 23
(January 1866), 1.
39. See Bascom, "The Relation of Intuitions to Thought and Theology," *American
Presbyterian and Theological Review* 4 (April 1866), 283.

source in God. "These intuitions above all products of the mind are," as Bascom put it, "certified by the seal of God."[40]

Thus also, Bascom depicted the human intellect as ever active, expansive, finding its way in the world of things and the world of spirit. To be sure, he preserved a clear dualism; these realms are qualitatively differentiated from each other. But in Bascom's presentation, in contrast to Hickok, their relationship is one of interaction and engagement. The intuitions of the mind do not, in Bascom's account, constitute static norms; nor are they passive receptors. They nourish themselves on the widening data of experience. The mind seeks and discerns a larger pattern of relationships, evident in an expanding horizon that our vision reveals to us. This process, he further assured, makes so many interconnections that we see the world as intelligent and rational, and purposeful in its movement. One gain builds on the other, "ever impelling the mind onward." "From beginning to end," Bascom certified, "there is implied, in each new resemblance brought to light, each fact of order disclosed, the presence of a harmonizing and thoughtful power, the nature and extent of whose action the mind takes pleasure in tracing." The human intellect thus seeks, and achieves in partial form, the primal causal ground of all things, their divine foundation.[41] This key process, this "harmonizing," would have extended significance for Bascom when he turned to subjects of social, economic, and political content.

There remains one point to make in concluding this section. We glimpse a rational universe and a God who holds it together, Bascom assured. However, our knowledge of the divine grows progressively, it advances in degree, and it makes its gains amid the flux and flow of life. For, Bascom wrote, "We cannot find out the Almighty to perfection."[42] In a close reading of Bascom's essay one notices, here and there, a vocabulary that distinguishes his writing from others', especially in the religious community. The world, Bascom wrote, seems always "liable to disturbance, and hence to new phenomena." "Equilibrium" never

40. Bascom, "Relation of Intuitions," 275, 287–88.

41. Bascom, "Intuitive Ideas," 31. Bascom's views here have some proximity to the "absolute idealism" of Hegel, which Bascom labeled an "extreme idealism." Hegel sought to overcome the Kantian dualism of nature and spirit by making both extensions of pure thought and its location in the Absolute. But Bascom found Hegel's idealism too prescriptive, too rigid in its logic, too overpowering of "variety and independence," and giving us not a God of personhood but one only of idea and process. Bascom, *Historical Interpretation of Philosophy*, 441–58.

42. Bascom, "Intuitive Ideas," 27, 47.

connotes stability, or stasis, he insisted; "the forces of life press on through an orbit of growth, or, failing of this, perish." A universe that revealed design did not mean one fixed and controlled, Bascom asserted. This universe also embodies chance and change, seeming at times to be "half-accidental, half-caused." The world confronts us, partly shaped, partly unformed, he explained. "There is neither complete implicit causation, nor yet absolute arbitrary liberty." And this because the spiritual and material constantly interact. And therein human life finds its drama, therein the human mind finds its great challenges and secures its gains. And these considerations precisely would now command from Bascom his most critical attention. For he had already come under the spell of evolutionary ideas, and out of them emerged his own form of liberal Christianity.[43]

So finally, one more intellectual engagement, of a different kind, prepared Bascom for his career at Wisconsin. New directions in philosophical thinking, the expanding appeal of science, and the responses from religious thinkers were widening the arena of intellectual conflict. France and England now also provided the new challenges. Auguste Comte, Herbert Spencer, and Charles Darwin, with their various disciples and protagonists, threw down the gauntlet to Bascom and many other American thinkers and compelled them to respond. Intellectual historian Franklin Baumer labeled the movement these thinkers represented as the "New Enlightenment." It registered and advanced the vogue of science that affected Europe in the middle decades of the nineteenth century. The new philosophes, as Baumer describes them, did not go in search of first or final causes or remote and invisible essences. We must confine our attention to observable things, they insisted. On them we build a certain knowledge, and on this basis of certifiable fact we assure human progress.[44] Much of the New Enlightenment Bascom was anxious to absorb; much of it he wanted to discredit. From his pen came scholarly, and indeed polemical, essays and a dense and weighty monograph, too.

The term "positivism" gained its first formulation from the Frenchman Auguste Comte. Beginning in 1842 he produced his six-volume *Cours de philosophie positive* and from 1851 to 1854 his *Système de politique positive*. Comte posited three stages of human history, denoted successively by a theological era with its highest expression in monotheism, a metaphysical era, which yielded notions of natural

43. Bascom, "Intuitive Ideas," 34, 35, 47.

44. Franklin L. Baumer, *Modern European Thought: Continuity and Change in Ideas, 1600–1950* (New York: Macmillan, 1977), 302–14.

law, liberty, equality, and brotherhood, and the positive stage. Each constituted a progression, an intellectual advance. Now in this highest stage, the positive, Comte believed, we need no longer concern ourselves with anything beyond the phenomenal world, with ultimate causes, or occult noumena. On these matters Comte pleaded agnosticism. Appealing to Kant and Hume, he asserted that the human mind has limited capabilities in these matters. And even if these transcendent entities did exist, it mattered not. Sociology would now replace metaphysics and its meaningless and irrelevant quests. Positivism restricted human knowledge to individual phenomena and their interrelationships.[45]

Bascom believed that the dangers of an excessive philosophical idealism had mostly passed; the reigning threat, and the more serious by far, came from positivism and the various doctrines of empiricism, naturalism, and materialism in the New Enlightenment. The Williams professor had the opportunity to place into a large treatise some of the ideas he had levied against these expressions in the journal essays he had written in the 1860s. The recognition he had gained led to his appointment as the Lowell lecturer in 1871. Endowed by the eminent industrialist family of Boston, the Lowell Lectures had earlier featured notables such as Mark Hopkins and Harvard's Francis Bowen, and the year previous to Bascom the young philosopher Charles Sanders Peirce. Later recipients of the honor included William James and Oliver Wendell Holmes Jr. The lectures Bascom presented became his book *Science, Philosophy and Religion* in 1871. In the first chapter he announced that "the chief force of our critical argument will throughout be directed against materialism."[46]

Bascom actually welcomed much in the New Enlightenment. It grounded attention on the facts of the moment and the here and now. He would always want religion to be thus focused, and that concern would underscore his developing liberal Christianity and social gospel. He wanted only to strike at positivism for its excesses, he said, and especially for what it overlooked.[47] Ultimately, positivism, in Bascom's judgment, had far too limited a vision of the world. It dangerously excluded the powers of mind that opened up our knowledge to unseen realities. But, it actually undermined science, too, Bascom believed.[48]

45. Charles D. Cashdollar, *The Transformation of Theology, 1830–1890: Positivism and Protestant Thought in Britain and America* (Princeton, NJ: Princeton University Press, 1989), 7–12.

46. John Bascom, *Science, Philosophy and Religion* [Lowell Lectures] (New York: G. P. Putnam & Sons, 1871), 24.

47. Bascom, *Science, Philosophy and Religion*, 18.

48. Bascom, *Science, Philosophy and Religion*, 23.

Science, Bascom insisted, relied critically on the intuitive powers of the
human mind in doing its work. In science, as alike in philosophy, Bascom
wrote, we are constantly working with supersensual notions, "purely mental
phenomena." The notion of causality, for example, is vital to science and
"wholly the offspring of the mind."[49] Here, of course, Bascom brought Kantian
philosophy into his judgments. Against the empiricist rendering of causality,
from Hume to John Stuart Mill to Spencer, Bascom upheld its status as a form
of intuition. "If the intuitive notion of cause and effect cannot stand," he wrote,
"neither can this ingenious scientific structure which rests upon it." But crucial
for Bascom was the fact that we reach causes through the mind and not through
the senses; causation represents how the mind responds to what arises from the
senses and the manner of its organizing those data.[50]

Bascom invoked science, and the new knowledge it was bringing, as an aid
to religion. Of critical value to the faith were the gains of intellect. "Religion,"
Bascom avowed, "is, and must be, amenable to reason . . . to instructed, liberal
thought." Spiritual insight will not come to us by a frozen and inflexible belief
or by "bigoted adherence to irrational dogma," Bascom wrote. And he welcomed the challenge of skepticism, too. Religious philosophy, he believed, had
made many gains as it took up the challenge levied by David Hume and others
in the previous century, and by the positivists now. Science, too, has also saved
religion from "dogmatic interpretation" and has given breadth to religious
thinking. "Fortunate it is for us," Bascom wrote, "if we can suffer our creeds to
be shattered, and preserve our faith entire." "Every cry of heresy assumes the
weakness of the truth, and implies that we are now about to retire from fair
inquiry and cogent presentation. . . . Religion is rational, and has nothing to
fear from all right reason."[51]

To those with Bascom's view of things, another threat had already made its
appearance. Charles Darwin published his monumental study of evolution, his
book *Origin of Species*, in 1859. It caused an instant sensation. As a reviewer for
the *Methodist Quarterly* observed, Darwin's grand work drew attention everywhere. "Perhaps no scientific work," the journal noted, "has ever been at once
so extensively read, not only by the scientific few, but by the reading masses

---

49. Bascom, *Science, Philosophy and Religion*, 62–63, 37–39.
50. Bascom, *Science, Philosophy and Religion*, 62–63.
51. John Bascom, "Buckle's History of Civilization," *New Englander* 21 (April 1862),
191–92.

generally."[52] In the United States most of the religious journals offered extensive reviews. They brought Darwin's main theory of evolution under close scrutiny and marshaled the scientific evidence that each contributor believed would make or break the case advanced by the British naturalist. Bascom joined the discussion late, just after Darwin published his *Descent of Man* in 1871. He took on Darwin in the pages of the *American Presbyterian Review*.[53]

Darwin had stated his thesis forthrightly. He made the commonplace observation that no offspring exactly replicates the characteristics of its parents and that, in some cases, a marked difference may be evident. He called these key changes mutations and believed that they occurred by chance. Darwin judged all previous theories of evolution inadequate because they could not account for why species change and evolve into new species; and much of the evidentiary side of his book tried to show that species do change. Unlike the many earlier theories of evolution, Darwin's supplied a plausible cause, the motor that drove evolution on its long course. He called it "natural selection." By natural selection Darwin meant that nature "selects," from the abundance of changes that occur, those variations that enable an organism to improve its chances of survival. That organism then passes the new or modified trait on to successive generations, and, over a long course of time, the differentiations yield a new species. Each newborn, as Darwin said, is potentially an "incipient species." As he reviewed the biological record, it convinced him that most forms of life visible to us today had experienced an extensive record of change.

Bascom, at the outset of his essay on Darwin, acknowledged a major scientific theory, of which few previously had offered so comprehensive a view of life. The fact, as he noticed, that so many in the young generation of scientists had endorsed Darwin made his contribution deserving of respect and wide attention. Bascom admired Darwin's candor and expressions of his own occasional doubts about his theory. But he also acknowledged that Darwin had assembled an abundance of very credible evidence to support his proposition; he had demonstrated powerfully the close connections of the many forms of

52. Anon., "Darwin on the Origin of Species," *Methodist Quarterly Review* 13 (October 1861), 605–6.

53. Herbert Spencer, who coined the expression "survival of the fittest," had earlier outlined a grand scheme of evolution. Bascom gave much attention to Spencer but dealt mostly with his views of force and the "Unknown," not with his evolutionary hypothesis. See John Bascom, "Evolution, as Advocated by Herbert Spencer," *Presbyterian Quarterly and Princeton Review* 3 (July 1872), 496–515.

life, the striking analogies between even the most remote members of the animal kingdom. Bascom thus made it clear from the beginning that he had no stake in the separate creation of each species, a fact on which strict biblicists, and even the renowned scientist Louis Agassiz, insisted. "To start independently in each new enterprise," Bascom wrote, "is certainly not the method of the human mind, nor do we see any good reason why it should be of the divine mind." Bascom clearly wanted to bring evolution into the framework of his philosophical idealism. The Reason, he said, delights to perceive a large integrated plan, as opposed to ad hoc and disconnected activity in nature. Evolution thus gives a new and larger view of God's great scheme, Bascom believed. Within this framework, however, Bascom prepared to make some corrections.[54]

On Darwin's idea of natural selection hung the overall credibility of his contribution to science. Many who insisted that they fully accepted the idea of evolution drew short of accepting Darwin's version because he made the struggle for existence, adaptation to the environment, and the consequent creation of one species from others, the driving force in evolution. Natural selection raised the critical matter of causation, shifting the weight to secondary causes, and, with Darwin's recourse to blind chance, discounting final causes, or teleology. Bascom did not quarrel with Darwin's natural selection as such; he wanted only to show that it did not contradict creation, order, or design. Bascom believed that both Darwin and Alfred Russel Wallace, for all their array of facts, had rushed too quickly to conclusions. But all the facts were not yet fully available, and Bascom would put himself in a position of only tentative assessment. He foresaw a long time ahead of constant revision to Darwin's theory "as it now stands," but he conceded that Darwin had already struck "new veins of truth" well worthy of everyone's attention.[55]

Naturally, also, Bascom addressed the critical question in Darwin concerning the gaps—"the wide spaces frequently found between family, genera, species," as Bascom put it. When we put together all the pieces of the evolutionary puzzle, many are missing, he pointed out. For religious critics especially, this fact provided their heaviest artillery against Darwin, and they cited the record especially in differentiating apes from humans. They could not acknowledge a genetic descent. Bascom himself believed that the evidence told against Darwin, at least for now. He observed that Darwin's defenders appealed to the imperfection of the geologic record, its incompleteness. Eventually, new data will complete the linear connections, they contended. Bascom exercised patience.

54. John Bascom, "Darwin's Theory of the Origin of Species," *American Presbyterian Review* 3 (July 1871): 349–52 (quotation), 362.

55. Bascom, "Darwin's Theory," 362.

"The mere absence of the desired connecting forms of life in the [fossil] deposits laid open," he wrote, "furnishes no evidence [against] development, but simply reveals the difficulty of firmly establishing the theory, if it be true." Bascom urged caution on both sides of the debate. And he said that even if the entire geological record that makes the case for evolution should show a full half to be missing, that fact should not prevent us from inferring a record of continuity. He saw the predominance of order, too, and blind chance, he insisted, cannot explain that fact of evolution. Altogether, Bascom's words do show his efforts to find some answers within the framework of natural selection, carefully qualified.[56]

On the matter of human beings, Bascom took a more conventional stance. Religious thinkers, but not they alone, sat uncomfortably with the derivation of homo sapiens from lower forms of life. Biblical considerations figured in the calculus, to be sure, but many critics took exception on other grounds. Bascom made his point this way: "In the appearance of man, we have a startling and extravagant result, if we consider the forms of life that have preceded him. He is not to be derived from the anthropomorphic monkeys of his own time." Nor can evolutionary naturalism explain the higher, spiritual faculties of human beings. Thus, Bascom could read evolution within the framework of his larger philosophical system. An idealism that intermixed the natural and supernatural, material and spiritual, found a vivid correlative in Bascom's understanding of evolution. Here, of course, Bascom read much more into Darwin than the biologist had ascribed to his theory. But, Bascom insisted, Darwin had opened up new vistas of scientific inquiry that will likely further confirm his hypotheses and provide a larger vision of an integrated life. And, in a manner that seems most to have distinguished Bascom from the other religious commentators, he suggested that the new knowledge will all the more demonstrate a governing rational process in evolution. If only Darwin himself could see it![57]

Thus also for Bascom evolution decertified fixity of truth, formulaic impositions on religious belief, static creeds, and dogmatic summaries. Evolution verified chance, growth, and progression. It did not replace God as governor of the universe, but made God an active presence in natural history. Increasingly over his academic career at Williams and at Wisconsin, Bascom took up other subjects—politics, economics, and sociology—and evolution gave him insights on these emerging academic disciplines. His writings in these fields also made Bascom the most radical of the college's faculty at Williams, and later at Wisconsin, an outspoken reformer.

56. Bascom, "Darwin's Theory," 365, 369–70.
57. Bascom, "Darwin's Theory," 378.

2

A Political Professor

Civil War was raging when John Bascom presented a baccalaureate sermon to the graduating Williams class of 1861. Bascom used as his text Matthew 9:17: "Neither do men put new wine into old bottles; else the bottles break, and the wine runneth out." Bascom explained to his audience that the scriptures here referenced wine bottles made of skins. At first they can expand, but then they become hard and crisp. Soon the fermenting liquor breaks them. "But they put new wine into new bottles, and both are preserved," the verse concludes. Bascom found in Jesus's admonition just the metaphor he wanted to express on this occasion. Everywhere he saw the fermentation of new ideas, new moral awareness, new forces waiting activation and effect. But everywhere, too, he saw brittle forms, inflexible institutions, stubborn old habits of thought. The Bible had it right, he knew. These old ways must expand, or they will break.[1]

John Bascom always had an optimistic outlook. His sermon to the young men of Williams expressed his conviction that civilization was advancing with new ideas and gaining in moral insight. "What was once pardonable error," he said, "is now glaring guilt." We no longer celebrate war as a high mark of manliness. We no longer fawn over the falseness of chivalry. The Christian church no longer finds its good in plunder. The world comes slowly but inevitably (quicker in some places than in others) to advance liberty and equality, the new ideals that now motivate and inspire. But the "new wine of liberty" must have "a new bottle," he urged. Bascom's sermon registered all that he had written, in matters of religion and church, about dogma, the nemesis, as he had often described, of a growing and progressing Christianity. Hard and fast

---

1. John Bascom, *Belief and Action* [Baccalaureate Sermon] (Boston: T. R. Marvin & Son, 1861), 1.

thinking and institutional conservatism, he lamented, always hindered progress. But "God has, from time to time," Bascom wrote, "sent the world new truths, and provided it a new religious life." The same situation applied elsewhere, too, as, for example, in law and politics.[2]

That focus brought Bascom to his concluding remarks, where he turned his attention to slavery. On this subject, his optimism mixed with frustration, and anger, too. The world had been fighting this evil for ages, he said, and "this reform is well nigh complete." But where does the evil yet thrive? In our own country, he lamented. In a Christian nation. Christianity has registered one moral gain after another, but here progress falters. "Slavery," said Bascom, "is the last slough of sin which a growing world is even now in the agony of casting off; the stronghold of Satan against which Christ to-day leads his elect." The moral ferment, to return to the metaphor, seeks to burst the old skins, but the old forms remain. The old sin seeks to preserve the world "with the dead husks of an old, unsanctified life." It "refuses the new gospel." Bascom thus saw the American Civil War in its largest terms and gave it the largest meaning he could. It thus held for Bascom the promises of both righteousness and redemption. He regretted the bloodshed of the battlefield, but, as if forgetting what he had said moments before about war, insisted that we must pay this price. Not again will this country undergo such "a baptism of blood in the cause of truth." A new "theocratic liberty is here," Bascom said, and he urged the Williams students to work for its advent. Should they also become martyrs to the cause we may still thank God for the call.[3]

Bascom made these points to a local audience, but the next year he went national. In an essay he titled "National Repentance," he found himself again in no mood to hold back. The United States today, he asserted, stood under severe judgment and must address its "national sin." Any reader would know that Bascom's short essay dealt with the subject of slavery. For decades Protestant pulpits around the country had condemned slavery and warned that God's wrath would not spare a guilty nation. Many in this frame of mind looked at the South exclusively where for many years they had seen a way of life marked by violence, cruelty, and lust. Bascom, too, saw a nation divided by culture and habit. "The South and North," he wrote, "are distinct in their interior life," and slavery marked the external manifestation of that divide. Like many other Northern ministers and politicians, Bascom decried the aggression of Southern leaders in their resolve to secure and expand slavery's hold, and by whatever

2. Bascom, *Belief and Action*, 7.
3. Bascom, *Belief and Action*, 21.

means.[4] Bascom, however, meant to do more than simply single out the South for its moral transgression. He saw sin and he saw it writ national.

No part of the country, Bascom believed, had a clean record on race. The machinery of the whole nation had from the beginning fed off the economics of slavery, he said. And, most damning of all, press and pulpit in all sections had promoted moral and political accommodation of slavery. Bascom specified: "In that wickedness which has striven to apologize for slavery and gave it the sanction of religion, the North has scarcely been surpassed by the South." In action, too, the North has done no better, and Bascom cited an Ohio law that denied its black population access to public schools. Repentance, which these united states needed, knew no sectional boundaries. But, Bascom urged, our repentance "is yet very partial if we do not feel our guilt to be strictly national—the despising of those whom God has not despised. In this hour of secession, let us no longer talk of divided responsibilities."[5]

Bascom offered his piece in February 1862, seven months before President Abraham Lincoln announced his intention to issue a proclamation freeing the slaves. Bascom's thoughts also anticipate those words from Lincoln in his powerful and moving second inaugural address. Bascom, too, saw a nation under divine judgment, suffering for the sins of slavery, and remaining under condemnation until it eradicated the evil. We may have days of fasting and confession, he said, but nothing will suffice but action. "If God has evoked the war out of and because of slavery, it follows by inevitable inference that under his government it can only be removed by that true repentance which removes its cause." Short of that action at the time he penned these words, Bascom, like Lincoln, saw no relief; the war goes on; we suffer still. Only one action will make any difference—"the utter putting away of this national sin."[6]

In practical terms Bascom saw only one means of the national redemption: the Union armies. National politics, indeed the whole apparatus of our democratic machinery, he asserted, has not lifted the moral burden from us. In fact, it has only compounded it. But God has delivered into our hands this "unprovoked war" and this war gives us the opportunity to do right. Bascom wanted the Union forces to conquer and occupy the Southern states and do so

4. John Bascom, "National Repentance," *Independent*, February 27, 1862, 2.

5. Bascom, "National Repentance," 2. Historian Larry E. Tise has observed the surprising number of proslavery books, sermons, and tracts that came from the Middle Atlantic states and New England. Indeed, in the 1830s New England outnumbered the Southern states in these publications. See his book *Proslavery: A History of the Defense of Slavery in America, 1701–1840* (Athens: University of Georgia Press, 1987), 130.

6. Bascom, "National Repentance," 2.

without political reservations. So strongly did he view the war in religious terms that he stated directly that God "has abolished constitutional bonds, and laid his own laws upon us." Bascom envisioned military occupation to compel liberation of the slaves, by which process also the master class in the South would lose its great political dominance. Nothing will come easily, Bascom knew, but "who has ever expected that we shall find our way out of this great sin without grave difficulty." Nothing else, though, will remove America from "the growing judgments of God."[7]

John Bascom thus pronounced on the American Civil War, its nature and purposes, in a manner parallel to that of the most radical of the Radical Republicans. Significantly, too, he placed his views in a religious newspaper, the *Independent*, and thereby joined a major outlet of religious liberalism in the United States. What began in 1862 with this piece would eventually yield an extended commentary by Bascom on the social and political issues of the day, and in this venue heavily. The *Independent* had made its debut in 1848, founded by Henry C. Bowen, son-in-law of abolitionist Lewis Tappan. No one better symbolized the connection of wealthy American capitalism to antislavery than the Tappan brothers, Lewis and Henry, powerful New York City merchants and members, later, of Henry Ward Beecher's Plymouth Church in Brooklyn Heights. The *Independent* came into great influence in the 1850s with its topical opinion pieces on hot-button political subjects. Beecher later became the newspaper's major voice and most visible association, and also its editor. Of course, slavery captured the paper's constant attention. The *Independent* had supported the Free Soil Party in 1848 when antislavery Democrats would not accept the "popular sovereignty" option sanctioned by their party, and like-minded "Conscience" Whigs would not endorse slave-owner and presidential nominee Zachary Taylor. Bascom, too, had favored the Free Soilers. The *Independent* rejected the Compromise of 1850 with its notorious Fugitive Slave Law in place, denouncing its violation of national ideals and Christian moral principles.[8]

So while Bascom was writing on metaphysics and evolution he was also addressing social and political issues. He felt a responsibility to do so. Religion, he believed, for too long has confined itself, limited its reach, protected its purity by cordoning off its truths from the world before it. Bascom detested "clerical propriety." Too much good Christian doctrine, he said, has been lying around "for generations" awaiting the right revolutionary moment that would give it

7. Bascom, "National Repentance," 2.

8. Gary Dorrien, *The Making of American Liberal Theology: Imagining Progressive Religion, 1805–1900* (Louisville: Westminster John Knox Press, 2001), 196–97, 201.

life.[9] To Bascom, religion and politics did not constitute separate, or disconnected pursuits. They blended together and reinforced each other, Bascom
believed. And then in the late 1860s a special opportunity came to Bascom that
helped him illustrate this point. He received an invitation, or otherwise arranged,
to write for the religious journal *Bibliotheca Sacra* a series of essays, all under
the heading "The Natural Theology of Social Science." These lengthy essays
amounted to seven in number and constituted a virtual book on sociology
and, indeed, one of the first on that subject in the United States. Moreover, they
seem to have had an unprecedented arrangement. The religious journal was
making available to a single author a unique opportunity to serialize a hefty
treatise, in effect, in the pages of its quarterly issues. Bascom's engagements
with religious and social questions essentially had begun with his book *Political
Economy* in 1859. His writings clearly had won attention and had moved *BS*'s
editors, Bascom's former teacher Edwards Amasa Park and George E. Day, to
offer this special opportunity for him.

Sociology" at this time in the United States had not yet acquired its standing
as an academic field or as a distinct mode of inquiry. Neither, however, had the
other disciplines in the modern humanities and social sciences. Thus, in collegiate studies, what passed for attention to matters of government and the state,
or family, or property, would have occurred within the larger subject of moral
philosophy, from the colonial era onward a mainstay of the undergraduate
curriculum in American higher education. Bascom's own approach reflects
that tradition, even though he now used the word "sociology" to represent a
subject he believed could claim its own identity, and to that end he employed
the term "social science" as well. But he wished also to ground this subject in
religion. Hence, as detailed in the first essay, the "natural theology" of social
science.[10]
    Bascom set his study in an evolutionary framework. God has built our
world, he wrote, by stages that began with primal forces. An era of higher inorganic life follows. Finally, life attains an "intellectual superstructure which
makes it the abode of a rational spirit." Human life gives the reality to this

9. John Bascom, *Secret Societies in College* [Sermon] (Pittsfield, MA: Berkshire County
Eagle, 1868), 3.
    10. Gladys Bryson, "The Comparable Interests of the Old Moral Philosophy and
the Modern Social Sciences," *Social Forces* 11 (October 1932), 19–27. For the larger history
of the social sciences in the United States, see Dorothy Ross, *The Origins of American Social
Science* (Cambridge: Cambridge University Press, 1991); John Bascom, "The Natural
Theology of Social Science," *Bibliotheca Sacra* 24 (October 1867), 722–44.

stage. Man, a spiritual being with spiritual ends, inhabits the earth and completes the cycle of life that preceded him. This last stage offers a new dispensation; however, it does not secure it. Bascom did not describe an easy path of rationalism and moral amelioration in the advance of human life. He bore too much the Protestant sense of sin and evolution's portrayal of aggression and struggle to place human life and society in a wholly benign trajectory. Human beings, as the link in creation to all that is above and all that is below, incorporate in their nature a hierarchy, he believed. At the first and lowest level, we exist as creatures of interest, our own interest. We enter life laden with appetites, passions, and tastes and seek to secure the means of their satisfaction. Self-love rules us; we cannot escape its grip, and we cannot rise above it. And selfishness sinks us. "The more debased men become, the more is this the sole force that rules them," Bascom wrote in the second essay.[11]

Although we cannot rise above self-love, self-love can raise us. It must, however, employ the proper means. Here we have recourse to a higher region, one that transcends in authority and impulse the total domination of interest. Bascom referred to morals, which furnish independent motives and give place to the laws of conscience in the way we choose to live. Moral forces thus counteract self-love; they direct, limit, and complete those inferior forces that govern self-love. So also do the affections, most importantly the love of God. Never do these forces overcome or supersede self-love. It abides always. Bascom, therefore, could write: "The highest spiritual life blends the forces beneath, and gives them their most complete expression." But we do arrive through this blended hierarchy of our full being to a state of new awareness, one in which self-love finds a higher realization in benevolence. Self-love can discover its own true interest when it sees everything only through the eyes of a wider love.[12]

So grounding his subject, Bascom took up first the subject of economics and opened it right away to the issue of wealth. Nothing more defines the human being, he said, because wealth supplies the means for realizing the highest and lowest in our makeup. We can use wealth to build churches and otherwise advance the kingdom of God, or we can make it an outlet for the brute within us, he wrote. Bascom thus did not espouse antimaterialism. He had written in *Political Economy* that wealth underlies all civilization, is the first step to social worth and national strength. Bascom had even to concede that

11. John Bascom, "The Natural Theology of Social Science, No. II," *Bibliotheca Sacra* 25 (January 1868), 6.
12. Bascom, "Social Science II," 6–10, 9 (quotation).

when we measure "the rank of nations," wealth factors heavily—from the comforts of an elegant life to the advancement of learning. Always the high and low mix in our activities, and even the purest of souls have in their work all the offices of ambition, ego, worldly recognition, or prospect of gain in the marketplace.[13]

In the variety of human beings brought to our attention by history and anthropology Bascom could locate few intrinsic differences. Barbarian man is not by nature really set apart from civilized man. One key factor, however, explains everything. The first type, he said, sees the world through only a narrow vision, a limited range of thought and imagination. At the same time the social realm in which he lives makes few claims and inspires few ambitions in him. No incentives drive this individual to anything but satiation of appetite. Bascom employed words like "torpor of thought," "sluggishness of desire," and "the indolent soul" to describe the static existence of the lower human life. But then at some time, the new prospect of wealth charges new energy, invigorates appetites, passions, tastes, and moral impulses all at once. They now range themselves "on the side of acquisition." Bascom almost celebrated this process. However, he anticipated a major distinction that would govern key points of his sociology. Only those who "have risen very high, or sunk very low"—the self-indulgent rich and the lethargic poor—stand removed from the energizing effects of the new vitality, and he pronounced them usually "the most worthless members of society."[14]

Bascom became almost lyrical when he associated the desire for wealth with one activity in particular: the pursuit of knowledge. Knowledge quickens acquisition. Acquisition in turn makes constant demands for new knowledge and becomes "the great school of the faculties of the mass of men." Here Bascom cited the vast reach of modern commerce and trade and the new global vistas that stimulate the intellect and the imagination. He revealed himself in these passages as an enthusiast for his age and almost Emersonian in his spiritual reading of material things. Here, in this passage, for example, he speaks about the steam press: "an almost mythical product of the brain, yet existing before the eye in solid iron, with perfect execution and marvelous performance; these wonder-working looms, with more fingers and a more precise thought to guide them than belonged to fabled monster of old; these sewing, knitting, and card machines; instinct with the omnipresent life of successive inventors; these reapers

---

13. Bascom, "Social Science II," 12–13; idem, *Political Economy: Designed as a Text-Book for Colleges* (Andover, MA: Warren F. Draper, 1860), 14–15.

14. Bascom, "Social Science II," 15–16.

and threshers, casting about them with the strength and execution of a squad of men; these rollers and crushers, Titans of power." Let us be astonished of poetry and philosophy, Bascom urged, but let us wonder, too, at the dazzling constructions wrought by chemistry and physics, mechanical invention, thermodynamics, and electricity, all these powers that make the world "a workhouse" of sensual and supersensual forces, the locus of empirical and spiritual awareness both.[15]

So Bascom as social reformer never wished that role to set him against the march of material progress. He wanted always to bring more people into its march—farmers and industrial laborers, and women more widely. However, whatever idealism he registered in these efforts he tempered it, he believed, by reality principles. Bascom, for example, insisted that no society could escape the constraints of the market. Inequalities will necessarily exist. But a society marked by glaring disparity of wealth and poverty, and the coarseness of character that sometimes prevails in producing them, could not sustain itself. Our civilization so marked, he avowed, would lapse into "a most savage and remorseless state; one of entire selfishness and heathenism," as we have witnessed in the social life of China and Japan, for example. His later thinking will show how Bascom searched for the opposing forces of correction. His prescriptions would become more coercive over time, and more radical, but here in these early essays the critical outlines of an emerging reformist philosophy do appear.[16]

Bascom made an important step in this direction by upholding the ideal of the social organism. It was emerging in his thinking as he involved himself in studying evolution and would gain in influence the more evolution became ascendant in his whole worldview. The idea of society as organic, as a unity of parts and not as a collection of autonomous pieces, gave Bascom a governing model. And it set his priority of the social interest over the individual interest. In his third essay Bascom writes: "The general good must override individual good, since the last is included in the first." Thus, one individual cannot claim a superior moral position against another, as in the distribution of wealth among members of a community, but the social organism can. Furthermore, "a member cannot set up a claim as against a whole body." In other words, personal liberty cannot become so powerful as to conflict with the needs of "a healthy social state." Restrictions have a clear legitimacy when needed as "the remedy of a public evil," Bascom specified. "Society is so far organic," he wrote, "that it

15. Bascom, "Social Science II," 18–19.
16. John Bascom, "The Natural Theology of Social Science, No. III: Value and Natural Agents," *Bibliotheca Sacra* 25 (April 1868), 287–89.

may . . . do what it can for its own good." Thus no society, cognizant of its collective interest as an organism, will allow "private rights" to rend or destroy that collective interest. "The common weal," Bascom wrote, "must give the form, and individual liberty the substance, of national prosperity; the two inseparably organized into a perfect social constitution."[17]

Bascom gave much credit to those who created wealth. They achieved success by vision and imagination; they took the measure of the larger society's needs and effected public good in the process. But Bascom issued warnings. Material success can readily create bad habits. The power acquired by the prosperous, he wrote, leads them the more to turn against the weaker, "to shift the common burdens back on those who have fallen behind." Avarice, arrogance, and tyranny take a hold and matters become more difficult for the abject classes, or in the world arena, the oppressed races. Now more oppressed people face conditions from which it becomes more difficult to break. Slavery provides the worst example, but Bascom also saw other illustrations among the industrial workers of his day. Too many of them, he said, have little opportunity for education, for acquisition of new skills, and, in short, for the exercise of intelligence that Bascom believed the sina qua non of any improvement. What seems so right in theory about the progress of the race turns out to have severe qualifications. Bascom, who believed very strongly—and in classic Whig fashion—that harmony should prevail between labor and capital, that each should advance in mutual interest, had to concede that this ideal constituted "a speculative truth rather than a practical one." It stood far from reality in the United States of his day, Bascom believed.[18]

Bascom wanted to dismantle the barriers between labor and capital that marked this regression. Labor needed new entrees into the field of capital, Bascom maintained. He pointed to joint-stock companies and copartnerships as possible means, but gave these prospects no elaboration. In a revealing statement, however, he showed the passion behind his reformist ideas. Bascom wrote: "Only as [the] Vandals of the workshop break in on the luxuries of the effete and effeminate, only as these Goths of the field bring sturdy and multitudinous powers wherewith to freshen and re-invigorate the pursuits and customs of society, rescuing to a new growth the seeds of civilization, shall we reach that later state, wherein the inheritance of kings and aristocracies becomes the

17. Bascom, "Social Science III," 303.

18. John Bascom, "The Natural Theology of Social Science, No. IV: Labor and Capital," *Bibliotheca Sacra* 25 (October 1868), 662–64, 673–4, 676.

abundant and sufficient possession of the people."[19] A later chapter will detail Bascom's fight for labor unions while he was president of the University of Wisconsin.

However much, then, Bascom looked with admiration and awe at the dazzling marks of material progress in his time, he always checked his enthusiasm by a countermeasure, the one that alone really mattered, he believed. For within these advances, he wrote, "it is, however, the march of the masses of men, of the rank and file of the great army of humanity, that is to be watched over and longed for." The homes in which they dwell and other comforts they might enjoy, the leisure and art available for their improvements: these incidents measure our progress. As he reinforced these points in the seventh and final essay in the series, Bascom referenced the "crowded, unclean tenements," where masses struggled to survive in the United States. Inattention to these debilitating circumstances, he believed, would check any hope of progress for the social organism. "Without lifting the lowest," he wrote, "those next above them cannot be much elevated in social well-being; and thus on to the highest rank." Christ's poor, he urged, will have a kingdom opened to them when "Christian leaders" exercise the moral laws designed so fittingly to assure the gains of all.[20]

John Bascom completed his essays on social science five years before he finished his academic career at Williams College and moved on to the University of Wisconsin. He offered forceful arguments for the consideration of his readers. Bascom endeavored carefully to integrate his subject with his other writings—on theology, philosophy, and natural science. He wanted to construct "the natural theology of social science." His effort conveyed distinct points of view that differentiated Bascom from other liberal Christians and social progressives of his time. Several themes demonstrate the integration of Bascom's philosophy with his sociology.

What stands out foremost is Bascom's debt to the German direction in American thought. To be sure, philosophical idealism, he believed, had its excesses. But it also signified for him a liberation—from religious dogma, outworn habits of thought in religion and metaphysics—and above all a way to

19. Bascom, "Social Science IV," 684.
20. John Bascom, "The Natural Theology of Social Science, No. VI: Credit and Consumption," *Bibliotheca Sacra* 26 (July 1869), 435; John Bascom, "The Natural Theology of Social Science, No. VII: Man's Intellectual Constitution, and the Growth of Society," *Bibliotheca Sacra* 26 (October 1869), 633.

experience the world. The life of the intuitions is a life of awareness and discovery, Bascom believed. It begins in the realms of material facts, of daily life and its mundane realities. But it always seeks out more. It perceives the spiritual amid the material and in so doing it ascends. It perceives a larger reality, a "supersensual" one. This vision, though, does not lose itself in transcendental remoteness from the world. A mind so removed impedes the individual as much as a mind lost in materialism. Bascom so preoccupied himself with this urgency that it dominated his sociology. He gave recurring attention in the essays to the plight of the poor, the workers. Their social condition reflects their intellectual. Their minds cannot empower them. Their neglect by others has left them trapped in a life uninformed by spirit and deprived of any large vision. These concerns made Bascom attentive to the way the masses lived, and it elicited his sympathy. He even made their situation the critical measure of social progress. Bascom did not have a program to address the crisis. His position remained a hortatory and not a practical one. What the *Bibliotheca Sacra* essays disclose is Bascom's lack, at this time, of a philosophy of government and of the positive state. His Wisconsin years will register a significant shift.[21]

The essays addressed subjects like capital and labor, but Bascom had an opportunity to apply his social philosophy, as outlined in the essays, to another issue: the condition of women. His feminism, so strenuously urged during his Wisconsin presidency, gave him much notoriety. Bascom, however, brought to Wisconsin ideas about women and gender culture in the United States that he had expressed forcefully at Williams. There the issue had emerged in the early 1870s, and now much discussion focused on whether the college should admit women students. The matter became highly contested, and Bascom, despite valiant efforts, suffered a very discouraging defeat.

Coeducation had made modest gains in the United States before the Civil War, in western state universities and in a few private colleges. Recently, some men's colleges in New England had become coeducational. Williams could not ignore the issue, although President Mark Hopkins would have preferred to. The idea had supporters among alumni and possibly among a few trustees, but

21. Writing in the *Independent*, Bascom drew attention to the poor as the primary concern of any genuine Christian man or woman. We must think of this class of people, he wrote, not with "the label of beggary and vice," nor must we discharge our obligation simply by handing over our money to agencies of assistance as our proxies. Only strong feelings of generosity and love meet the Christian test. "Good Will," *Independent* (September 14, 1871), 1; also in *Friends' Intelligencer* 28 (October 7, 1871), 501–2.

a full sampling would have found these preferences to be minority ones. In 1871 the Williams Society of Alumni decided to give coeducation a closer examination. It appointed an investigative committee to report its recommendations. When the majority voted not to endorse the admission of female students, a minority report emerged that gave full support for the proposal. The student newspaper the *Williams Vidette* published the two reports in their entirety in summer 1872. They make for very interesting reading.[22]

The majority report, arguing against coeducation at Williams, had three signatures. Francis H. Dewey was a Williams graduate of 1840, a very prominent attorney in Worcester, and member of the state supreme court. He had become a railroad president as well and served on the college board of trustees. Clement Hugh Hill, a graduate of Williams in 1856, served as clerk of the federal district court for the district of Massachusetts and acquired a reputation for his law practice and legal scholarship. Henry Hopkins, the son of the college president, graduated in 1858, joined the ministry with service as chaplain in the Civil War, and in 1902 became the college president. This majority began its report by conceding that women in America had suffered injustice in the comparative lack of opportunity available to them for education. The country, however, was now awakening to this deficiency, and the signatories recorded with pleasure the efforts other colleges were making for coeducation and also the "munificent endowments" recently offered by wealthy benefactors in promotion of women's colleges. The report also recognized that coeducation had its place—in high schools and academies, where it seemed to work well. However, these trustees said, "we cannot admit that it naturally follows that the same system should be continued after students arrive at years of maturity, and enter upon their university course of study." For one thing, the writers said, proximity of male and female students would require a stronger disciplinary regime than now exists at Williams, one that the students would not tolerate.[23]

Other reasons argued against coeducation at Williams, according to the majority report. The authors observed that the new practice prevailed only in the western part of the country. But "habits, feelings, tastes and prejudices" differed in all the other sections so that while public opinion in the West might support coeducation it would not elsewhere. The East in particular appeared not to be "ripe" for the bold experiment. Beyond the geographical relativism

    22. Frederick Rudolph, *Mark Hopkins and the Log: Williams College, 1836–1872* (New Haven, CT: Yale University Press, 1956), 231.
    23. "The Majority Report," *Williams Vidette* 6 (July 6, 1872), 1–2.

that weighed on the minds of coeducation's critics, they also cited one reason particular to Williams College: money. Williams, the majority remarked, had never aspired to university status; it had opted not to establish medical or law programs. It remained a small, rural college. Admitting women, the report said, would require the school to have a separate female curriculum. This arrangement, they argued, had enabled pioneering Oberlin College to have and keep women students. Williams, however, could not afford the costs of an added curriculum, and without one sufficient female applicants would not materialize. We probably would not get more than a dozen or twenty, the three trustees believed. A bit of circular reason prevailed here, but the majority opinion had no trouble reaching its conclusion: "The arguments, therefore, in favor of admitting women to Williams College, which might apply elsewhere, do not apply to an institution like ours, limited to one department of instruction." So the report urged caution. We should not hastily abandon the original intention of Williams's founders, the majority urged. Coeducation here should await another day.[24]

The dissenting minority report on coeducation bore two signatures: John Bascom and David Dudley Field. Field had become Williams's most prominent alumnus. He had grown up in Stockbridge, a youthful companion and later classmate of Mark Hopkins. Suspended for his part in a campus riot in 1824, he never rejoined the student body. He went on nonetheless to a successful career in the law and played an important role in New York State legal reform. He used his acquired wealth to good ends for Williams, especially in executing a program of new buildings on the campus in the 1850s and afterward. In 1862 this wealthiest of Williams's donors also steered the college toward the Union's efforts in the Civil War by military training of its young men.[25] Field joined Bascom in the minority report, but the document reflects on every page the social philosophy and the literary style of the professor. Very likely Bascom wrote all of it himself,[26] though very happy he was to have this important trustee on board with him. Bascom alone of the Williams faculty seems to have made an unqualified commitment to coeducation at the college. He submitted

---

24. "Majority Report," 2–3. That day arrived in 1970.

25. Rudolph, *Mark Hopkins*, 231.

26. In one part of the report the narrative falls into first-person statements, to wit, when it uses the testimony of college presidents and professors outside of Williams College—from Cornell, Michigan, Oberlin, Antioch, and Ripon. "I have received" and letters "to me" exemplify the first-person form. Bascom certainly initiated the correspondence.

a remarkable statement in the process. The report has thrice the length of the majority's—eight long, double-columned pages. Bascom used this opportunity to focus not solely on the provincial matters relevant to the college, but also to take an expanded look at the gender culture of nineteenth-century America. Expressed with vigor, often with passion and anger, it is a compelling document.

Had anyone been following what Bascom was writing about the situation of women in the United States, the minority report he authored would have come as no surprise. It simply gave its author an opportunity to reinforce by local references points he had made about sexual equality just two years previously in a substantial piece he had written for *Putnam's Magazine*. This one also, in its breadth of vision, described a very unhappy situation. With the title "The Foci of the Social Ellipse," Bascom employed a clever analogy. This geometrical figure, this ellipse, he said, gives us a model spatial relation, one with two points, two conjoint centers. A diameter equidistant from them divides the curve into two equal and complementary parts, and the sum of the differences from the two points to any point on the perimeter is constant. Let us think of the points, Bascom said, as male and female, and let us think of how they might stand to each other in "a true social ellipse." We would have equality and we would have complementary and reciprocal relations. It's just a way we might think of our ideal society, he wrote. "We affirm that men and women occupy equal, balanced social positions." But the model should also help us understand that our society today wholly fails to reflect this just proportionality. It fails in a hundred ways.[27]

Bascom's essay addressed matters both obvious and subtle. In the first category he observed that woman has no equality in the law. She makes no laws and enforces no laws. She has no equal possession of property or of inheritance or of entitlement to dispose of her property if married. The law assures women no equal access to occupations and professional careers.[28] Bascom considered these facts as symptoms only. He wanted to explore why women remained locked in social subjugation to men, why progress, so manifest in much of recent history, had not advanced for females. Men's attitudes, he believed, lay at the heart of the situation. Men have always held women in contempt, he attested. What began in physical domination took on sundry other forms, he explained. Consider language and the many words of insult applied to females. "Shrew,"

27. John Bascom, "The Foci of the Social Ellipse," *Putnam's Magazine* 14 (December 1869), 713.
28. Bascom, "Foci," 718–19.

"vixen," "slut" flow freely in men's talk, but where are the male counterparts of these words? "There is scarcely in our language an epithet of disparagement that belongs exclusively to man." Bascom saw more than contempt at work here; he also saw fear.[29]

The essay gave attention to other matters, for example, women's dress. Bascom decried the braces, buckles, and bustles that dominated women's fashion in the post–Civil War era. Bad enough, he said, that female dress was unhealthy, uncomfortable, and inconvenient, but worse it meant for a woman "a life rejected from service." The restricting vestments locked the female out of useful work and trapped her in "contemptible" wages for the little work available to her. It all conspired, thus, to enhance women's already too great state of dependency on men, Bascom lamented. This tyranny of fashion— "ridiculous," "irrational"—served also to confirm women in behavior that fortified inequality, Bascom argued. They suffered from vanities, by the infinite forms of stylistic effects that constituted social standards of beauty. Further-more, in the prevailing model of the "voluptuous woman" Bascom saw a cor-ruption of "beauty," one detached from moral purity and associated with lust.[30]

Bascom also located other incidents of female deprivation and male con-trol. One came in the form of gallantry and the related social habits that men used to incur the favor of women. He saw this behavior as a residual of medie-val chivalry, a mark of a barbarous era, and an instance of a society that had failed down to the present to liberate itself from these insidious habits. This gallantry, Bascom did not doubt, perpetuated women in dependency. He con-sidered it a disingenuous celebration of women's virtues, virtues that serve only to keep her "in close vassalage." This noxious custom turns women into orna-ments, but they adorn only the "links of servitude." Gallantry, Bascom wrote, "is one of the more mischievous ways in which man asserts his position, then stoops gracefully from it to hawk up his prey." The social culture of gender re-lationships, its codes of manners and courtly ritual, Bascom denounced; they conspire to keep alive a vicious dualism: woman weak, man strong. Bascom deplored the socialization of females, their training in an excessive femininity, "a giggling girlishness, or a simpering sentimentality." These traits projected signals of weakness and dependency that men readily exploited. And in Bascom's

29. Bascom, "Foci," 716.

30. Bascom, "Foci," 720, 721, 723. The term "voluptuous woman" comes from Lois W. Banner's use of it as the descriptive norm of the feminine ideal in the early Gilded Age. See her *American Beauty* (New York: Alfred A. Knopf, 1983).

view, they sustained a family structure marked by the "coarse authority" and patriarchal arrogance that typically rule it.[31]

Bascom foresaw no hope for women's improvement save through an intellectual reconstruction. First, he believed, we must rid ourselves of the arcane and debilitating notion that there is a "female nature." Bascom did not deny different intellectual characteristics in men and women, but he did believe that this idea had very bad effects. Specifically, "female nature," a male construction in itself, he claimed, had allowed men to keep women in servitude and dependency. "Nature is against you," men say, and around the notion of female weakness they have constructed institutions and laws that reify that fiction. Bascom denounced these "alleged provisions of nature." But ideas control reality and thus these normative notions of female identity have perpetuated the numerous social ills to which Bascom wanted his essay to draw attention. He stated: "We have had man's idea of woman's place and power a long time, organized into fixed institutions; suppose we have for a time woman's notion of her own capabilities."[32]

Bascom looked for a solution to these problems and returned to the subject of women's education throughout the essay. On it he placed his greatest hopes for women's improvement in the United States, and he carried his case for reform directly into the debate at Williams College. Bascom wanted to establish at the outset the fact of women's intellectual powers. Whether in literature, with the examples of the Bröntes and Harriet Beecher Stowe, or in philosophy, with Harriet Martineau and Margaret Fuller, the record speaks for itself, he affirmed. Prejudices against the education of women, and especially against their obtaining the highest education available to men, he said, made no sense. "It is strange," he wrote, "that any wise man should wish to set limits to the powers of any portion of the race." To diminish this education for females would hold from society all the good that education offers it. Here again male attitudes, "the jealousy of a blind selfishness," obstructed the wheels of progress. Bascom related the subject of women's education to his larger sociology, as indeed the essay came as a kind of addendum to his long series on the social

---

31. Bascom, "Foci," 717, 719, 720. On the other hand, Bascom showed sympathy toward husbands and fathers. They work themselves to the bone to answer the demands of wife and daughters for more and more of the earmarks of conspicuous consumption. The harried man then cannot easily summon the kindly sentiments that should soften the home life (720).

32. Bascom, "Foci," 722–23.

sciences. To deny women's intellect, he insisted, is to work against the way society naturally improves. "Everywhere, and at all times," he reiterated, "[society] is searching up and down through its various members for power. . . . [Natural] society does not fear power, it fears dependence."[33] With this larger perspective in mind, Bascom easily showed how the American system of education had it all wrong.

Bascom illustrated his complaint mostly by reference to what passed for women's advanced education—the female academies and "finishing schools." They constitute a training in domesticity and preparation for the condition of women as ornament, he stated. If women function as commodities, as Bascom believed they did, female education only fortified that situation. It threw a woman into the marketplace of marriage, enhancing her purchase price, and it equipped her for "the frivolous part which fashionable society assigns her." Bascom called for an education designed to improve women's intellects; it would for that reason also constitute an education in power and in independence. "Women must be at perfect liberty to acquire, and at perfect liberty to use power," Bascom implored. Furthermore, that education would differ not at all from what men received at Harvard or Yale, where, Bascom believed, women should also sit in the classrooms. As it is, he said, they are excluded "from anything approaching a liberal education." Women, in Bascom's program, must break from that excessive femininity that holds them back. "Sober, sedate strength is wanting, and wanting because broad, deep knowledge is wanting." An acculturation that thrives in sentimentality and results in weightlessness needs the counterforce of intellect. Bascom wrote: "As woman, above all, is deeply freighted with feeling, so, above all, does she require the ballast of weighty purpose and profound thought." Bascom even avowed that such an education would equip women more effectively to confront those who are too often her adversaries, that is, the men in their lives.[34]

Equality in education thus signified to Bascom the most critical step toward equality of the sexes in America. Without that change we will not have the true social ellipse, the foci will not locate themselves where they form the balance and harmony of that geometrical shape. Balance and harmony, Bascom maintained, would help bring about an improved society—in the workplace, and especially in the family and home. They would help the institution of marriage. For women, marriage should not mean, as it does now, a condition of

33. Bascom, "Foci," 722.
34. Bascom, "Foci," 720–21, 723–24.

"surrender," but one of growth and true union. Without the change, Bascom warned, we shall continue in the ways of "unchristian and barbarous society." And ultimately Bascom did judge the gender relations of his time from a religious perspective. His essay thus also reflected his "natural theology" of social science that prescribed the path of human advance. With special urgency he placed the subject of women's education in stark religious terms: "He who shuts to me the gates of opportunity, stands between me and God, me and life, me and the fulfillment of that heavenly destiny which is upon me."[35]

In their minority report, Bascom and Field immediately placed the subject of coeducation into a large context. Two concerns clearly reflected Bascom's own long-standing priorities, prevalent in his philosophical writings and in the recently completed essays on social science. First, he embraced the cause of intellect, purely and simply. It should have no restrictions of any kind. It knew no gender differentiations. "God forbid," said the report, "also that we, as an assembly of educated men, discussing the interests of education, should put any unnecessary restriction on any human being in gaining knowledge." Second, the matter concerned progress, and the report also reflected what Bascom had come to understand about the human record over a long history. We have advanced slowly up from "barbarism," he stated, but relics of "a dark and savage past" remain. He hoped that "this exclusion of women from our highest seats of learning is among the remnants" of that past. The two dissenters called for equal enjoyment for both sexes of every opportunity to acquire knowledge.[36]

The needed corrections, Bascom and Field believed, would come in part from a new kind of education for females, an education in "self-reliance." "Strength is the quality we miss in women," they stressed. If along the way of a new education they may "shed some languid graces" and "molt a few of the feathers of fashion," so be it. Close reading of the report also disclosed some language that further connected it to Bascom's social science essays. The best education that women might receive, the report asserted, would advance women in society through "more depth and breadth of knowledge, by larger and more urgent relations, and profounder sympathies." Bascom, of course, appealed anew to that expanse of insight and connective thought that marked the intellectual progress of all humans. This empowerment must include women in the quest as well as men, the more so as the modern world challenges

---

35. Bascom, "Foci," 721, 723–24. See also his "Reaction of the Ideal," *Independent*, October 3, 1872, 2.

36. "The Minority Report," *Williams Vidette* 6 (July 6, 1872), 4.

us with "the urgent and delicate social problems that are now thrown upon us for resolution."[37]

Also, separate education of men and women, the minority writers argued, has justification only on the grounds that men and women have different minds and different intellectual capacities. Those notions they rejected wholly. The separate women's curriculums, they insisted, mostly register that "invidious" notion; they "proceed almost always on the idea that the same grade of intellectual discipline is not called for in the training of young women as of young men." Some therefore argue, they noted, that admitting women into the men's colleges would lower the standard of scholarship in those institutions. Or they insist that colleges cannot accommodate females because their minds work differently, or are simply unequipped for the intellectual rigors of a collegiate education. Those assumptions, said Bascom and Field, have no persuasion. "That which strengthens one mind strengthens another mind," they asserted. There followed another of their forceful statements in the report: "It remains no longer a fact that one *curriculum* belongs to the one sex and another to the other." What an "outrage" it is then, the report added, to say to a young woman that you are a woman and for that reason alone we will not admit you to this college. "Language," the writers added, "may be more contemptuous in form, but never more contemptuous in substance than this."[38]

Bascom and Field here were attacking and ridiculing what passed as conventional wisdom in most of the United States at this time. The views prevailing in America that they wanted to counter flourished just as much at the college itself. Additional discussion in the *Williams Review*, for example, dismissed the notion that similar education for men and women served any public need. We ought not let "Amazonian femininity" turn the world upside down, said one contributor. Here and elsewhere opinion reflected the normative standards of the Cult of True Womanhood in the United States and other modern, industrialized nations. Woman, this voice in the *Review* said, "was not made to dabble in politics . . . not designed to shine in the pulpit, at the bar, or in the forum, but to create and transfigure *home*, to manage the kitchen, to instruct and tranquilize

---

37. "Minority Report," 5. Some student opinion strongly favored admission of women to the college, somewhat along the lines of the minority report. An editorial entry warned against stereotyping of sex roles, and asked, for mothers, what could have greater importance than intellectual and moral cultivation? If one inquired why teach a girl algebra, one might ask the same question of boys. "Shall Girls Have Colleges?," *Williams Review* 2 (November 6, 1871), 34.

38. "Minority Report," 6.

the nursery, and to preside over the drawing-room with greater dignity and queenly grace."[39]

The minority reporters themselves, however, did not wholly avoid gender normalization. Bascom, who again appears to be the voice here, tried, though, to use the dual standards to good effect. He conceded to woman's nature a superior degree of intuitive power and asserted that young men suffer from too laborious a training in reason. Both sexes, then, stand in need of the other's strengths. Precisely that "interplay of diverse powers," which Bascom recommended as a major support for coeducation, for the growth of individuals and of society derives from interaction and mutual influence. "Young men want more sentiment, young women more sense." Bascom asserted that God intended this healthy reinforcement as the natural way of things. We raise boys and girls together and educate them together through the high schools, he observed; then at the time of their critical intellectual and spiritual maturation, we separate them. "What sufficient reason," asked the minority report, "can be given for cutting out four years of life, and distinguishing it from every other portion of it in its method of discipline?"[40] So Bascom drew on his philosophical thinking and his sociology to make the case for female education in America. But he also had the example of three sisters who had broken the prevailing gender roles at Emma Willard's academy in Troy, New York.

The news came to the Williams College community late in 1873 that John Bascom had accepted a call to become president of the University of Wisconsin. He was heading "west." The student editors of the *Williams Review*, well aware of the recent controversies that had divided the campus and the alumni, pronounced Bascom's resignation as "a loss that the college can ill afford to sustain." The editors considered Bascom the college's main resister against the false friends of the institution whose actions and words checked its progress and growth. The paper the previous year, in a biting satirical piece, had railed against "antiquated conservatism" and all its proclamations of loyalty to the "Old Williams."[41] The student writers and all at Williams knew, too, that

39. Theodore W. Friend, "The Williams Man and His Women," *American Quarterly* 6 (Spring 1954), 47. See "Shall Williams Change Her Policy?," *Williams Review* 2 (February 26, 1872), 202. See also "Shall Williams Change Her Policy?," *Williams Review* 2 (November 27, 1871), 49–50.

40. "Minority Report," 8–9.

41. *Williams Review* 4 (December 6, 1873), 39; *Williams Review* 4 (February 26, 1872), 103–4.

Bascom had fanned the flames of controversy that year in an event coincident
with the debate on coeducation. That incident will bring to an end Bascom's
tenure at Williams, but before considering it, a look at another side of his legacy
at Williams.

A young student named Washington Gladden arrived to Williams College
in fall 1856. A raw farm youth, he had been living in Owego, New York. Gladden
remembered from his early rural years a lively religious environment, marked
by revivals and his family's faithful attendance at a Presbyterian church. But
he remembered also some unsettling aspects of this experience—horrible de-
pictions of hell and the constant reminder to the youth that he must have signs
of divine assurance or know that his soul was lost forever. It troubled young
Gladden to think himself an outcast from God. Later in his own church ministry he encountered many others with like anxieties at an impressionable age.
Gladden later became a major voice of liberal Christian theology in the post–
Civil War decades and of the Social Gospel, which he conjoined in his own
stellar career. Along the way he met John Bascom.[42]

His first encounter, as Gladden later related it, began awkwardly. The
student met with Bascom to discuss a paper he had written. The professor criticized it rather severely, too severely, the student thought, "seriously disfigured
it," with his blue pencil, Gladden said. Reconsideration, however, led Gladden
to change his mind and "confess that the points were well taken." Ensuing
years gave him an even higher estimate of his former professor. Gladden would
remember with fondness from his Williams years the president Mark Hopkins,
his brother Albert, and Arthur Perry as classroom stars at the college. "Of all
the instructors, however," Gladden wrote, "the one to whom I am most indebted
was John Bascom." He found in Bascom a "brave and veracious soul," and he
grew in appreciation for him as they continued in correspondence for years
afterward. The student gained reinforcement from Bascom in the liberalizing
religious views he had brought from home. Gladden offered this assessment of
Bascom's significance: "The score of volumes of which Dr. Bascom is the author
have had but a limited circulation; but there are few books of the last half-
century, dealing with the applications of philosophy to life, which are better
worth knowing." Gladden's biographer writes that "Bascom was Gladden's
mentor as long as he lived."[43]

42. Washington Gladden, *Recollections* (New York: Houghton Mifflin Company,
1909), 26, 32–33, 35–36, 38, 46–47, 63; Jacob Henry Dorn, *Washington Gladden: Prophet of
the Social Gospel* (Columbus: Ohio State University Press, 1968), vii–viii, 10–11.

43. Gladden, *Recollections*, 74; Dorn, *Gladden*, 18–19.

Another intellectual leader who came out of Williams, later in the 1860s, was G. Stanley Hall. Hall pioneered in the field of psychology in the United States. The first student to win a doctorate degree in that subject, he helped establish psychology as an academic discipline and initiated its major professional journal. He made significant studies in child psychology, but he also worked actively for educational reform. When Clark University in Massachusetts opened its doors in 1887 Hall became its first president. Hall grew up in Ashfield, Massachusetts, and entered Williams College in 1863. He remembered President Hopkins and Professor Perry as engaging teachers and among the few active scholars at the school. But Hall valued Bascom especially, and for specific reasons. "As I look back on my four years here, it is to Bascom that I owe most. He alone suggested to me reading, criticized personally and in detail my literary efforts." Bascom set Hall in the direction of John Stuart Mill, Henry Longueville Mansel, and others, not all of whom Bascom himself approved.[44]

A third student offers a different angle on the Bascom years at Williams. James Abram Garfield, the future president of the United States, arrived at the college in 1854, slightly ahead of Bascom's return there as professor. Garfield had spent two years at Hiram College, where he returned later as president before beginning his political career. Garfield became a devoted alumnus of Williams College and was serving as president of the alumni society in 1871. That year Bascom addressed the group in New York City, and, according to a New York paper, his remarks "created a sensation." The meeting took place three days after Christmas at the famous Delmonico's restaurant. A round of speakers preceded Bascom, including alumnus William Cullen Bryant, the noted poet, and Washington Gladden, now editor of the *Independent*. Bascom did not intend to echo the sanguine summaries and salutes to the college that others were offering that night. Instead, he addressed the matter of Williams's inability to compete with other colleges in attracting students. The college was located too far from Boston and New York, he said. But Williams had other problems. Its professors had low salaries and that fact made for bad relations between them. The college needed more buildings and better facilities and equipment, he added. Bascom also made an oblique reference to the political divisions that impaired Williams's progress. Its trustees were too old and too

44. G. Stanley Hall, *Life and Confessions of a Psychologist* (New York: D. Appleton, 1927), 157. Hall's biographer also believed that Bascom had a transforming impact on Hall, encouraging his independence and building the self-confidence of the student. See Dorothy Ross, *G. Stanley Hall: The Psychologist as Prophet* (Chicago: University of Chicago Press, 1972), 25.

conservative, he complained. Its alumni did not fulfill their responsibilities. And last, he lamented, Williams suffered because for too long one man had exercised an ascendancy, towered above all others at the place, and gave the impression that the college depended on him for its reputation and effectiveness. In fact, though, Bascom believed, President Hopkins lacked the business skills that could address the school's monetary plight.[45]

General Garfield (the title came from his Civil War service) followed Bascom at the podium. He began with a "glowing tribute" to President Hopkins. He went on to say that Williams graduates could compete in any field. He assured that although Harvard, Yale, or Princeton had great names among their faculties, one year with grand old Mark Hopkins was worth them all. Here Garfield offered the remark that became legendary. Garfield said that he would define the ideal college as "a student on one end of a log and Mark Hopkins on the other." With so great an asset at hand, Garfield went on, Williams did not need more brick and mortar to fulfill its goals. Well, these words gained wide circulation and over time fostered the wrong-headed romanticism that has long affected popular thinking about American higher education in the nineteenth century. But Garfield appears not to have made his defense of the college quite this way. Washington Gladden remembered it differently, and assured that he was there at the banquet when Garfield actually said: "A pine bench, with Mark Hopkins at one end of it, and me at the other, is a good enough college for me." We note for our purposes that, however the matter stands, Bascom was the catalyst for the famous words. More important, though, a larger context explaines this incident.[46]

For some time Bascom had felt a growing estrangement from Hopkins. Bascom did not approve Hopkins's philosophy and apparently had faulted the second set of the Lowell Lectures that Hopkins had delivered in 1868. A kind of intellectual rivalry thus had existed between the two, and the students shared in it. Hall remembered how he and his colleagues found it amusing that Bascom diverged so much in his philosophical instruction from that of the college president and that "most of us took sides with one or the other." Many students also appreciated Bascom for his forceful, partisan viewpoints; he left them no doubt

45. *Williams Review* 2 (February 5, 1872), 89; Rudolph, *Mark Hopkins*, 226.

46. *Williams Review* 2 (February 5, 1872), 90; Gladden, *Recollections*, 72–73; Rudolph, *Mark Hopkins*, 226–27. Years later, upon the tragic assassination of President Garfield, President Bascom held a memorial service for the fallen leader in Madison. The student paper reported that Bascom dwelled at length on Garfield's excellent qualities: "Intellectually strong; warm hearted; ambitious, but not selfish" and "owing his greatest strength to his moral power." *University Press*, September 30, 1881.

where he stood on any issue. This kind of teaching they preferred. They cited Arthur Perry and his tirades against protectionism, and Bascom and his declamations against utilitarianism.[47]

Shortly before the controversial banquet in New York, Bascom, apparently desperate to leave Williams, wrote to now Congressman Garfield asking an appointment to the Federal Labor Commission in Washington. The professor poured out his feelings to his former student. "My religious liberty," he said, "has led the authorities to look upon me with distrust, and my opportunities are so straitened, that I can do comparatively little for the college. . . . I am out of sympathy with the present languid *executive* administration, and am unable to quicken it. Hence I am willing to withdraw as an impotent minority." Bascom wrote Garfield just two weeks before the New York event, so Garfield certainly might have anticipated the words from Bascom that rocked the meeting. And he certainly had Garfield ready to respond with his unqualified praise of Hopkins.[48]

Even as the event in New York City was taking place at the end of 1871 another issue loomed. It concerned the imminent resignation of President Hopkins and the decision about his successor. Two among the faculty seemed the most likely candidates—John Bascom and Paul A. Chadbourne. Chadbourne had arrived at Williams only recently, having served as president of the University of Wisconsin in Madison. A product of Maine and of Methodist parents, he graduated from Williams in 1848 and pursued a teaching career in botany and chemistry. Bascom and Chadbourne had moved along distinctly different intellectual paths. Chadbourne had subscribed to the liberal, Arminian doctrines of his parents, but then rejected them and turned to Calvinism. Perry said that Chadbourne adhered to these views in an extreme and superficial way, making him also "effusively if not offensively orthodox." A teacher of science though he was, Chadbourne expressed his debt to the Book of Genesis, for without it, he said, we would not know the order of the creation.[49]

That religious orientation gave Chadbourne the lead over Bascom in the mind of the only man who mattered in this succession issue. Mark Hopkins considered it his proprietary right to name his heir apparent and to protect his own intellectual and religious legacy at the college. And he would not turn his

47. Hall, *Confessions*, 157.

48. Rudolph, *Mark Hopkins*, 225–26. Bascom wrote to Garfield shortly after the event and said he had actually "softened my real opinions very much" in his criticism of the college (227).

49. Arthur Latham Perry, *Williamstown and Williams College* (published by the author, 1899), 650–51, 656.

Williams College faculty, 1866–67. Bascom seated far left. President Hopkins seated center. (Williams College Archives and Special Collections)

college over to Bascom. Hopkins considered Bascom far too liberal in his theology, even referring to his views as "odium theologicum." On the board of trustees sat a majority of like-minded religious conservatives, "narrow and bigoted theologically," in Perry's estimation of them. "This alone cut off all chance of Bascom's preferment," he wrote. Bascom had the full support of the faculty, and Perry may not have been the only one of Bascom's colleagues to believe that Bascom "was not equaled by any man at Williams during the first century of the College." Bascom earnestly wanted the job. He asked Perry to rally the faculty for him. Perry taught economics at the college and although he and Bascom disagreed profoundly on matters such as free trade, they had great respect for each other. Perry held a meeting at his home to organize the faculty's support for Bascom. Nearly all of that group attended. But the die was cast. Hopkins offered the presidency to Chadbourne, not even bothering to gain the endorsement of the trustees.[50]

50. Perry, *Williamstown*, 651, 623, 654.

Chadbourne's inauguration took place in July 1872. John Bascom spoke and welcomed him on behalf of the faculty, but he also used the occasion to state that the age of presidential tyranny must end and that the faculty must assume more rights and more authority in running the college. "Petty tyrannies, absolute powers, secret counsels belong to an army or a man of war, in which the barbarous creed of force still prevails, not to the College."[51] All knew the context of Bascom's words, but not everyone—Chadbourne and at least one trustee especially—appreciated them. The address registered again Bascom's festering discontent at Williams. Then only a little while after this event, an emissary came to talk to him about becoming the University of Wisconsin's new president. Chadbourne felt little inclination to dissuade Bascom from accepting the offer. He, like the former president, sat uncomfortably with Bascom's liberal views on religion and on women's education, too. Nor would it have mattered. Bascom eagerly accepted the offer and the new opportunity that came with it. So John Bascom headed west, out to the institution that Chadbourne had also served as president.

51. "Address of Prof. Bascom in Behalf of the Faculty," *Williams Vidette*, supplement, July 6, 1872, 208–9; Perry, *Williamstown*, 658, 678–79.

3

Wisconsin:
A State and Its University

Wisconsin had just completed its first quarter century of statehood the year before John Bascom traveled west to head its university. The years that followed marked a critical turn in Wisconsin history, as the Civil War and Reconstruction faded from front-page attention and yielded to news from the business world. Politics made a corresponding turn and confronted the new era of powerful corporations, individual wealth, and the greater disparities of money among the populace. In the arenas of reform, race still mattered, but labor and the rights of women now gained more attention. Old alliances stayed pretty much in place, and the battle lines of reform and resistance reflected familiar religious and ethnic fault lines. Wisconsin registered these divisions as much as any state in the union, now fully restored in 1877.

Bascom, as noted, had not shied from engagement on these fronts. Nor did he do so in his new position. Headship of a state university placed him in the public arena. Of course, he might have opted to make his office one of academic retreat, removed from the low political strife of capitol politics and partisan struggles. Most university presidents of his day did so. Not for a moment, however, did Bascom so choose. His administration embroiled him in politics from its very outset. It ended in bitterness. But Bascom's presidency has an equal importance in the continued intellectual advances he made. Here also Bascom distinguished himself as few university presidents did, maintaining a prodigious level of scholarship. In fact, Bascom brought into full statements his initial forays into liberal theology and the Social Gospel, evolution, and sociology. Indeed, in the years of his Wisconsin presidency these subjects found a large integration, as Bascom provided them an inclusive intellectual framework. What makes all these efforts the more interesting to observe is Bascom's application of his system

58

to the reform efforts in Wisconsin and to issues of national concern during the 1870s and 1880s. This subject requires a brief look at this state's history in its first twenty-five years. Bascom's intellectual career now placed him squarely into the religious and ethnic configurations that drove the cultural and social politics of Wisconsin.

The 1870 census showed that Wisconsin had a population of about a million people. Its American-born portion constituted only two-fifths of that number as Wisconsin stood second only to California in foreign-born percentage. It remained overwhelmingly rural, nearly 90 percent, with Milwaukee its largest city. Wisconsin had become a territory in 1836. White settlers had entered, occupying lands of the natives—Chippewa, Menominee, Winnebago, Sauk, Potawatomi, Fox, Miami, and others. Even by this time, however, the white presence had changed the Indians' ways of life. Some of the native tribes had been abandoning older ways—agriculture, hunting and gathering—as the Europeans encroached on their lands. Many had moved to single-family farming. Disease, as it had from the time of the Spaniards, took a heavy toll among the natives, and liquor proved all too tempting, leaving dissipation in its wake. The French had earlier tried to win the natives to Catholicism, and later American missionaries offered the Protestant faith. None had much success.[1]

Later came the Yankees and from them territorial Wisconsin. In these years before statehood Wisconsin experienced what historian Alice Smith called "the Protestant era." That label derived from the inrush of easterners, coming overwhelmingly from New York, and most of them with New England family backgrounds. Religious identifications showed a heavy portion of Presbyterians and Congregationalists, now fortified by growing numbers of Baptists and especially Methodists, the largest Protestant group in Wisconsin at the time of Bascom's arrival. The missionary efforts that described the early work of Bascom's father continued farther west as the American Home Missionary Society assisted the development of new churches on the distant frontier. Among the Presbyterians a large majority of New School loyalists prevailed and gave Wisconsin politics much of its moralistic content. They brought to the territory a familiar resolve to fight sin wherever they saw it. It wasn't always easy. Smith quotes a typical pastoral lament from among the early Protestant clericals as this person surveyed the Wisconsin scene: "We have course and clamorous infidelity, petty grog shops becoming numerous, much profane

1. Robert C. Nesbit, *Wisconsin: A History* (Madison: University of Wisconsin Press, 1973), 341, 12–14, 21–22; Richard N. Current, *The Civil War Era, 1848–1873*, vol. 2 of *The History of Wisconsin* (Madison: State Historical Society of Wisconsin, 1976), 151–52.

swearing, contempt of the Sabbath, and of all religious institutions. . . . A strong, sweeping current of worldly enterprise, a rush and scramble after wealth."[2]

Observers of early Wisconsin have labeled it "New York's Daughter State." Wisconsin did not stand alone in this identity. As New Englanders had reshaped the early "Yorkers," the New York migrants now brought a special moral fervor to states like Ohio and Michigan. Here one found "centers of pure New England culture," and here also commitment to temperance, Sabbatarianism, and abolitionism. In many instances the areas of moral politics, well warmed by revivalism, "fostered a view of the world in which compromise with sin was itself a sin."[3] Temperance provided Wisconsin its first reform movement. It would be a big issue for Bascom. This program took root right away: "It was among settlements of descendants of New England," Smith writes, "—in Milwaukee, Racine, Walworth, Waukesha, and Rock counties—that the movement was most vigorously promoted." Wisconsin also had Sunday "blue laws" in place during its territorial era. The town of Southport (later Kenosha) flourished with these reform activities, but also with a cultural and social energy that engaged people in experimental projects like Fourierism, phrenology, and vegetarianism. One should not be surprised that so many of Southport's citizenry had migrated there from the "burned-over district" of New York State, joined by a smaller number who had come directly from New England.[4] Around the state the popular lyceums, appearing first in Milwaukee in 1839, assured that interested audiences could meet and hear distinguished voices from the East— Horace Greeley from New York, James Russell Lowell from New England. Early Wisconsin colleges like Lawrence in Appleton, Carroll in Waukesha, and Beloit reinforced the institutional likeness to New England.[5]

But demographics were changing in Wisconsin, and changing fast. The Germans led in this transformation, their immigration reaching a high tide in

2. Alice E. Smith, *From Exploration to Statehood*, vol. 1 of *The History of Wisconsin* (Madison: State Historical Society of Wisconsin, 1973), 618–19.

3. Edward P. Alexander, "Wisconsin, New York's Daughter State," *Wisconsin Magazine of History* 30 (1946), 11–30; Eric Foner, *Free Soil, Free Labor, Free Men: The Ideology of the Republican Party before the Civil War* (New York: Oxford University Press, 1970), 106–9.

4. Smith, *Exploration to Statehood*, 626–27, 640–41; Current, *Civil War Era*, 43, 142.

5. Joseph Schafer, "The Yankee and the Teuton in Wisconsin, III: Some Social Traits of the Yankees," *Wisconsin Magazine of History* 6 (June 1923), 394–95; Current, *Civil War Era*, 171–72; Smith, *Exploration to Statehood*, 562–63.

the 1850s. German communities stretched in number along the Lake Michigan coast north of Milwaukee, and by 1860 they constituted one-third of the population in Wisconsin.[6] They brought heavy numbers of Catholics at first, and then large numbers of Lutherans. But neither group of Germans identified with the Yankee Protestants, for reasons that quickly found their way into state politics. The Irish had been here longer and their Catholicism held steady. The newly arriving Scandinavian and Swiss populations in the state found it easier than the Germans to work in harmony with the Yankees. Wisconsin was looking increasingly like a patchwork of ethnic communities, each quite self-contained, each sharing its own language and customs. The foreign-born constituted well more than half the state's population now. And diverse as they were, most of them would observe, and many of them feel directly, the push of the Yankee moral imperium in Wisconsin. For a long time Yankees dominated the power structure of the state, in business and government.[7]

Wisconsin entered the Union during the era of the "Second Party System"—the era of Whigs and Democrats. At the outset, Democrats had the edge. Southerners had moved into the lead mining region of southwestern Wisconsin and brought strong Jacksonian leanings with them. When, in the proposed constitution of 1846, they inscribed a Jacksonian economic program—against banking and internal improvements—Yankee elements fought back. Rufus King, editor of the strongly Whig *Milwaukee Sentinel* newspaper, with allies among the city's commercial elite, effected a resounding defeat of the proposed constitution. Voting showed numbers against it from Yankee counties like Rock and Racine, heavily Whig areas, and strong support from German counties like Washington. Already Wisconsin had in place the ethnocultural lines that would shape its politics for several decades.[8]

6. Smith, *Exploration to Statehood*, 609.

7. Herman J. Deutsch, "Yankee-Teuton Rivalry in Wisconsin Politics of the Seventies: Section II: Christian Morals and Political Aptitude," *Wisconsin Magazine of History* 14 (1931), 412–13; Richard Nelson Current, *Wisconsin: A Bicentennial History* (New York: W. W. Norton, 1977), 36, 38–39; Alexander, "Wisconsin, New York's Daughter State," 24–25, 26–27; Nesbit, *Wisconsin*, 153.

8. Nesbit, *Wisconsin*, 116, 215. For an important study that shows the incidence of these ethnic-religious lines in Wisconsin politics during these years, see Robert Booth Fowler, *Wisconsin Votes: An Electoral History* (Madison: University of Wisconsin Press, 2008). Fowler writes: "Class issues do not seem to have been important." "Instead ethnic and religious variables are the key to understanding Wisconsin voting behavior" (24, 25).

The Yankee Wisconsinites generally took the lead in establishing the state university. In fact, Wisconsin had the unusual distinction of founding a state university before it was a state. Going back to its territorial days in 1838, a bill establishing a university at the first state capital, Belmont, located it there, but then shifted it to Madison the next year. No efforts emerged to give the institution life, but the Constitution of 1848 carried a provision for establishing a university "at or near the seat of state government" and for naming the university with its state identity when statehood did occur. The outcome registered the work of the Committee of Education and School Funds, which consisted almost entirely of Wisconsinites who had come from New York or New England. They included Rufus King and also Eleazer Root, a graduate of Williams College. And for its first chancellor (later retitled "president"), too, the university regents selected a Yorker, John H. Lathrop, born in 1799 in New York and graduated from upstate Hamilton College. He brought extensive experience in education to his new post, including recently his presidency of the University of Missouri. His inauguration in May 1850 presented Madison with a gala and splendid affair. The celebratory ball did not break up until two o'clock in the morning. But the extravagance did not play well in provincial outposts. The aspect of luxuriance and social display, some said, did not bespeak an institution disciplined in religious restraint. Some judged Lathrop himself a "skeptic in his religious views."[9]

Those concerns had no foundation. But they do point to one of the difficult and challenging questions in the history of American higher education in the nineteenth century and particularly of the nature, character, and purpose of the state universities. Few knew exactly what the term "state university" meant. Histories of almost all the state universities point out that founders usually had no experience in public higher education. In Wisconsin's case individuals came from a part of the country where private colleges prevailed and in which they themselves had received their collegiate educations. Now they took the reins of the new public university. To be sure, well before the Morrill Act of 1862 reformers had called for a break from the long-standing classical curriculum. They called for practical education—mechanics and agriculture—suitable for a modern economy and for working-class students. When the Morrill legislation passed, attention to these subjects became requisite, but the act clearly specified that the new curriculum should not exclude attention to traditional

9. Merle Curti and Vernon Carstensen, *The University of Wisconsin: A History, 1848–1925*, 2 vols. (Madison: University of Wisconsin Press, 1949), 1:4, 6, 39–40, 48–49, 62–63, 63n; J. F. A. Pyre, *Wisconsin* (New York: Oxford University Press, 1920), 85.

subjects. The whole business proceeded place by place in an unformulaic manner, each state institution finding its own way.[10]

Wisconsin stayed traditional almost by default, as did the new state schools generally. In its early years the university looked very much like an old-time college. Thus, Chancellor Lathrop took up the standard role of teaching seniors in ethics, civil polity, and political economy, as those subjects kept their place within the moral philosophy rubric, "Theoretic and Practical Morality" in this instance. If the early curriculum had any new departures from the old it found them in German and French foreign language courses. One could also gain some practical education through courses in the sciences. Engineering and agriculture entered into the program of studies, and students did enjoy considerable freedom of selection in their educational preferences. But the Madison institution also reflected continuity with the past in its quite emphatic religious culture. Students attended required chapel services in these years. A university chaplain arranged these services as well as Sunday afternoon religious lectures. Professor Daniel Read taught a course titled "Evidences of Christianity," a standard offering in American colleges from the early century and the vogue of the British theologian William Paley. Nothing in these practices distinguished the University of Wisconsin; the state universities in general perpetuated the religious substance of American higher education into the emerging university era.[11]

President Lathrop, who had many ideas about advancing the university, proved ineffective in giving them life. He did not show a forceful leadership and lacked aggressiveness in getting from the legislature the money needed by the university. Well liked though he was, when he submitted his resignation no one on the board of regents tried to talk him out of it. Then the trustees brought in a man of large reputation and much promise, or so they thought. Henry Barnard ranked second to Horace Mann as American champion of education. Now Wisconsin gave him the opportunity to have practical consequences in implementing his bold ideas. So, much anticipation accompanied Barnard in his arrival to Madison in 1865. But Barnard never delivered; he seemed to ride serenely above the fray of institutional politics and gave most attention to working with the expanding public school system in the state, and less to university

10. Curti and Carstensen, *University of Wisconsin*, 1:4, 29; Pyre, *Wisconsin*, 161–63.

11. Curti and Carstensen, *University of Wisconsin*, 1:79, 83–84, 176, 182. For examples of religion's presence and influence at midwestern state universities at this time, see Bradley J. Longfield, "From Evangelicalism to Liberalism: Public Midwestern Universities in Nineteenth-Century America," in *The Secularization of the Academy*, ed. George M. Marsden and Bradley J. Longfield (New York: Oxford University Press, 1992), 46–47.

matters. He lasted but one year. Nor did the university flourish under the next two presidents. Paul Chadbourne, Williams graduate, professor, and Bascom's colleague there, came to Madison in 1866. Despite some accomplishments at Wisconsin, he accepted the invitation that came from his alma mater back east, replacing Mark Hopkins at Williams, and, as noted, defeating Bascom's efforts for the same office. John H. Twombly replaced Chadbourne. A Methodist minister and superb orator, he had no scholarly achievements. He did not work well with the regents. In 1873, the stage was set for Bascom.[12]

There is no information about how Bascom came to the attention of the board. Chadbourne, now at Williams, had a connection back to Wisconsin, as his presidency there had ended only a few years before. And he may have welcomed the chance to lose to Wisconsin the man who had challenged him for the Williams presidency. Chadbourne did recommend Bascom for Chadbourne's former position. No other names seem to have emerged with Bascom's as the regents eagerly sought to move out of the brief and unhappy Twombly era. The university's board of visitors took up the search and sent an envoy to Williams to meet with Bascom. The report that followed described Bascom as "a man who has earned a national reputation as an original thinker, able writer, and ripe scholar." It highlighted as well his "long experience and peculiar aptitude in teaching," cited his "executive ability," and suggested that this asset might end the prevailing disarray in the administrative operations of the university. His personality, too, had a recommendation: "an instinctive hatred of all pretense and sham." The visitors knew that Bascom strongly supported coeducation and women's rights and that he had a clear and progressive record in matters of social justice. So Bascom received the unanimous approval of the regents. They, the university community in general, and the State of Wisconsin, whose interested citizens had viewed with frustration the faltering progress of the state institution to this point, now looked for great things to come of the new appointment. New Englanders and Yorkers in the state welcomed Bascom as a favorite son. One historian of the university, writing from the perspective of a half century later, rendered this conclusion: "The time was ripe for an individual of power who, infusing intensity and distinction into the academic temper of the institution, might simultaneously and by that very act, clarify the popular will and transfuse it with purer hopes. John Bascom proved to be the appointed spirit."[13]

12. Curti and Carstensen, *University of Wisconsin*, 1:163, 165, 221–22, 236–45; Pyre, *Wisconsin*, 119–20, 122.

13. Curti and Carstensen, *University of Wisconsin*, 1:247; Pyre, *Wisconsin*, 192–93, 191 (longer quotation).

John Bascom arrived at Madison in June of 1874. He got there three months before his appointment actually started, so happily liberated was he now from Williams College and Mark Hopkins. Bascom, serving as president into 1887, began a term of presidential leadership at the University of Wisconsin second in length only to that of his student Charles Van Hise, university president from 1903 to 1918. The rest of the family joined Bascom in August. John Bascom had married Emma Curtiss three years after the death of his first wife. She came from Sheffield, Massachusetts, the daughter of Owen and Caroline Curtiss, and taught school in the area. Emma and John Bascom had five children, all born in Williamstown. George, the only son, was born in 1857 followed by Jean (Jennie) in 1859, and Emma in 1861. Another daughter, Mabel, was born in 1867, but died within the year. Emma died in 1879 and a large audience attended the funeral on the campus. That same year George and Jennie graduated from the UW, classmates of Robert La Follette and Charles Van Hise. Daughter Florence, born in 1862 and later a pioneering geologist, remembered a campus sweltering in summer heat, as the family prepared the president's home, situated on a hill that sloped down to Lake Mendota. One wonders if the new president, soon to be known around the state as a champion of prohibition, had any idea that the family's new property had "an orchard on the northern slope just west of the house and a vineyard of Concord grapes on the southern slope"![14]

As a new student at the University of Wisconsin, Florence Bascom remembered an instructional program rooted in the old pedagogy of memorization and recitation. Few of the faculty had any ambition for scholarship, she recalled. That situation changed under Bascom's leadership as the university moved gradually from the era of the college to that of the university in American higher education. Bascom sought and secured new academic chairs: pharmacy, teaching, agricultural chemistry, and botany numbered among them. He also tried to raise faculty salaries, but the regents balked. Wisconsin marched in step with the new directions taken by other American universities, though not necessarily at a faster pace than comparative schools. President Bascom became a powerful presence among the faculty and not all of the instructors felt at ease with him. But Bascom did follow the standards of democracy and academic freedom that he had urged in his departing speech at Williams. The president did not interfere with the professors' teaching; he recognized their expertise in their fields of study and wished to assure their growth.

14. Florence Bascom, "The University in 1874–1887," *Wisconsin Magazine of History* 8 (March 1925), 300–301. On the career of Florence Bascom, see Jill S. Schneiderman, "A Life of Firsts: Florence Bascom," *GSA Today*, July 1997, 8–9.

Florence Bascom. (Wisconsin Historical Society, WHi-121044)

And especially, Bascom has received a lot of credit for changing the intellectual tone and atmosphere of the campus. A new seriousness about study and a delight in intellectual inquiry took hold. Already, however, one can see a problem for Bascom. He wanted academic recognition for the university and knew that it must come from the work and prestige of its faculty. On the other hand, he disliked intellectual narrowness. All areas of learning, he strongly believed, give us access to the great universality of design and purpose, that great integrated wholeness and unity of all things that motivated and described Bascom's intellectual system. And in this large framework we must teach all the fields of learning, he urged. But the American intellect was moving the other way. Specialization defined the emerging research university.[15]

Bascom himself helped promote it. The president embraced the German research model, and on more than one occasion he urged the matter on the board of regents. He wanted Wisconsin professors to be masters in their fields of learning. But they could not attain that goal, he suggested, when they had to teach in different subjects (he referenced the instance of Latin and political economy) and when their obligations had them in the classroom three hours a day throughout the instructional week. So the university must subdivide the curriculum, Bascom said, to the extent that "each professor should have the opportunity to thoroughly master his topic" and gain recognition through scholarship. "If a professor is to do really superior work," Bascom said in a report to the regents, "his entire labor must be confined to a single department, and he must have sufficient time at his disposal to make himself a master of his chosen field." Furthermore, Bascom promised that classroom instruction would gain immeasurably by the shift in emphasis. New learning, "original work," will promote greater interest, more enthusiasm, more intellectual inquiry by professor and student alike, he avowed. And Bascom believed that the university was progressing well in this direction. In 1882 he claimed that Wisconsin could compete with Harvard, Cornell, and other pacesetters in the new university era. The strength of its faculty, indicated by its scholarship, will decide the outcome, Bascom told the regents.[16]

15. Florence Bascom, "University," 305; Curti and Carstensen, *University of Wisconsin*, 1:1, 252. See chap. 13, 1:327–63, for details of curricular change. Pyre, *Wisconsin*, 234, 236–37.

16. John Bascom, "Report of the President of the University to the Board of Regents," in *Annual Report of the Board of Regents of the University of Wisconsin, for the Fiscal Year Ending September 30, 1878* (Madison, 1878), 27–28. Hereafter, "President's Report," with the appropriate year. "President's Report, 1879," 25–26; "President's Report, 1882," 27–28; "President's Report, 1887," 37. Regrettably, a fire in 1916 destroyed the building later named Bascom Hall and with it the private correspondence of the president.

In other quarters, however, things went badly for Bascom. A protracted embroilment with the regents, beginning early and worsening throughout his administration, became a legendary part of the University of Wisconsin's history. Most of the details will receive attention later. They involved politics. But core issues of educational philosophy and practice also played a role. Bascom complained that the regents did not spend enough money on the strictly educational purposes of the university, barely more than half of the budgets. Worse, they did not give him the room he needed to shape the university, expand its programs, and move it upward in academic reputation. The regents never troubled themselves to provide the president with any secretarial assistance. He had to address catalogues and commencement programs by himself. At a time when Bascom urged the faculty toward individual expertise in their fields, the regents made a statutory requirement that they themselves approve all textbooks. Bascom seethed. The president also wanted to have the initiative in academic appointments, with the board giving consent. The president insisted that he must have charge over all matters of a strictly academic nature. The board said no. But late in his administration, when Bascom's activities on behalf of the Prohibitionist Party in the state had created hard resentment among some powerful regents, the board told him to cool it on politics and stick to academic business! Bascom, in his memoir, came down hard on the regents. The board, he said, consisted "almost exclusively of those interested in politics." "Rarely, indeed, was any man granted the position of Regent who had any special knowledge of the methods of education, or interest in them," he lamented. "The result was that questions of management were settled on narrow grounds, and trifling and personal interests gained the ascendancy."[17]

The plenary details of John Bascom's presidency at the University of Wisconsin have their full record in excellent institutional histories, the two cited previously in this chapter. This study, however, pursues a different enterprise. Curti and Carstensen wrote: "President Bascom was a dominant influence in the life of students from the time he came in 1874 until he left Wisconsin in

17. Curti and Carstensen, *University of Wisconsin*, 1:252, 272, 250, 266–67; Florence Bascom, "University," 308; John Bascom, *Things Learned by Living* (New York: G. P. Putnam's Sons, 1913), 70. Pyre says quite properly that Bascom overreacted in this criticism. The university, Pyre states, is a public institution. It must have the good will of many from the public and enlist the interests of those from outside it. Neither the University of Wisconsin nor any other major university at this time could have fashioned a governing body of educationalists only. Furthermore, through powerfully connected businessmen like William F. Vilas and John C. Spooner, both graduates of the university, it could gain influence and good results from the state legislature. Pyre, *Wisconsin*, 220–21.

1887." That dominance came at first from Bascom's rather daunting presence in the midst of the students: "A figure tall, erect, and strong; a face at once massive and mobile; a curt, incisive, and direct address; a mind powerful far beyond the ordinary measure . . . a dominating personality." So recalled Dean Birge. Edward A. Birge had joined the Wisconsin faculty in 1875, beginning a long career at the institution that included deanship of the College of Letters and Science and service as acting president. Birge, also a Williams graduate, knew Bascom well as a teacher there. Charles Van Hise remembered that many students at first did not know how to react to Bascom: "without popular qualities, cold in manner, severe in face, austere in intellect." But slowly, Van Hise stated, Bascom's qualities revealed themselves. Students came to recognize the president's sincere interest in them. "Toward the close of his career here," Van Hise recalled, "mingled with their respect was a touch of reverence. When he left it seemed to them that irremediable catastrophe had befallen the University."[18]

Bascom exercised moral and intellectual influence above all. A Puritan strain in him found special appeal among Wisconsin's New England population. It came from the books he wrote and the classes he taught. Bascom instructed all the seniors in philosophy throughout his presidential term. He had personal meetings with the students and addressed the university community regularly. These occasions had small reinforcements from the senior and faculty receptions that the president and Mrs. Bascom held at their home. The Bascoms' daughter Florence had no doubt about the large impact of these closer encounters, especially the Sunday meetings with the seniors: "Our student meetings were held at first in the chapel of University Hall and later in the assembly room of the Library Hall, where also on Sunday afternoons we were addressed by the president on themes of ethical import with a vigor and potency. . . . Our obligations to the state were made exceedingly plain, and the seed was sown which later fructified in the 'Wisconsin Idea.'"[19]

University historian J. F. A. Pyre assessed Bascom's influence similarly. Bascom, he wrote, presented his ideas whole, each part a particular within a massive unity that gave it its special import. "He was preëminently 'a great teacher.'" Everything about Bascom and the intellectual evolution of the

18. Edward A. Birge, "President Bascom and the University of Wisconsin," in *Memorial Service in Honor of John Bascom*. . . . (n.p., n.d.), 16, 24; Charles Van Hise, "Introductory Address," in *Memorial Service*, 8.

19. Curti and Carstensen, *University of Wisconsin*, 1:247; Florence Bascom, "University," 307.

University of Wisconsin class of 1876. (Wisconsin Historical Society, WHi-27195)

university in his years there, Pyre believed, derived from that fact. Bascom moved from broad philosophical outline to social applications of that larger outline. Thus he charged his classrooms with high intellectual seriousness and with the agenda of social reform for which he fought there and beyond the campus. Pyre observed that Bascom published eight books during his Wisconsin presidency, more than a book every two years on average. Some of them— *Ethics, Natural Theology, The Science of Mind*—he wrote for the textbook market, and they came directly from his classes. The others continued his explorations in philosophy and religion and came piecemeal into his teaching, too. And finally, from Birge comes another testimonial that opens up what the rest of this book will explore. Dean Birge spoke at the special memorial service held for Bascom on his death in Williamstown in 1911. Birge said of Bascom: "He found in philosophy the principles which made life coherent and intelligible. . . . From philosophy came the revelation which correlated life's scattered experiences and corrected its partial views." Birge concluded: "*I question whether the history of any great commonwealth can show so intimate a relation between the forces which have governed its social development and the principles expounded from a teacher's desk as that which exists between Wisconsin and the classroom of John Bascom.*"[20]

The university realized Bascom's goals only slowly. Birge believed that they did not come into fruition until late in the century. But Birge did say of Bascom that "the faculty felt the inspiration of his leadership" and all saw the intellectual tone and standards of the college rise. The reforms necessary to move Wisconsin from the facsimile of the old-time college to a university where research and scholarship would have more prominence became "a rallying point" for the faculty. Altogether, though, Birge believed that Bascom's educational achievements had the greatest impact at the undergraduate level.[21]

John Bascom, anxious to leave old, stagnant Williams behind and throw himself into the young life of the "Middlewest," this land of democratic promise and change as he saw it, had arrived in Madison, as noted, even before his contracted term of service was to begin the next fall. Bascom used the early arrival to make his debut in giving the baccalaureate sermon, an address to the graduating seniors. He spoke to students whom he had never met and to a public audience seeing the new president for the first time. He titled his sermon "Freedom of Faith." The tradition of the sermon itself confirms the perpetuation

20. Pyre, *Wisconsin*, 198, 229–31, 230 (quotation); Birge, "President Bascom," 37, 41 (italics in original).

21. Birge, "President Bascom," 20, 21.

of religious forms at the new state universities, and Bascom's address had clear religious content. Moreover, the sermon provided a kind of intellectual review of Bascom's thinking to this point and a glimpse of the administration to follow.

In this baccalaureate sermon Bascom talked about John Calvin. (Yes!) What he admired in the great reformer, he said, came from his bold spirit and independence; what he disliked came from the long and harsh conformity that his system had created in the life of the churches. Opposed to the intellectual retrenchment that had reigned too long, the new president raised the standards of wide inquiry and fresh thought in all realms of human experience, religious and other. "Much of our religious faith," he told the seniors, "is purely conventional, a tacit concession to the sectarian spirit that envelopes us . . . [and not] a direct perception of the truth. . . . Such a faith deadens, if it does not destroy, the religious life." Anyone familiar with Bascom's career to this point would have found these words familiar. The churches have succumbed to dead belief and abandoned intellectual adventure in yielding to "stern dogmatic conditions." Bascom called for a "new religious revolution." It would come from an "iconoclastic attitude," the truly religious one, he asserted, the spirit of Christ himself.[22] From the distant perspective of later years, we see in Bascom's first words at the University of Wisconsin a preview of his presidential career there. In the wake of his address came Bascom's "new theology," his continual opening to science and evolution, his adventures into the new social sciences, his own version of the Social Gospel, and his applications of all these new departures to the politics of the 1870s and 1880s.

Thirteen years later Bascom gave his last address as president of the university. In a remarkable statement, his "farewell," as it were, Bascom spoke on the subject of "A Christian State." He pronounced in a way that no one of his peers, no president of a major state or private university in the United States, was doing. He summoned into one powerful statement the governing social philosophy he had elaborated throughout his presidency and some of the particular issues to which he applied it. Only a summary is given here; the later narrative will have many references to this last word at Wisconsin.

Bascom meant to make some hard judgments. At the outside he described the Christian state as one based in an organic view of society. All that he had written and all that he had taught his students at Madison came together here. The state, he said, represents "the common ground on which nature, man and God meet." That view came from his understanding of true Christianity, as

22. John Bascom, *The Freedom of Faith* [Baccalaureate Sermon] (Madison: Atwood & Culver, 1874), 10–12.

reinforced by evolution. All things relate to one another and all individuals belong as citizens to a political community, a state, he said. So, "the Christian state will be completely organic." But as the president surveyed the United States of 1887, he saw that ideal in utter ruin. American values had gone wrong on every front, religion, too, warped and twisted to false application. Everywhere, Bascom protested, we see the rights of powerful interests overriding the common good. Whether it emanates from private wealth or corporate privilege or from the libertarian excesses of the drunkard, society and laws stand enfeebled against "the full swing of individual assertion." We have wholly misunderstood the true meaning of liberty, Bascom pronounced. We have developed little sense of what constitutes the public interest, the common good. We have no laws to support the interests of the larger society against the recklessness of individuals who erode the collectivity.[23]

Bascom had throughout his tenure at Wisconsin tried to reify the state, as an entity, live, like the corporation, with its own interests, and quite properly, with its own power to realize them. Here in his final public appearance as president Bascom offered details aplenty, and more will emerge anon. But for now, a question: what had transpired between Bascom's first baccalaureate sermon in 1874, with its correctives on religion, and his last one in 1887, with its correctives on "the social question," that specter that haunted Gilded Age America? The remainder of this study will answer that question.

23. John Bascom, *A Christian State* [Baccalaureate Sermon] (Milwaukee: Cramer, Aikins & Cramer, 1887), 4, 5, 10.

4

New Theology, New University

American higher education experienced significant transformation in the middle and late nineteenth century. Colleges became universities and in the process expanded their academic offerings and redefined their purposes. Many motivations spurred the process. Mostly, academic leaders took stock of their situations and found them unencouraging; colleges were just not popular places. They seemed to some ill suited to the shifting economic life of the nation, irrelevant to an age of new technology, commerce, industry, and finance, to say nothing of democracy itself. One could look almost anywhere to register the laments. Most frequently remembered over the long history since its utterance were the words of Francis Wayland, president of Brown University: "We have produced an article for which the demand is diminishing. We sell it at less than cost, and the deficiency is made up by charity. We give it away and still the demand diminishes." And should that fact surprise us? he wondered. How can a curriculum of ancient classics, a little math, and a little science help develop the vast resources of this nation, as the general population wanted to do?[1]

Others had loftier reasons for moving the "old-time college" out of its long and static history into a new university era. They judged that the colleges simply could not keep up with the explosion of new knowledge and that the old schools, structured as they were in their curricular arrangements, could not accommodate the new branches of learning that this proliferating new knowledge was creating. Year by year the situation became more frustrating. American students traveled the Atlantic to attend European universities, the German ones especially, where research and scholarship brought the excitements of

---

1. *Report to the Corporation of Brown University, on Changes in the System of Collegiate Education, Read March 28, 1850* (Providence, 1850), 34.

new discoveries, the advancement of learning as opposed to the passing on of an acquired body of knowledge. Students so infected returned to their home country and became the vanguard of a new, reforming generation of educators in the United States.[2]

The record of this transformation received its most thorough outline in Laurence Veysey's now classic treatment, his book of 1965, *The Emergence of the American University*. Veysey, as he studied a vast literature of academic reform, described the history in terms of three themes: utility, research, and liberal culture. Each had a role in leading the colleges away from the older norms of "mental discipline" and "piety" that had for a century or more supplied these institutions with their pedagogical, which is also to say their religious and moral, purposes. These new ideals did not necessarily compete with each other. More often leading educators invoked all of them to advance new designs and ambitions for their colleges. Veysey read the literature with much sensitivity and described how American higher education generally formed a habit to "blend and reconcile" as it moved into its new future. And each institution took up the challenge in its own way. Cornell looked like Harvard in many ways, but in many ways did not. Princeton looked like Yale in many ways, but in key ways it differed. Wisconsin followed Michigan in important ways, but also made significant departures. And so it went. Some of the smaller colleges moved away from their denominational beginnings; others perpetuated sectarian habits.[3]

Since Veysey's great effort, others have looked for different perspectives by which to frame this era of change. Most importantly, Julie Reuben, in her study *The Making of the Modern University*, published in 1996, set the transformation of American higher education within a large intellectual context. Here a story of continuity emerges, of careful evolution as opposed to revolutionary shift. The emerging universities did not abandon the religious identities and purposes that had long described them. Rather, she describes, key leaders of the new era, an important group of academic reformers, sought to make the transition to modern universities by adapting religion to a new age of learning and by redefining religion in their institutions. Thus, stalwarts of this new generation— Charles William Eliot at Harvard, Daniel Coit Gilman at California and Johns

---

2. See Carl Diehl, *Americans and German Scholarship, 1770–1870* (New Haven, CT: Yale University Press, 1978).

3. Laurence R. Veysey, *The Emergence of the American University* (Chicago: University of Chicago Press, 1965). See also Roger L. Geiger, *The History of American Higher Education: Learning and Culture from the Founding to World War II* (Princeton, NJ: Princeton University Press, 2014).

Hopkins, Andrew D. White at Cornell, James B. Angell at Michigan—
"believed they could alter the position of religion in higher education to make it
consistent with modern scientific standards of intellectual inquiry." With enthusiasm and confidence, these academics helped shape the "modern American
university," incorporating the German model in great measure, but giving it an
American look. In the process they, and their new expanding faculties, brought
their institutions into an exciting intellectual discourse. They entered, even as
they enriched, the great era of Protestant liberal theology and the challenging
era of Darwin and evolution.[4] And more recently Andrew Jewett has described
continuity more than revolution as the transition pattern from the college to
the university era. Especially, he finds, liberal Protestantism, to which Bascom
contributed significantly, explains the critical connection.[5]

Into this discourse John Bascom entered, and quite prolifically at that. The
new academic literature that addressed the relations of science and religion
yielded much rethinking. It rejected as the essence of religion its dogmatic
content and creedal formulations. The reformers wanted another way of affirming religious truth. They cited the need for a different way of studying and
understanding religion. In 1876, during his third year at Wisconsin, Bascom
published his massive book *A Philosophy of Religion*. He also formulated the "new
theology," the key term that brought all these subjects into one catchphrase for
a reform agenda.

One does not easily locate patterns in the literature of academic reform,
but it helps to highlight two different habits of thought. One should not label
them categories, because here too the tendency to blend and reconcile prevailed.
This study has given attention previously to the two traditions of empiricism
and idealism, in great part because they provide the most useful parameters for
understanding John Bascom's intellectual career to this point. But differentiation along these lines also appears among the academic reformers, one line
continuous with the salient features of Scottish Realism and the other with
German philosophy. Two examples will illuminate the distinctions.

Francis Wayland authored several books, including the most popular of all
the moral philosophy texts that flourished in the antebellum college. Wayland
came from New York City and had his collegiate education at Union College
in Schenectady. He also had a year of study at Andover Theological Seminary.

4. Julie A. Reuben, *The Making of the Modern University: Intellectual Transformation and
the Marginalization of Morality* (Chicago: University of Chicago Press, 1996), 4–5.

5. Andrew Jewett, *Science, Democracy, and the American University: From the Civil War to
the Cold War* (Cambridge: Cambridge University Press, 2012), especially 34–39.

Wayland's popular textbook *The Elements of Moral Science* stood effectively in the Scottish tradition, as he and the other academic authors spun variations of Thomas Reid and Dugald Stewart. Scottish Common Sense thinking, as noted, reflected many norms of the eighteenth-century Enlightenment. It saw the world in mechanical terms and universal laws, the work of a great designing creator, and thus affirming meaning and purpose in the universe. The American moral philosophers also adapted from it a "faculty psychology" that posited a complex of functions at work in the human mind—reason and intellect, will, emotion (or sensibility), and the moral faculty (or conscience). Mental philosophy instructed in the right interplay and balance of these faculties. Also, thinkers like Reid and Stewart had won their stripes in the battles against speculation, against the aberrations of David Hume and skeptics who led philosophy into doubt about the existence of real things and the possibility of knowing them. It checked intellectual excess then and still had use in the nineteenth century to thwart the new aberrations coming from Germany. And finally, the Scottish thinking, rooted in Francis Bacon and inductive methods of verifying truth, thrived within the data of experience, both of consciousness and a real self within and of the the world and its objects without.[6]

A different view of academic reform had its sources in a different intellectual tradition. As Americans engaged the universities in Germany they absorbed, too, the intellectual atmosphere in the German states. Indeed, as George Marsden stated, "The rise to preeminence of German universities coincided with the rise of German Idealism and must be understood in terms of that broader romantic movement." German philosophers like Johann Gottlieb Fichte celebrated the university for its spiritual role, "the most holy thing which the human race possesses" and thriving "far above everything transitory."[7] Idealism had much opposition to overcome in American academe, but in individuals like Laurens P. Hickok, Bascom's own mentor, it made some gains.

In terms of the academic presidency, however, it made a bold appearance in an unlikely place—the new state university of Michigan. Its leader: the singular and remarkable Henry Philip Tappan. Tappan deserves a special look. His career in many ways parallels John Bascom's. Born in 1806, Tappan

6. See Wilson Smith, *Professors and Public Ethics: Studies of Northern Moral Philosophers before the Civil War* (Ithaca, NY: Cornell University Press, 1956), 36–41; D. H. Meyer, *The Instructed Conscience: The Shaping of the American National Ethic* (Philadelphia: University of Pennsylvania Press, 1972), 35–42.

7. George M. Marsden, *The Soul of the American University: From Protestant Establishment to Established Nonbelief* (New York: Oxford University Press, 1994), 104, 105.

also came from New York, but in this instance from the old Dutch area of the Hudson River. He grew up in Kingston and, like Wayland, studied with Eliphalet Nott at Union College. And like Bascom, Tappan enrolled at Auburn Theological Seminary. This contact brought Tappan into loose allegiance with New School Presbyterianism. He received ordination in the Congregational Church and became minister in Pittsfield, Massachusetts. But Tappan had only tangential loyalties to the Presbyterian and Congregational denominations. Much in Protestantism troubled him. A man of high aesthetic tastes and, increasingly, an enthusiast of European culture, he recoiled from the severity of Protestant worship and wanted religion to ally with music, art, and literature. All the more, too, did he want the pulpit not merely to serve the interests of creeds and dogmas. Tappan's liberal Protestantism, like Bascom's, saw those preoccupations as impediments to religious growth and progress. Tappan perceived even in the churches of his day too much residual Calvinism, too much concern with sin, too much wrath and bitterness. We need more, he believed, preaching that "quickens dead souls by the power of love in the cross of Christ, and binds together all who believe in the blissful fellowship of the heavenly Comforter."[8]

In 1832 Tappan became professor of moral and intellectual philosophy at the University of the City of New York (later CUNY). Now he could put on paper many of his doubts. Like Bascom he became a strong champion of free will, a critic in particular of Jonathan Edwards's determinism. Tappan had become a Platonist, and, once rooted in that tradition, he opened up to modern extrapolations of it, especially that of Kant. And, as they did with Bascom, these influences liberated Tappan from the chain of causation familiar to more logical strains of thought. By the 1840s Tappan clearly identified himself with the Kantian critical philosophy. A trip to Europe in 1851 sealed matters for him. He became enthralled with the system of education in Prussia, which all the more enhanced German Idealism's status in his thinking.[9]

The year before his European excursion Tappan accepted an invitation to become the University of Michigan's first president. His famous inaugural address gave a fair preview of the administration that would follow, especially in holding forth the model of Prussian education that he so much admired. Advancement of leaning and use of the lecture system by professors to convey new knowledge gained the endorsement of the new president. And even before this offering Tappan had issued a landmark document in the history of

8. Charles M. Perry, *Henry Philip Tappan: Philosopher and University President* (1933; New York: Arno Press and the New York Times, 1971), 1–8, 35, 42–43, 47–48, 67, 114–15, 122.

9. Perry, *Tappan*, 126, 152, 158.

American higher education.[10] The university, Tappan believed, must become a counterforce to the prevailing commercial ethic in America; it should not yield to or seek to find its place immersed in society and drifting with its trends. Tappan stood empathically for scholarship, for research in all avenues of learning, as the only reason and purpose of the university. Tappan wanted it to study every branch of knowledge "in full," and pursue "all scientific investigation; where study may be extended without limit, where the mind may be cultivated according to its wants." Tappan had no desire to turn higher education over to "the merchant, the gold digger," and he set himself squarely against Wayland's proposals for utilitarian reform. True education, he proclaimed, does not exist as "a mere preparation for the facile doing of the business world."[11]

Tappan sought to formulate the "philosophical idea of the university," and his efforts reflect a recourse to German Idealism that registered in a contrasting manner to Wayland's extension of the Scottish system. Research, scholarship, and new learning had for Tappan virtually spiritual qualities and religious power. Given the opportunity for the right kind of university in America, these new norms would spread their good effects throughout the society. They would serve, Tappan believed, not only as counterforce to "the excessive commercial spirit"; they would have good effects everywhere—in eroding social prejudice, in moderating partisan politics, in exposing demagoguery and ideological extremism (e.g., socialism). Careful reading will detect the inroads of philosophical idealism in Tappan's rhetoric, as when he referenced "breathing the spirit of scholarship" into all branches of learning and in "the self-creative force of study and thought." Education, said Tappan, should have as its major concern "the nurture of souls."[12]

Bascom saw much of the challenge before American higher education in philosophical terms and came down for idealism in the Tappan mode in preference to the common sense mode of Wayland. By the time he was teaching at Wisconsin, Bascom had grown more critical of the Scottish thinkers, especially

---

10. *Discourse Delivered by Henry P. Tappan on the Occasion of His Inauguration as Chancellor of the University of Michigan, December 21st, 1852* (n.p., n.d.); Richard Hofstadter and Wilson Smith, eds., "Henry P. Tappan on University Education, 1851," in *American Higher Education*, 2 vols. (Chicago: University of Chicago Press, 1961), 1:491; Howard H. Peckham, *The Making of the University of Michigan, 1817–1967* (Ann Arbor: University of Michigan Press, 1967), 36; Marsden, *Soul of the University*, 109.

11. Hofstadter and Smith, "Tappan," 1:492, 493, 495; Perry, *Tappan*, 214 (longer quotation).

12. Perry, *Tappan*, 213; Hofstadter and Smith, "Tappan," 1:492; Henry P. Tappan, "Soul-Growth," *Christian Parlor Magazine*, May 1, 1849, 51.

Reid. True, they had done yeoman service in upending the skepticism of
Berkeley and Hume, but at some expense of larger truth. "The dogmatic assertion of common sense was put in the place of complete analysis," Bascom
wrote. Making the mind's great faculties the function of common sense, he
explained, yielded to "dogmatic assertion." Certainly the Scottish thinkers had
no business making the Reason a function of common sense, for that operation
confined our knowledge to the domain of perceptions and the objects to which
they attach. Bascom and the idealists wanted more from philosophy. They
wanted a bolder play of intuitions, a more confident speculation, a larger intellectual reach. The Scottish methodology worked in tepid fashion, Bascom
complained; it still rested too strongly in the Lockean empirical mode. "The
sensationalism of Locke," Bascom asserted, "cast a cold, benumbing shadow
on many forms of belief that were striving to escape it."[13]

Bascom addressed this subject, using more common parlance, in a baccalaureate sermon, "Common Sense and Spiritual Insight." We owe much to
"common sense," he said. "Common sense stands for shrewd, sagacious, fox-
like power." It's a great endowment if one has it. Business supplies its natural
outlet, and so does politics, because in these activities "the cunning touch"
yields advantages. Bascom did not dismiss the value of this asset for the common
good or for sound philanthropic work that aids social progress. Common sense,
however, too often gives us only a microscopic view of things. We need more,
and here Bascom made the contrast with "spiritual insight," the gift of Reason.
That faculty enlarges our vision, brings the parts into a whole, and above all
perceives those invisible forces—spiritual and moral—that thrive in and rule
physical nature. "The man of simple common sense," Bascom said, "knows
nothing of these forces." In the end, he believed, spiritual insight has more
practical value than common sense, because it envisions the larger needs of the
human community. So "true statesmanship . . . requires also the rarer, much
larger gift of insight." Had spiritual insight prevailed over common sense,
Bascom asserted, we would have ended slavery much sooner than we did. He
urged his audience to apply the same vision toward the social ills of the day: the
plight of the poor, the toll of liquor, the inordinate power of money. Ultimately,
Bascom said, we need both qualities of mind. "We must be able to unite and
harmonize these two things, spiritual insight and practical sagacity."[14]

13. John Bascom, *An Historical Interpretation of Philosophy* (New York: G. P. Putnam's
Sons, 1893), 292–94.
14. John Bascom, *Common Sense and Spiritual Insight* [Baccalaureate Sermon] (Milwaukee: Cramer, Aikens & Cramer, 1886), 4–7.

Bascom's address had large implications for university education. In 1881, in the pages of the *North American Review*, he had taken on the subject of "Atheism in Colleges." Like others, Bascom saw the question in terms of philosophy, and he led with an attack, once more, on the empiricist tradition. He began his essay with a glance at the British universities, which both Wayland and Tappan believed the American colleges had too long emulated. Bascom claimed that they were in far worse condition intellectually than the American. That country's long tradition of philosophical empiricism had prepared the way for a bad situation there, he believed. "A philosophy of sensationalism, materialism, skepticism, and agnosticism," Bascom wrote, "has formed the deepest and strongest current of English speculation. Atheism is the necessary upshot of such a line of thought." "The English mind," Bascom warned, "has striven to draw the supply of its spiritual life so long out of the dry roots of sensationalism." We have a rather direct path then, he asserted, from Locke and Joseph Priestley, to John Tyndall, Thomas Huxley, John Stuart Mill, and Herbert Spencer. The long and bad effects, Bascom asserted, registered empiricism's disparagement of rational thought, by which Bascom meant the idealist's sense of Reason, denoting the mind and its expansive powers that provide "avenues to the spiritual world."[15]

American higher education, Bascom stated, faced many intellectual challenges. It could not meet them, though, through a course of reaction. "No regression and no resentment" against modern ideas will do. Religious dogma will not suffice. The small colleges could retrench in their old sectarian ways, Bascom said, but the large-scale university, open to avenues of new knowledge, could not. And in these colleges, Bascom noted, even in the late date of 1881, the Scottish philosophy still enjoys its vogue. To be sure, Bascom allowed, it stands in "dogmatic opposition" to English sensationalism and positivism, but it comes out of the same empiricist workshop. Thus, he said, "it does not fully trust or give clear explanation of those rational powers by which mind rises beyond the world of sensible impressions into that of spiritual truths." The Scottish philosophy, then, affords only "a temporary support to faith." Ultimately, the American universities will win or lose the battle on the grounds of philosophy. "The evil is intellectual," Bascom affirmed, "and admits only of an intellectual remedy." Philosophy is key.[16]

15. John Bascom, "Atheism in Colleges," *North American Review* 132 (January 1881), 32–33, 35.

16. Bascom, "Atheism," 34 (first quotation), 35–39. On this subject see also, John Bascom, "The Degeneracy of Empirical Philosophy," *Unitarian Review and Religious Magazine* 15 (April 1881), 342–50.

As Bascom pressed this matter he gave much attention also to science and religion, a main focus of his "new theology." The whole new course of higher education in the United States would reflect the responses to the questions posed by that relationship, he believed. Protestant liberalism everywhere embraced an opening to science. Amid the attempts at reconciliation, Bascom maintained the distinction between the natural and the supernatural, but always emphasizing their interrelationship. He would say many times over, as he did in his book *Natural Theology*, that science always informs our understanding of God, and guides us in a progressive revelation. Bascom wrote this book from his classroom lectures at Wisconsin, and it served afterward as a text for his classes. "Science," he said, "is constantly subserving [a] great purpose; it compels us to reshape our conceptions of the divine nature, and give them more fulness and proportion."[17] On the other hand, an erroneous understanding of science, he believed, threatens to lead us wholly astray. Bascom had never relented in his war against positivism. Ultimately, he asserted, one had to have clearly in view the distinctions between the natural and the supernatural. Error went in two directions: in confusions that followed from merging their identities, and in the misconceptions of a theological dualism so sharp as to contain these realities in separate spheres. The new theology understood the world in terms of the dynamic interrelationships of the natural and the supernatural, above all in their evolutionary patterns of interaction.

Bascom fought to make these points in his Wisconsin classroom and beyond. Thus in 1883 he assumed the public podium and gave his baccalaureate address on the subject of "The Natural and the Supernatural." The seniors in the audience would have found his remarks very familiar. Bascom had made the major points in more detailed outline previously, in 1876, in his publication of *A Philosophy of Religion*. In all places Bascom emphasized that a sound philosophy of religion depended greatly on a correct understanding of science. He always wondered at the technological marvels of his day and called science "the great, distinguishing good of our time." In fact, Bascom charged that often the great threat to religion really came from religion's most dogged defenders; they betrayed it by intellectual inflexibility and closed thinking. Theology must pay attention to science, he affirmed. At the outset of *Philosophy of Religion*, his first book written as president at Wisconsin, he said that he wanted to speak for those religious-minded people who felt the need to reopen old questions, to give Reason more room in which to work, and to engage in "freer, bolder, more critical" approaches to the faith. The quest will lead into philosophy,

17. John Bascom, *Natural Theology* (New York: G. P. Putnam's Sons, 1880), 80.

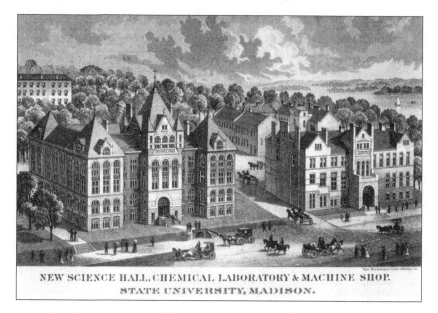

NEW SCIENCE HALL, CHEMICAL LABORATORY & MACHINE SHOP.
STATE UNIVERSITY, MADISON.

New Science Hall, 1887. (Wisconsin Historical Society, WHi-3604)

Bascom asserted. Philosophy underlies religion and "we wish to see exactly what that philosophy is which underlies religion."[18]

First, he would dispense with the positivists. We can study nature, he said, and perceive fact after fact. We can accumulate a large composite of data from the rich sensory life of the world. These "slow-plodding steps of empirical inquiry" supply the facts that fill the mind and build knowledge. But we cannot stop there, Bascom urged. And the best scientific thinking knows why. Here the president posited two considerations. First, he said, modern science has advanced to where it sees beyond mere data. The advanced knowledge and new theories

18. Bascom, *Natural Theology*, v; idem, *A Philosophy of Religion, or The Rational Grounds of Religious Belief* (New York: G. P. Putnam's Sons, 1876), ix, 3, 13. Bascom requested the construction of a new science hall upon his arrival to the presidency. One was built, and when it burned a second followed, in 1887. Science expanded significantly in the UW curriculum and even to the point that Bascom believed it had too much emphasis. Merle Curti and Vernon Carstensen, *The University of Wisconsin: A History, 1848–1925*, 2 vols. (Madison: University of Wisconsin Press, 1949), 1: 311–12, 321–22, 362–63. The authors write: "It was clear that by 1887 the University of Wisconsin had become a center of scientific investigation that could not be overlooked in any evaluation of the scientific resources of the nation" (1:362).

are showing us that nature discloses more than sensory manifestations; it reveals an underlying reality of forces and powers. We can no longer regard material things as static, inert, passive. This age of the atom demonstrates that invisible, active, occult realities describe nature in its true and ultimate condition. "The deadest things thus contain the liveliest energies," Bascom wrote. He used terms like "supersensual substratum," "inscrutable force," and "inexplicable to the senses" in convening this large, invisible reality. The old static view of nature and the universe, inheritance of the Enlightenment, now yields to a more dynamic representation. "The analogy of a building is seen to fail, and that of a living organism takes its place." That reference led Bascom to attribute to this hidden world a spiritual presence, an intelligence, an "omniscient power." Modern science delivers us to a new and firmer foundation for theological thinking, he assured.[19]

But Bascom feared that religion itself failed to exercise this intellectual outreach as much as science also failed. He went public with a statement in the *Independent*, addressing the question "What Is the Trouble with Religion?" Some people, Bascom wrote, say that nothing is wrong with religion, and that we should have no trouble if everyone simply accepted the established truths that religion has given us. Were religion that simple, Bascom replied, the problem would not exist. But this view casts religion too narrowly. Bascom insisted that we have multiple means of approaching religion, which, like a large mountain, can be assailed from many sides. "The spiritual world," Bascom wrote, "is a large world and a strange one to the feet of men; and it cannot be known by traveling along a single, defined path." He also hastened to characterize religion as "a living experience." He likened it to a fine art; "it is a peculiar and high experience into which the soul half sees, half feels its way." Religion, like science, Bascom believed, must loosen the reins of the vision that drives it. His remarks in the *Independent* concurred with a large project that had been engaging him for some time, for he had concluded that Christianity in America needed a "new theology."[20]

19. Bascom, *Natural Theology*, 97–98; idem, *Philosophy of Religion*, 98–102, 109–10.

20. John Bascom, "What Is the Trouble with Religion?," *Independent*, June 16, 1881, 3. D. H. Meyer, in his study of American moral philosophy, credits Bascom with helping to break from the idea of fixed moral truth, secure in its independent ontological status. He finds a key passage in the textbook Bascom wrote at Madison: "As controlling circumstances are always changing, as social life is ever unfolding, the moral law never remains the same for any considerable period, and is hardly twice alike in its application. . . . An absolute and unchanging right in action is illusory." Meyer, *Instructed Conscience*, 128; John Bascom, *Ethics or Science of Duty* (New York: G. P. Putnam's Sons, 1879), 354.

The "New Theology" became a mantra of the liberal theology movement in the post–Civil War period, the era in American religious history that Sydney Ahlstrom called "The Golden Age of Protestant Liberalism."[21] Bascom introduced his New Theology formally in his baccalaureate address at Madison in 1884 and had the address reprinted in the *Christian Union*. (A year earlier, theologian Theodore Munger of Andover Theological Seminary had titled an essay "The New Theology," in his book *The Freedom of Faith*.) Bascom outlined key points that he expanded in other places and ultimately into his book of 1891, which has this name. Bascom, as did much of the liberal movement, gave considerable attention to Reason and revelation. Partisans of one or the other in the churches, Bascom noted, had quarreled bitterly over the primacy each side favored in Christian theology. But Bascom judged the dispute unecessary; Reason and revelation, he proclaimed, "culminate at one point; are gathered up in the same clear and serene light." Bascom, however, effected this union only by severely diminishing the weight of "Revelation" as understood by the conservative theologians, that is, as the revealed word of God in scripture. For true revelation really signifies Reason. "Reason," Bascom, explained, "stands for all our powers of knowledge in their full, harmonious, successful action." Revelation does not constitute something distinct from Reason; it is Reason. Bascom, however, gave Reason all the trump cards over Revelation. "Revelation so far as it is not addressed to reason, or grasped by reason, is not Revelation."[22]

The New Theology had yet more to offer. For Bascom it signified a God in history, whose governance occurred procedurally, in progression, and in an unfolding revelation. Bascom, however, did not speak merely of a gradual disclosure of a remote inspiration. A God in history meant for him a God in the world. Progression bore along with it renovation, reconstruction, social amelioration, and advancement toward the earthly Kingdom of God. Bascom thus asserted that "the new theology does not separate itself from this work of regeneration in society as we actually find it." Here for Bascom and many other liberals theology found its fullest application in the Social Gospel. The work of improving the world gathered hope from the idea of God's progressive manifestation in human history. A theology of immanence became normative to the new liberalism. But for Bascom, one new idea especially gave the imprimatur of science to this new theology, the idea he called "the great thought of our time": evolution. Evolution brought everything together for Bascom. It assisted

---

21. Sydney E. Ahlstrom, *A Religious History of the American People* (New Haven, CT: Yale University Press, 1972), chap. 46.

22. John Bascom, "The New Theology," *Christian Union* 30 (July 10, 1884), 37.

him crucially in solidifying his world view but also in deriving the social agenda that marked his career at Wisconsin. And it underscored the curricular purposes of higher education in the state, the new education, as Bascom was presenting it. Thus Bascom could write passionately at the end of his address to the Wisconsin students: "We seem to see the kingdom of heaven coming along these very lines of union between scientific research and religious insight; man and God, nature and the supernatural working together for a perfect individual and social life, redeeming the present and by it marching victoriously into the future." Of course, that promise also depended on a correct understanding of evolution.[23]

The idea of evolution gave liberal Protestantism new leverage in the later nineteenth century. By its appropriation the liberal theists found a ready means of accommodating modern science. Evolution also gave new and compelling expression to Christian ideas about the unity of creation. It gave inspiration to those liberals who saw their faith active in the world, advancing Christian ideas of benevolence and social improvement. And, to many in this group, evolution suggested a teleological promise that God had designs for the realization of the earthly kingdom.[24] Consider some of the publications that emerged from the new preoccupation with evolution: Minot J. Savage, *The Religion of Evolution* (1876); Henry Ward Beecher, *Evolution and Religion* (1885); Lyman Abbott, *The Evolution of Christianity* (1892) and his *The Theology of an Evolutionist* (1897); James McCosh, *The Religious Aspect of Evolution* (1890); George Harris, *Moral Evolution* (1896), and Bascom's own *Evolution and Religion* (1897).

An earlier chapter reviewed Bascom's first encounter with Charles Darwin's thesis. When he took up the subject again some eight years later, Bascom had reason to think that a facile theistic accommodation of Darwin had placed Christian thinking at risk. Bascom said that he wrote his textbook *Natural Theology* in order to make clarifications and corrections concerning evolution. Darwinism and other naturalistic versions of the idea, Bascom feared, were having the effect of turning attention back to creation and away from divine intervention. But such a shift, he protested, deprives evolution of its sustaining harmony, its wholeness, those features that we find not so much in an original deed but in an ongoing activity and oversight that takes in all the vast and impressive data that science supplies. Bascom here sounded a major theme in Liberal Protestantism's

23. Bascom, "New Theology," 37–38.

24. Gary Dorrien, *The Making of American Liberal Theology: Imagining Progressive Religion, 1805–1900* (Louisville: Westminster John Knox Press, 2001), 299–30.

endorsement of evolution.[25] Focused on that process, he also assured, we must not allow evolution to lapse into merely physical laws. Some kind of progressive deism, such as a theory that would posit all the future history of earth and man in some original nebula, gives in fact only a mechanical rendering of evolution.[26]

Bascom believed that evolution enhanced theism, but only when seen through the mind of philosophical idealism. The empiricist may see design, but only in each work as a separate creation. Theologian William Paley described a man finding a watch and from its intricate parts posits a watchmaker. But evolution, Bascom argued, affords a vastly more magnificent view of things, of design, expansive in scope, but also reflecting ongoing work over immense stretches of time. And throughout we see patterns and forms perpetuated, modified, but withal showing a unity, even across species transformed over millennia. These broad relations, Bascom affirmed, "disclose the lines of rational construction." And for Bascom, furthermore, no other doctrine or theory could better illustrate the dynamics of the two great realities of life: the physical and the spiritual. Bascom said that in the past, human error lay in exaggerating the supernatural; today error lies in exaggeration of the natural at the expense of the other. Evolution, however, perfectly restores the balance. Now we see the world as the critical interplay of the two forces, and we no longer perpetuate the rigid dualism that has led us astray.[27]

Bascom's contribution here gave further visibility to the significant intellectual role he was playing at the University of Wisconsin. He made that institution a citadel of Protestant liberal theology among the universities of the United

25. Or, as Henry Ward Beecher put it cryptically: "Design by wholesale is grander than design by retail." James R. Moore, *The Post-Darwinian Controversies: A Study of the Protestant Struggle to Come to Terms with Darwinism in Great Britain and America, 1870–1900* (Cambridge: Cambridge University Press, 1979), 221. Bascom's former student Washington Gladden subscribed enthusiastically to evolution as the new and sure foundation of religion. He offered an immanentist conception of divine reality "by which all these fragments are knit together in unity." Science, Gladden asserted, was supplying a surer foundation for religious understanding "far more firm and broad than that on which men rested their souls in what were known as the ages of faith." Dorrien, *Making of Theology*, 317.

26. Bascom, *Natural Theology*, 125–26; idem, "Philosophical Results of a Denial of Miracles," *Princeton Review*, n.s., 8 (July–December 1881), 88.

27. Bascom, *Natural Theology*, 147–48, 190–91, 194–99; idem, *The Natural and the Supernatural* [Baccalaureate Sermon] (Milwaukee: Cramer, Aikens & Cramer, 1883), 15.

States and the most important location of evolutionary theism among the state universities of the nation. Bascom did even more. He addressed religion, and he examined Christianity in all its many parts. He gave attention to subjects such as "inspiration," "interpretation," "miracles," "atonement," "sin," and "immortality," in far greater breadth and substance than any of his presidential peers. His writings in these subjects offer intriguing material and impose on this author the question of how much attention to give them. The brief review that concludes this chapter represents a selective reading and one that looks for clues to the next chapter, that is, Bascom's version of the Social Gospel, his early formulation of the Wisconsin Idea, and the reform politics of the later nineteenth century.

For at least three reasons Bascom wanted to take up matters of Christian belief. For one, he never believed that natural theology sufficed in itself to describe the life of true religion, or all of its intellectual content. Too often the God drawn from nature looks like nature, he said. That God, author of physical laws, submits to physical laws. Then the Divine Mind, put in back of the natural regime, becomes superfluous to it. Bascom would insist on seeing God as a personality and a being of supernatural powers. No other God can inspire true devotion as opposed to mere appreciation. Religion, furthermore, needs the rituals of worship, Bascom believed, as appropriate to a God so experienced. But the God of natural theism, Bascom feared, does not yield a God to be prayed to.[28]

Second, Bascom wanted to bring important aspects of Christian theology under review, and to revise them. He castigated the doctrine of vicarious atonement, the notion of Jesus's taking on all the sins of humankind, because, he said, it corrupted and diminished the true process of redemption. That process, Bascom said, leads through a slow course of repentance and regeneration. It not only requires of us careful nurture of our inner spiritual nature, but roots us in an organic life that includes the world outside, in short, society. Redemption demands our reorientation toward "living forces." God does, to be sure, work for the redemption of the race, but never by divine fiat. In vicarious atonement, Bascom objected, "a single achieved result is substituted for a living, ongoing, organic process." That process rebuilds the world, it fights against the evils in it, it looks for moral amelioration; in short, it builds the earthly Kingdom of Heaven. One can anticipate readily here that Bascom's strenuous faulting of vicarious atonement had much to do with his own effort to define and apply a

28. Bascom, *Natural Theology*, 228–30.

social gospel. Thus, he insisted, this errant doctrine "contravenes the work of God in the world."[29]

And third, John Bascom did believe in miracles, and wished to make the case for them. The idea won an easy acceptance in his thinking, for good philosophy pointed right to it. In fact, there was really nothing miraculous about a miracle at all, he believed. By this term, he said, we mean the intervention of a higher power in nature, with results that do not fall within the strict chain of physical forces. A miracle, Bascom wrote, "is but a disclosure of the supernatural beyond its ordinary limits." The act registers the work of those other forces not within our sight, not accessible by our sensory faculties. He called it "an overbearing power before which the laws and forces of nature give ground." We may label the phenomenon an intervention, a disruption, or a transcending of natural law, but it always signifies the essential nature of reality itself, as dually constituted by the natural and the supernatural. "If we include mind as well as matter in nature," Bascom wrote, "we then have in nature two laws, one of necessity and one of liberty." Bascom did not discuss the miracles of scripture. He felt no need to, though he did acknowledge that some reports of them reflected an age too much given to the supernatural. Bascom wished only to show to the modern intellect the ontological reasonableness of miracles. On that truth, Christianity secured its own credibility, he insisted. Christianity, from the early New Testament and in its understanding of the Incarnation, speaks most authentically to a correct philosophy, Bascom maintained. Writing in his *Philosophy of Religion* he spoke in a way that carried a conviction that he first embraced in his study with Laurens Hickok: "Christianity stands or falls through philosophy, a philosophy of liberty and spiritual intuitions."[30]

All of John Bascom's writing that this chapter has examined came from his Wisconsin years. They give substance to what J. F. A. Pyre and Edward Birge said about Bascom's affecting the intellectual life of the University in his years as president. But Bascom also created an atmosphere and set a tone for the institution. As he did in his philosophical system, Bascom upheld freedom as

29. Bascom, *Philosophy of Religion*, 457–58, 473, 452. Bascom also addressed the matter of immortality, which he affirmed. *Philosophy of Religion*, 480–81, 522, 528–29, and in relation to evolution, 183, 185, 190; idem, *Natural Theology*, 289.

30. Bascom, "The Gains and Losses of Faith from Science," *Christian Philosophy Quarterly* 1 (July 1882), 15–16 (first quotation); idem, *Philosophy of Religion*, 268–70 (second quotation), 322 (third quotation).

the lifeblood of the university. Another student remembered: "He knew and maintained that freedom can thrive only where there is intellectual independence, and where there is absolute freedom of inquiry and investigation." Bascom wanted each student to have as much choice of courses as possible at the university, free to support his or her unique nature. Truth always remained a high ideal for Bascom but he insisted on an open-ended pursuit of it. He made that point using, again, one of his favorite podiums, the baccalaureate sermon. "Inquiry," the president told his audience, "is a continuous, living, process. It is not the work of one man, or generation, or period." And so must the modern university approach its work. In philosophy, he believed, we work to arrive at "the provisional opinion." And that standard applies to all fields of learning, as it did, most importantly for Bascom, to theology.[31] And from Bascom's theology came his sociology and his version of the Social Gospel.

31. Justice Robert G. Siebecker, "Address on Behalf of the Alumni," in *Memorial Service in Honor of John Bascom*. . . . (n.p., n.d.), 14; [John Bascom], "Report of the President of the University to the Board of Regents," in *Annual Report of the Board of Regents of the University of Wisconsin, for the Fiscal Year Ending September 30, 1878* (Madison, 1878), 35; idem, "President's Report, 1882," 29 (electives); idem, *Truth and Truthfulness* [Baccalaureate Sermon] (Milwaukee: Cramer, Aikens & Cramer, 1881), 20.

5

The University and the Social Gospel

For John Bascom, an idealist philosophy that described the interaction of material and spiritual things in dynamic relations always had social extensions. He had made that connection clear in the essays he contributed to *Bibliotheca Sacra* in the late 1860s and early 1870s, but it became a major preoccupation for him after he became president of the University of Wisconsin. Now social and political questions took a higher ground in his thinking. His baccalaureate sermons, for one, take up one issue after another. He increased his contributions to the *Independent*, the most widely circulated voice of religious progressivism in the United States. Then, too, he had his classroom. Lectures he presented there found their way into a book he published in his last year at the university, one simply titled *Sociology*. He had much by way of theory in it, but, as Bascom hastened to emphasize, "there is a predominant interest in questions of immediate moment to society" also.[1]

This chapter builds from the previous one and carries Bascom's liberal Protestantism into his construction of a social gospel. That project, insofar as Bascom applied it to matters of state and university, constitutes his rendering of the Wisconsin Idea. Bascom's social gospel also carried into his specific social reform causes: temperance, women's rights, and the labor movement, each detailed in successive chapters.

Sociology and other social sciences, as noted earlier, grew out of academic moral philosophy. The subject retained much of that origin well into the late nineteenth century, but along the way, and more earnestly after the Civil War,

---

1. John Bascom, *Sociology* (New York: G. P. Putnam's Sons, 1887), v.

University of Wisconsin Campus, 1876. (University of Wisconsin–Madison Archives, S03079)

social thinkers sought to detach it from ethics. At Harvard, for example, President Eliot replaced Francis Bowen, who continued in moral philosophy, with Charles F. Dunbar, who in 1871 now became specifically professor of political economy. In an essay five years later Dunbar made clear that he, too, wanted to detach his subject from its longstanding connection to ethics and to establish it on its own basis. "The United States," he wrote, "have, thus far, done nothing toward developing the theory of political economy." For Dunbar and others, the social sciences would gain when they became just that, sciences. Hence one heard frequently the call to root these subjects in facts, and often with an accompanying endorsement of positivism. At the Sheffield School at Yale, Francis Amasa Walker placed in his *Political Economy* book of 1884 an exhortation that economists shun all moral axioms and sentiments. He purported at least to welcome in a new imperium of fact.[2]

Bascom would no more yield to this imperium than he would yield to the empiricists in metaphysics. If thinkers went wrong on the philosophy, they would go wrong on the sociology. Thus, said Bascom, "a sound philosophy

2. Dorothy Ross, *The Origins of American Social Science* (Cambridge: Cambridge University Press, 1991), 78–79.

must always be of leading importance in Sociology." And for him sociology was moral to the core. It could no more restrict its field of inquiry to observation of social conditions and reporting of empirical data than could the scientists restrict their vision to material substance. Bascom brought to sociology, indeed extended from it, his philosophical idealism. And when fortified by his growing appreciation for evolutionary theory, his sociology became the location of God's growing presence in human history. It recorded the advancing of the species in moral awareness, and disclosed a progressive revelation. Evolution illustrated the immanent presence of the supernatural in a historical trajectory. Under these conditions, and these alone, Bascom believed, did a tangible agenda of political reform make any sense or have any relevance. Furthermore, Bascom always insisted that the moral substance of sociology did not descend from afar onto the arena of human behavior; we move toward apprehension of it as we find our way through the social data and grasp by observation and intuition those moral realities. In this way Bascom might be said to have reversed the emphasis of the Scottish moral philosophers: "Sociology," he wrote, "culminates in moral philosophy." Sociology is an exercise of Reason.[3] In this particular combination of idealist philosophy and social science Bascom stood out among his American peers in the late nineteenth century.[4]

In another critical way, Bascom's sociology cut against the grain of academic thinking in the middle and late nineteenth century. He questioned the foundation of economic theories that posited an automatic mechanism for social improvement and that gave credence to laissez-faire formulae. That position emerged in Bascom's Williams years. He was no statist, though, at that point in his career. Nonetheless, his writings placed him at the outer limits of a prevailing orthodoxy. Bascom wrote at a time when free-market thinking still dominated what passed for economic thought in the United States. From Thomas Jefferson and Jacksonian advocates like William Leggett, faith in natural laws that governed the world had gained a clear ascendancy. And they had powerful

3. Bascom, *Sociology*, 257, 57.

4. American intellectual historians have not generally appreciated Bascom's effort. Robert A. Jones is an exception. He writes of Bascom: "What *is* extraordinary is the development of sociological theory out of such an intuitionist epistemology; . . . there is, to my knowledge, no comparable development in late-nineteenth century American sociology." Jones, "John Bascom 1827–1911: Anti-positivism and Intuitionism in American Sociology," *American Quarterly* 24 (October 1972), 506. And for this unusual combination of Kantian epistemology and social theory, Bascom became the most "influential" in this generation of idealist thinkers. Herbert W. Schneider, *A History of American Philosophy* (New York: Columbia University Press, 1946), 242.

reinforcement from European thinkers who claimed an American readership and often gained entry into American college classrooms.[5] Francis Wayland, for example, equated the laws of economics to the laws of God. By an all-wise oversight God coordinates the private ambitions of even the greediest of individuals and in a manner that increases the general welfare, said Wayland and the academic philosophers. As Harvard's moral philosopher Francis Bowen wrote, it is "the reconciliation of private aims with the public advantage" that this grand design achieves. From the Americans, too, came warnings against interference in this marvelous scheme. In Wayland's judgment, for example, poor laws deprived private citizens of the right to use their money as they saw fit and fostered the illegitimate notion that the rich have any obligation to support the poor.[6]

Bascom had as a colleague at Williams one of the foremost defenders of free trade in the United States: Arthur Latham Perry. Perry had published his *Political Economy* in 1856 and it became "a bible of the free trade movement." It went through twenty-two editions. And Perry did not stop there. He traveled the country to support the cause, delivering more than two hundred addresses on behalf of the American Free Trade Association, in his crusade against protectionism. He differed from others of similar views, and from Bascom most definitely, when he insisted that political economy had nothing to do with morality and that economics and moral science were "incommensurable."[7] But moral or amoral, laissez-faire orthodoxy and antistatism stood triumphant and barely challenged at the time Bascom was writing on social science. Historian Sidney Fine observed that "in 1865, though Americans saw a new industrial society emerging, they were without an adequate philosophy of state action to cope with the problems of that society." In fact, in the years that followed the Civil War and down to 1901, Fine says, "laissez faire was championed in

5. Sidney Fine, *Laissez Faire and the General-Welfare State: A Study of Conflict in American Thought, 1865–1901* (Ann Arbor: University of Michigan Press, 1965), 8, 10.

6. Fine, *Laissez Faire*, 8, 10, 52, 53–54. To be sure, state activity had some allowances granted by most political economists: public education, the postal service, provisions for the deaf, dumb, blind, and others in need of protection (58). Wayland, however, said of public provision for the poor that "it is taking from the industrious a portion of their earnings and conferring them, without equivalent, upon the idle." Francis Wayland, *The Elements of Moral Science*, ed. Joseph L. Blau (1837; Cambridge, MA: Belknap Press of Harvard University Press, 1963), 348.

7. Frederick Rudolph, *Mark Hopkins and the Log: Williams College, 1836–1872* (New Haven, CT: Yale University Press, 1956), 55.

America as it never was before and has never been since." Books by Wayland and Perry continued as texts in American colleges down to 1900.[8] Why did Bascom not go this same way? As previously observed, Bascom engaged the subject of evolution—Spencer, Darwin, and the naturalist interpretation of it generally—and gave it a reading that reflected idealism. In turn, evolution governed all of his sociological thinking and the social reform commitments he drew from it. Evolution provided Bascom certain insights that enabled him to advance his case for the state. He looked to the health of the species. Evolution signified to him the priority of the community over individuals, against the Social Darwinists of this time who inverted that priority. That standard also shaped Bascom's model of the organic society. He described it as an emerging ideal in human history, one embracing the principle of inclusiveness. The organic society opened to individuals and groups excluded from locations of power and participation in the larger social whole. Bascom will invoke repeatedly his notion of "harmonized powers" that combine individual freedom with collective strength. Individual liberty that turns into the power and interests of the social organism marks a gain for civilization, he insisted. Liberty not of this nature—self-contained, private, rooted in self-interest alone—becomes "suicidal" for the commonweal. Bascom faced a difficult challenge in explaining a possibly paradoxical idea of individual liberty and social good, but the ideas came through in every topic of contemporary politics he took up.[9]

Evolutionary language found its way into Bascom's descriptions. Because he saw each situation as but one instance in a large temporal extension, he rendered every situation as so located. He would not therefore appeal to universal laws or hard-and-fast moral maxims to measure that situation's legitimacy. One finds very little recourse in Bascom to "natural rights." Impermanence rather than fixity described reality. "Each phase of [growth]," he wrote, "prepares the way for another; each equilibrium for a higher and more complex equilibrium." Complexity for Bascom denoted integration, harmony. "Evolution in life is nothing more than an increase in comprehensiveness and completeness." Equally important, that pattern assures a greater place for the ethical. For moral insight gains, grows, must grow as it takes in a larger vision of life. Bascom had urged this understanding in his essays for the religious press. But at Wisconsin all his writings reflected a greater invocation of an evolutionary

---

8. Three presidents of the Free Trade League had been Williams College students, including David Dudley Field. Fine, *Laissez Faire*, 25, 29; Ross, *Origins*, 77.

9. Bascom, *Sociology*, 33–34.

framework. "Harmonized power," he explained, discloses the moral substance of human relations, raises moral insight into higher consciousness, and conjoins intellectual acquisition with ethical awareness.[10]

These thoughts led Bascom directly into discussion of the state. He gave a broad outline of his statism in *Sociology* but also addressed the subject more urgently in baccalaureate sermons and other public venues. Statism derived from the priority of the collective over the individual and that perspective in turn came from Bascom's critique of individualism. He judged contemporary discussion of the matter, especially as applied to economics, as weighing heavily for rights of the individual "in his primitive endowments." Each individual, says the prevailing notion, is a separate universe wherein specific rights reside, and it becomes the business of the state to see to their protection. These rights seldom bear any reference to others or to the priority of a larger common good, Bascom observed. But for that reason, he went on, we fail terribly in fostering the higher value of the whole, of the organic society. Moreover, and more dangerously, this abstract theory of personal rights, he asserted, assumes an original equality that has never in fact existed. "In the organization of society," Bascom wrote, "individuals have never counted as equal units." They never had an original equality to begin with. And "men do not to-day count as equal units. They never will so count." That fact leaves the matter of justice in a very tenuous situation.[11]

Social contract theories of societal formation often sustain the idea of natural rights theories. Bascom never embraced these theories, whether in Hobbes, Locke, Pufendorf, Rousseau, or Jefferson. He called them "pure fiction," and believed that they badly skew the discussion about rights in general. They begin with individuals and make the state nothing more than the loose amalgamation of these autonomous units. This traditional formula of individual rights fails because "it does not recognize the powers which society itself possesses." And, "A state constructed on this law is not organic," he emphasized. Social contract theories make a fatal miscalculation about the state. "The state," Bascom urged, "is organic, and not composite." It does not consist merely of identical and theoretically equal units. Bascom indicated that individual rights have a legitimate imperative and must demand protection, but his sociology, as evidenced in the *Bibliotheca Sacra* essays, properly postulated that individual rights gain within the viability and power of the larger social organism. Thus wealth and power originate and advance within a large, extended network on whose interconnections they depend. But so recognizing, Bascom insisted, we then

10. Bascom, *Sociology*, 79, 80.
11. Bascom, *Sociology*, 37–38.

must have as strong a conception of civil rights as we do of individual rights. The one needs the other, but a proper distinction between the two has much importance. In a modern community, Bascom pointed out, "the state immensely extends the field of possession, and makes it, through its enlarged domain, far more efficient than it previously was in its narrow bounds." From patent law to corporate law, he illustrated, the state creates protections and helps coordinate the extended transactions that foster economic exchange. These protections constitute civil rights; they derive from the power and action of the state, Bascom explained.[12]

Civil rights thus create new powers, but new responsibilities, too. Powers that grow from state protection can easily and do almost inevitably grow to monolithic size. Wealth feeds on wealth, and stark inequalities become visible. Such an imbalance, Bascom urged, impairs the organism. Concentration of power erodes conditions of wide opportunity, social disparities grow, and the social organization no longer functions in a healthy equilibrium. The state, Bascom insisted, has every right to correct the imbalance. To be sure, it would err dangerously, he said, in trying to effect an exact equality. Bascom took care to warn also of excessive state power. The ethics textbook he wrote for his university classes made that point clear. The state, he said, is not "a controlling organism in which the individual is swallowed up." But it would also err in ignoring inequality. A doctrine that recognizes only individual rights will deprive the state of any ability to address the "extreme inequalities" that result. "The state must also by every just device restore the conditions of renewed organization. . . . This is the very difficult task of government. In this movable equilibrium the justice of to-day becomes the injustice of to-morrow." The interests of the social organism, then, call for constant adjudication, may even require transfer of advantage from group to group. The state's constant adjudication of powers, fine-tuning as it were, is what Bascom meant by a "movable equilibrium." It is the organism's way of adjusting to its changing environment.[13]

This situation assigned a major role to the state, which became for Bascom the primal agency of freedom and equality. His narrative in *Sociology* inscribed this point in what appear almost like a series of maxims. Hence:

- "The state must find its power in the individual, the individual must command the full powers of the state. This is a government of the people for the people."

12. John Bascom, *Ethics or Science of Duty* (New York: G. P. Putnam's Sons, 1879), 211–12, 224 (first quotation); idem, *Sociology*, 40–42.

13. Bascom, *Sociology*, 44–45; idem, *Ethics*, 217.

- "The race is to be renewed, morning, noon and night, on equal terms."
- "The state must thus be benevolent as well as just. While it takes from no man what he has, it must not allow any man such an exercise of his powers as will ultimately swallow up the powers of other men."
- "The widest and most inclusive diffusion of power, issuing in the largest aggregate of power, is the aim of society."
- "All social movement, left to simply primary, natural tendencies, gravitates toward tyranny."[14]

Bascom advanced his views amid a turn in Protestant thinking. Whereas one challenge to religious orthodoxy issued from modern science and evolution, another emerged from social issues. In increasing numbers after 1830 or so, religious individuals spoke out against slavery. But when they engaged religious defenders of the vile institution, they found themselves at quite a disadvantage; they simply could not have recourse to the Bible for intellectual ammunition in their cause. If not positively defensive of slavery, the scriptures stood otherwise indifferent in the matter. But the progressive religionists knew that Christianity could not coexist with slavery. And they found their best strategy by effecting new, liberal understandings of Christian revelation. So finds historian Molly Oshatz in her study of this critical shift. Liberals now looked to the moral substance of God's word, as opposed to literal biblical statements; they asserted that the Bible's full meaning breaks out in the long path of human history. The key factor in that trajectory lies in humans' growth in moral awareness, over time and with experience, so that they could better discern God's true intentions. God also had a preparatory role, these theists maintained. The societies of Old Testament times and even those concurrent with Jesus's life could not fully discern a divine judgment against slavery. But they could do so in 1850. Albert Barnes, a leader among the New School Presbyterians, spoke for all the liberals when he wrote in 1857: "The *spirit* [my emphasis] of the New Testament is against slavery." And if one taps and applies its true principles, slavery will die.[15]

14. Bascom, *Sociology*, 44, 45, 46, 48, 210.

15. Quoted in Molly Oshatz, "The Problem of Moral Progress: The Slavery Debate and the Development of Liberal Protestantism in the United States," *Modern Intellectual History* 5 (August 2008), 227–28. See also her larger study, *Slavery and Sin: The Fight against Slavery and the Rise of Liberal Protestantism* (New York: Oxford University Press, 2011). See also Mark A. Noll, *America's God: From Jonathan Edwards to Abraham Lincoln* (New York: Oxford University Press, 2002), 367–445; and E. Brooks Holifield, *Theology in America: Christian Thought from the Age of the Puritans to the Civil War* (New Haven, CT: Yale University Press, 2003), 494–504.

John Bascom could endorse all these readings. They reinforced his liberal theology. Now some of the liberal theologians, but by no means all, took the matter beyond slavery into the social crisis standing starkly visible in the Gilded Age: the problem of wealth and poverty, class antagonisms, the labor movement. Bascom looked there to find new outlets for the Social Gospel; it had a very big field in which to work.

His ideas about government and the state provided a linchpin for Bascom as he addressed these reform issues. Here he cut directly against the grain of academic orthodoxy and its laissez-faire and free-market standards. What he said about the importance of the state in the era of big business and class tensions in the late nineteenth century placed him in line with the rethinking being done by the more visible reformers at work in the political system: the Populists of his day and the Progressives who were beginning to organize by the time Bascom left Wisconsin. The idea of the positive state grounded the Wisconsin Idea. But it bore with it a religious, moral, and spiritual content that marks Bascom's special contribution to the Wisconsin Idea in its origins.

One could list a large number of reformist intellectuals in Gilded Age America, and they would offer comparisons with Bascom. But one in particular has a suggestive parallel to the Wisconsin president—the sociologist Lester Frank Ward. He, too, employed a Darwinian perspective to the social issues of the time, especially in his monumental work, *Dynamic Sociology* (1883). Ward contrasts emphatically with Bascom, however, in his wholly secularist framework. Nonetheless, the views of government and the state that Ward advanced in his "Reform Darwinism" register the same views of Bascom. Each contributed to the important intellectual shift in American liberalism, from its classic laissez-faire libertarianism to its statist position in the Progressive Era of American history that followed. Among philosophers John Dewey played the most important role in effecting this transition.[16]

Bascom fully understood the obstacles to the reconstruction he sought to effect. America, after all, was the land of the free, of individuals given the gift of inalienable liberties, protected against the constriction and control of state and society. Secured in the Enlightenment thinking of the eighteenth century and inscribed in the founding document of the nation, the priority of the individual seemed triumphant and normative in the American ethos since the national

16. On Ward, see Edward C. Rafferty, *Apostle of Human Progress: Lester Frank Ward and American Political Thought, 1841–1913* (Lanham, MD: Rowman & Littlefield, 2003). Bascom wrote a substantial review of Ward's two-volume work. See his "Dynamic Sociology," *Dial* 4 (July 1883), 59–61.

birth. To be sure, mainstream American politics, especially in the Whig and Republican Parties with whom Bascom usually identified, had assigned important powers to the federal government, especially in endorsing a national economics that made the government a partner with business in economic growth that benefited all.[17] But Bascom feared that in the new era of powerful capitalism, of immense personal and corporate wealth, Americans had insufficient intellectual resources to prevent its worst social consequences. As he said in his last address at the university, "We are in the full swing of individual assertion. Unbridled enterprise is our controlling temper." Anything that government or public power sought to do by way of redressing the disparities of wealth and power, the deprivation of so many people excluded from integration with the larger community, simply brought suspicion and raised the cry of state tyranny, Bascom observed.[18]

Bascom also saw another conspirator against the state in the blind optimism Americans had about nature and country. According to the maxim, the unfettered course of nature assures that matters will work out well in the long run. Nature, or Providence, has certified that pursuit of individual interest somehow conspires to assure the common good, which needs no boost from interfering government. Bascom judged these uncritical theories of individual self-interest, and the canon of individual rights in the business arena built on such conviction, as dangerous thinking. Against such hardened prejudices, he feared, the state struggled for legitimation. Progressives like Bascom and Ward had to find ways to convince people that public power befit ideas about evolution and human progress even more worthily than did anarchic notions of unrestrained individual rights. Until the state wins this needed authority, Bascom urged, it will languish in weakness and helplessness and all the manifest social ills of the day will intensify unabated. Bascom often cited the great conservative Edmund Burke to reinforce his point. If we allow each individual to seek what he regards as his own liberty and without regard to the public measure, we have a result that Burke greatly feared. "The commonwealth itself in a few generations crumbles away," Burke wrote, "is disconnected into the dust and powder of individuality, and is at length dispersed to all [the] winds of heaven."[19]

17. Bascom, *Ethics*, 290–91.

18. John Bascom, *A Christian State* [Baccalaureate Sermon] (Milwaukee: Cramer, Aikens & Cramer, 1887), 10 (quotation), 4; idem, "The Functions of the State," *Independent*, January 31, 1889, 4; idem, "Fealty to the State," *Independent*, January 6, 1876, 3.

19. Bascom, "Functions of the State," 4; idem, "What Do the Members of a State University Owe to the State?," *University Review* 1 (December 1884), 92; idem, *Christian State*, 25 (Bascom is quoting Burke from his *Reflections on the Revolution in France*, 1790).

Burke surely had an easier time in England than Bascom did in the United States in trying to make a case for the state and its long and legitimate place in the national history. Like Burke, Bascom wanted people to think of the state as not merely an ad hoc assemblage of functions put in place to address quotidian matters and make the needed improvements. Fear of government, he said, often left it with only these "mechanical" functions. Like Burke, Bascom wanted the state to have a certain hold on people's imagination, to carry within themselves ideas of a transcendent good, a higher ideal to which all, as a collective unity, may claim a connection. Bascom also valued in Burke that statesman's notion of the higher social self. As individuals struggle against their low and base instincts and seek to realize their true moral and spiritual natures, so should society itself aspire. This higher ideal, Bascom hoped, would translate narrow self-interest into public awareness and social goodwill, would enlarge the "narrow, astute and unscrupulous impulses of commerce," the drive to individual power and wealth, and the "cunning of men" into a vision of the social organism's own special identity.[20]

Bascom wanted to instill in American thinking a feeling for the state as a real entity, a self, a living creation that had its own interests, its own needs, all of which drew directly from the individuals, the collectivity, that made it. Where should we direct our attention? Bascom asked, in one of his first baccalaureate sermons at Wisconsin. Not so much to the individual but to those points of our lives that constitute our common, social selves, he answered. He then evoked a norm, an ideal that he wished to have a large place in people's thinking: "the permanent life of the race, this pervasive life of the whole human family." In our immediate lives, and in this age of nations, he added, the state best acts as agency of this great truth. Bascom often used language that helped reify the state in people's imagination. "The state itself," he wrote, "is the repository of a grand aggregate of powers . . . which belong to all citizens in common." It must have its own identity, built of its many components but serving to promote justice between them, and thus requiring an independence, too. "Society as a whole," Bascom added, "is a third party in all inquiries concerning what is just and unjust in conduct."[21]

Once we begin to think of the state in this manner, we justly acknowledge its own rights, powers, and opportunities to adapt and thrive as the world about

20. Bascom, "What Do the Members?," 98; idem, *Education and the State* [Baccalaureate Sermon] (Madison: Democrat Co., 1877), 8.

21. John Bascom, *The Seat of Sin* [Baccalaureate Sermon] (n.p., [1876]), 14; idem, *Christian State*, 21.

it changes, Bascom asserted. To think of the state, to imagine the state as an organism, takes a first big step in that right direction. Bascom's understanding of evolution taught him to describe human progress in terms of greater integration of parts, the interrelatedness of them all in operations and actions that protect the whole, that is, what we should label the social organism. But he feared that American social thinking had not kept pace with modern science. We do not think of the whole, he lamented, and we exercise an "unreasonable timidity" toward the social organism. We must acknowledge that the state has its own legitimate interests, the common good, and thus the right "to complete its own organization," the integration that assures a healthy, functioning organism. Bascom wanted to place these considerations in an expanded evolutionary schemata. So again we must think of "intelligence," as always for humans the agency of their collective adaptation, as necessary for the social organism as it is for the individual. "Intelligence," Bascom said, "should be fruitful in collective as well as in individual effort." This conception makes the state society's brain, its agent of adaptation. The state is not a passive entity. It, too, must work by trial and error, by experimentation in legislation and bureaucratic initiatives. It must be active.[22]

But Bascom wished to do even more by way of defending the right principles of statism and to advance the idea of public power and authority at a time when all honor seemed to fall to powerful individuals. So he fortified his case, as he always did, by bringing these matters into moral and religious contexts. Once Bascom invoked evolution, and within it the organic nature of society, he had done the important contextualizing. For, as seen earlier, evolution made sense to Bascom only as a spiritual phenomenon, one that reflected philosophical idealism's ideas about the relation of the spiritual and the material. The organic idea in human society, Bascom believed, advanced and grew as a reality along the trajectory of evolutionary progress. Perfection of the social organism, which for Bascom necessitated an enlarged domain of authority and the expanded application of collective intelligence, had theological import. "Society is truly organic," Bascom wrote, "and that too, under a divine life." In the theology of divine immanence that Bascom drew from evolution, the state had a particular place. It registered the progressive immersion of God into human society.[23]

It registered morality, too. Bascom placed the moral intuitions into a social context and gave them the largest field of operation he could. Moral experience

---

22. Bascom, *Christian State*, 21, 28; idem, "Functions of the State," 4 (quotation).
23. Bascom, *Christian State*, 10.

grows as it embraces more and more of its field of operation. Enlarged connections energize moral power. Bascom easily followed this thinking into the state
and the diverse realms in which government works. "The State," he wrote, "is
perpetually passing into new fields of activity." For the state thrives as the critical
locus of the social organism, its head, its conscience, its will. Often Bascom took
familiar religious language, particularly that of the Protestant evangelicals, and
gave it a social rendering. Thus, he urged, "redemption in ourselves and in
society—this is our watchword." "The conversion of the individual is of small
amount save as it leads to the conversion of society." "Society is, in its sentiments,
the seat of sin. It must be made in its sentiments the seat of righteousness."
Morality centered increasingly and progressively in the state, a state self-
consciously aware of its own identity as protector of a real public interest.
Bascom was already applying that principle to public policy. He would allow
no individual and no group, and no theory of individual or corporate rights, to
rend the social organism.[24]

All these pronunciations Bascom made in the name of a "Christian Society"
as well. Jesus's teachings also supplied his idea of the state. Whig and Republican
political culture had long mixed religion with political agendas, especially in
assigning to the state a moral function in enhancing the health of the nation.
Bascom certainly endorsed that kind of politics, as in temperance and antislavery. But he also took the Whig and Republican moral outreach much
further, into the social class issues of the late nineteenth century. When he did
so, he amplified his activism, as the successive chapters will show.

In his own effort to enlarge the meaning of a social gospel, and to give his
version an application especially suited to a changing America, Bascom added
a new ingredient: the state university. Religion, as observed in the last chapter,
still occupied a substantial place in American higher education. Bascom never
doubted that religion should have such a place. But he also carefully articulated
how the large debate about the new curriculum and the new scholarly purposes
of the university would not only secure a religious substance to its academic
work, but also, in the case of the public university, serve a larger social, reformist
purpose.

Like Henry P. Tappan before him and like others in his own time, Bascom
had to refute charges that the state university embodies a secular culture and a
standard of scientific neutrality that make it irreligious and amoral. Rivalries

24. Bascom, *Seat of Sin*, 14, 14n, 16; idem, "Functions of the State," 4; idem, *Christian State*, 20.

between the new state universities and the older religious colleges fueled these charges of "infidelity" and challenged presidents and other defenders of the state schools to show otherwise. Bascom came to Wisconsin from a struggling, small college, and yet one far better off than literally hundreds of similar schools, most of them with Protestant denominational affiliations. He believed he knew firsthand the academic deficiencies of these places and would engage in no sentimentality such as now President Garfield had done in celebrating Mark Hopkins and the log. Again he used the baccalaureate sermon as his bully pulpit. The colleges serve a useful purpose, especially to their sponsoring religious groups, Bascom allowed, but they "drag on in poverty" and cannot bear the burden the nation requires from higher education today.[25] Bascom had two large points to make on the greater usefulness of the new state universities over the small colleges.

For one, Bascom believed that the state universities served as harmonizing agencies in a United States where diversity—ethnic, religious, and more increasingly social class—challenged its national identity as never before. In the era of new immigration this challenge to assimilation intensifies, he pointed out. Many in this group and in the nation generally have no attachments to religion and find the sectarian schools "distasteful," Bascom observed. Many other people, however, still wanted public funds to go to these colleges instead of to their state university. Bascom deplored that preference. He contrasted the states of Ohio and Michigan. The first, he observed, has small colleges in proliferation. They have a poor record in scholarship and have kept its state university in mean condition. Michigan showed a different pattern; it had fewer sectarian colleges but, it had the University of Michigan, which Wisconsin had long emulated. That institution had wide state support. The University of Michigan, Bascom indicated, "commands an influence and concentrates an educational energy compared with which the power of any one of [the private] institutions is insignificant." That state university, furthermore, had helped unify the state through the whole system of public education and had a record of superior scholarship. Altogether, Bascom believed, Michigan's state university promoted an "organic" growth for the state.[26]

In a national forum Bascom made a plea for state universities the year after his arrival in Madison. The United States, he said, cannot let so crucial a matter as its advanced education rest on the goodwill and charity of those loyal to the

25. Bascom, *Education and the State*, 9.

26. Bascom, *Education and the State*, 9–11, 15–16 (quotation); idem, "The State University," *Independent*, August 26, 1875, 7.

small sectarian colleges. If nothing else, they serve only to perpetuate the fragmentation of our social body. They ill serve its organic needs, the harmonization process. Thus the happenstance situation that prevails now, he added, "is egregiously unjust to the state itself" and to the nation as a whole. The demands of the day turn our attention to science and technology, keys to economic progress. We need institutions that can promote research in these fields, and the small colleges, overburdened as they are, cannot possibly meet the demands. The state has a duty and an interest in sustaining its university. "Higher education is not a branch of business," Bascom urged. "It does not directly pay for itself. It is not right that its burden should be thrown as a charity on a few, rather than as a duty upon the many. It is unworthy of a great state to do this."[27]

Bascom's conception of the state university fit very well with his entire social philosophy, especially its organic ideals and evolution's scheme of advancing harmony and integration in the human race. The whole idea of "the public" appealed to Bascom. Therefore, he pleaded in the *Independent*: "The state university is a general and common possession." It serves the public in a way that the small colleges cannot. "It exerts a correspondingly broad, universal influence." Bascom wanted that influence to begin in the state's program of public education, from the lowest to the highest levels. He spoke often on the need for integration, and urged that the lower schools orient their instructional programs so as to make a continuous line of subject matter preparatory to the university at Madison. As it is now, Bascom indicated, "Our education in all or almost all of our states lacks completeness, organic dependence, the ministration of all parts to each and each to all." So did Bascom implore in his baccalaureate sermon in 1880, titled "Tests of a School-system." "Does [the] system build up the state in all its powers, and harmonize it in all its interests, and strengthen it in all its liberties?" he asked. Here Bascom stated another recommendation for public education, one that he would give broad application to social issues. Public education should enhance the public spirit. It should give life in our thought and imagination to the reality of the state and the common good. It will need such a vivid sense to meet the designs of powerful, private interests that injure the social organism.[28]

Meeting the charges against them, Bascom had to address the religious and moral pedagogy of the state universities. Here he seized an opportunity and

27. Bascom, "State University," 7.

28. Bascom, "State University," 7; idem, "The State University," *Independent,* July 22, 1875, 2; idem, *Tests of a School-system* [Baccalaureate Sermon] (Milwaukee: Cramer, Aikens & Cramer, 1880), 10 (quotation).

here he placed the last component in his comprehensive social gospel as related to higher education. Simply stated, his position asserted the superior ability of the state institution to instill a truly religious education. And by religious Bascom meant everything that one would expect from his lengthy writings on theology and religious practice. Thus, on the many occasions in which he tried to address the current ills of religion, he cited its dogmatism, its attachment to creeds, its obsession with asserting and enforcing fixed truth. Insofar as the sectarian colleges have denominational loyalties and are under the sponsorship of religious organizations, Bascom believed, they suffer from a static intellect, "instruction that is narrowed down to a single dogmatic system, and enforced on all sides as an authoritative belief."[29]

Bascom had three reinforcing points to make on behalf of the state university. First, he asserted that it could advance religion in religion's best and most common character—its service to morality. Morality, Bascom affirmed, underscores all religious teaching; it provides the common core that thrives amid the theological fine points that have so long fostered disunity in the Christian churches. The state universities, then, may not promote a particular religious faith or creed, but "only the more strongly and clearly may their attention be turned to a beautiful and fruitful ethical life—the culmination of religion." Bascom had always placed religion in the world, its purpose to foster social ideals of love and harmony. This role, he claimed, conjoined the religious life and God's great work for the human race in its collective needs. For Bascom, university education, insofar as it advanced moral knowledge, also advanced a social ethic, one that sometimes stood athwart the counter ideal of individual rights, when that ideology became dangerously ascendant and threatening to the organic society. Bascom, of course, saw that reality dominant in the United States of the 1870s and 1880s.[30]

Second, the state university could serve this ethical need in line with the modern intellect. It would do so through those new curricular advances coming into the university—the social sciences especially. Bascom had made sociology central to his own teaching program at Wisconsin and had given it a religious

---

29. Bascom, *Education and the State*, 18. Bascom was not entirely fair in making this point; the small colleges had always offered broadly humanistic programs of study, and denominational affiliation barely showed through in their instructional programs, including the important course in moral philosophy. Nor did they impose religious tests on students.

30. John Bascom, "What Do the Members?," 99–100, 92; idem, *Tests of a School-system*, 22.

foundation and a moral substance. Bascom's own instruction marked his commitment to the new academic discipline and carried his conviction that the social sciences bore the means of human progress more helpfully than static religious belief. In the social sciences, Bascom proclaimed, we find the means of "social redemption," for these disciplines supply that enlarged view of the whole that the social organism needs for its means of adaptation and survival, and its moral progress. Bascom gave the social sciences a large embrace and included in them the subjects of political economy, civil law, constitutional law, sociology, and international law. These new intellectual fields expand our understanding of the many parts of the social whole and their precise interconnections. They are to that extent indispensable to an enlarged moral vision. Here, Bascom said, "moral truths have their seat." Of course, Bascom had just as much faith in humanistic learning. Right philosophy, as he said repeatedly, underscores all the social sciences.[31]

And third, Bascom urged that the state university can best meet the needs of the modern intellect and so serve the state as well. We must have no restraints on full access to all the gains the world is making through new ideas. "It is also the privilege of public instruction to handle freely the great truths of our lives," he wrote. Two important points followed. We should have no restrictions on what is taught at the state university. We must legitimate all new knowledge. And we must sanction all methods of pursuing it. "The state," Bascom specified, "is responsible for a truly liberal method, and for that only." In fact, open pursuit of the truth makes the state university a large asset to the state itself. "The state may, in each branch of instruction and in each school, avail itself of all the freedom the specific time and place will allow." And to that extent, he averred, "the freedom of instruction is worth more than any one thing taught." Bascom inscribed these principles into his classroom instruction at Wisconsin, from which he derived his textbook on ethics.[32]

So considering the good role of the new education, Bascom envisioned further gains to come from it. In words remembered by many of his students, most importantly Robert La Follette, Bascom urged from the graduates of the state university a large loyalty to the state and a life of service to the state by those who had benefited from the state's sponsorship of their education. And when he spoke to the graduating students at Madison in 1877 he offered one of his most hopeful and urgent pleas. The state university graduates, as he foresaw their role, would function almost like a new force, a fourth estate in the state's

31. Bascom, "What Do the Members?," 100; idem, *Tests of a School-system*, 22–23.
32. Bascom, *Ethics*, 306–7.

public life. Directly or indirectly they would extend to the life of the state a certain influence; they would provide a leavening effect in wider and wider circles of the state. "The time will come," Bascom said in his baccalaureate, "and public education will hasten it, in which educational men will gather influence within their own field, and become the servants of the State to counsel action as well as to carry it out." Bascom wished to impress on the university graduates a sense of patriotic duty. "The State has educated you for yourselves and for it," he told them. He followed with lines familiar to all his social ethics: The two purposes are not in conflict, he said, "but they can only be harmonized by a noble life. To such a life, at least in its social bearings, you are pre-eminently bound. You have no right to seek your own weal, if your own weal does not include the public weal."[33]

One might find such encouragement of public service not uncommon among the commencement speeches of the day, but these words do have a particular Bascom theme. Bascom had special reasons for explaining why university graduates might take on these roles and exercise this influence. He judged these students especially equipped for these purposes because of the kind of education they had received. They above all others should know and support the moral forces that advance humanity; they above all others should have the wide, inclusive vision of life and of society so as to advance the harmonizing process. Here Bascom contemplated an emerging intellectual elite. For what the university graduates owe above all to the state, Bascom believed, is ideas. They must act as an intellectual vanguard that will usher in a new age of Reason. "It will be your office," Bascom said to graduates on another occasion, "to make these ruling ideas clear, sound, and suitable." The graduates of state universities have a duty to carry into action, through state offices or through a large public influence, the ideas that will bring about the just state and usher in the new era of collective power. Trained in philosophy and the social sciences, the preeminent moral subjects, this cohort owes to society the full force of moral conviction, Bascom asserted.[34]

The Wisconsin Idea, under John Bascom's first conception of it, thus had a powerful moral urgency in its message. Above all, it derived its great hopes from humanistic education and the social sciences. In an age in which demands for "utility" caught the ears of so many university presidents and in which demands for higher education to fuel the engines of industrial growth motivated educational change, Bascom resisted. Mere practicality narrows our

33. Bascom, *Education and the State*, 17, 19.
34. Bascom, "What Do the Members?," 96, 94.

educational vision, he said. Our education should be "free and full and humanitarian." When Bascom told the audience at Madison that "the University of
Wisconsin will be permanently great in the degree in which it understands the
conditions of the prosperity and peace of the people, and helps to provide
them," he meant no narrowly practical instruction. True education included
other elements: "revelation of truth, the law of righteousness and the love of
man."[35]

Bascom thus spoke in his typical fashion. All issues for him, and especially
the grand subject of state university education, reflected the core of his religious
liberalism. Bascom offered the following remarks as the concluding words in
his last public address as president of the University of Wisconsin in 1887. He
spoke to the graduates:

> Standing in this open space of thought between the past and the future, in
> full view of what has been done, in full view of what may be done, I bid
> you good-bye, pledging you, one by one, with extended hand, to a faithful
> adhesion, within your life and beyond it, to all the great issues discussed by
> us in common, and in common held by us as our inheritance from our
> fathers—issues that give amplitude and scope to our own love, and are the
> commitment of the divine hand to us in the gracious and everlasting
> government of Christ.[36]

"All the great issues discussed by us in common." Many students from the
University of Wisconsin long remembered those discussions.

35. Bascom, "What Do the Members?," 93.
36. Bascom, *Christian State*, 32.

6

Progressivism I:
Temperance

The movement to ban the manufacture, sale, and consumption of alcoholic beverages seems bizarre from the vantage of the twenty-first century, or from any time after 1919. It probably strikes most people today as an aspect of irrationality, of puritanical moralism, of misplaced idealism. Why would a whole nation vote to deny itself one of life's simple pleasures? For a full century or so, however, temperance, and then the legislation to prohibit all traffic in intoxicating drink, shared center stage in American social movements and political party politics. The issue just wouldn't go away, and ultimately it found its way into the United States Constitution. Significantly, the temperance movement had critical attachments to other aspects of American life—to religion and denominational differentiations, to ethnic cultures, to the party ideologies of Whigs and Democrats and then of Democrats and Republicans, and to the role and power of women in the larger society. The movement has given historians much to ponder. But temperance provided John Bascom a cause to which he remained committed all his life.[1]

Alcoholic drink pervaded all aspects of American society in the early nineteenth century, de rigueur for nearly all events.[2] The situation began to

1. Joseph F. Kett, "Review Essay: Temperance and Intemperance as Historical Problems," *Journal of American History* 67 (March 1981), 878–79. See also Joseph R. Gusfield, *Symbolic Crusade: Status Politics and the American Temperance Movement* (Urbana: University of Illinois Press, 1963).

2. W. J. Rorabaugh, *The Alcoholic Republic: An American Tradition* (New York: Oxford University Press, 1979), 18–20.

moderate by the middle of the 1830s, a change owed greatly to a vigorous temperance movement, underway from the earlier century, and fortified by other changes in American life. Religion, as one would expect, weighed in early. Congregationalists and Presbyterians, acting within the emerging evangelical revival, spoke for abstinence as a form of self-purification. Evangelicals sought to promote reform through groups like the Connecticut Missionary Society, as local groups formed. Temperance had its largest registration in rural areas of New England and in the western sections of New York State. Bascom's father very likely had some participation in this activity. These efforts briefly predated the creation of the American Temperance Society (ATS), formed in 1826, and they brought the movement into the Benevolent Empire of Protestant evangelicalism and the liberal shifts in theology associated with it. Nathaniel William Taylor, Charles Finney, and Lyman Beecher gave it support.[3]

Temperance leaders never made the defeat of liquor a single cause. Nor did John Bascom. They always joined it to other objectives. One ATS leader called temperance "the foundation of all reform" because if you could defeat liquor you could defeat poverty, and crime, and gambling, and Sabbath-breaking. You could almost empty the insane asylums and hospitals. Thus, the temperance movement drew to it reformers of all kinds and cut across social classes, too. Some leaders in the labor movement attached their hopes for the improvement of workers to an image of a sober, disciplined body of laborers who could march in progress with the rest of the nation and contribute to its expanding wealth. The Washingtonian movement had an important role here. It came out of Baltimore in the 1840s, among reformed alcoholics in the city, who spread their message among the artisan classes. More secular than the ATS, it also flourished with mass entertainments—picnics, concerts, dances— that did not sit well with evangelicals. They insisted that the purpose of temperance was to save souls.[4]

Ian Tyrrell's valuable study of the temperance and prohibition movements argues against views that see them as conservative in nature and nativist in outlook. To make his point he stresses especially the complicated nature of the movement. Nativism thrived in cities like Philadelphia and New York, and

3. James R. Rohrer, "The Origins of the Temperance Movement: A Reinterpretation," *Journal of American Studies* 24 (August 1990), 228–35; Ian R. Tyrrell, *Sobering Up: From Temperance to Prohibition in Antebellum Reform, 1800–1860* (Westport, CT: Greenwood Press, 1979), 54–55, 60, 63, 72–73. See also Norman H. Clark, *Deliver Us from Evil: An Interpretation of American Prohibition* (New York: W. W. Norton, 1976).

4. Tyrrell, *Sobering Up*, 4, 41, 162–63, 176, 196, 207–8.

violence occurred in such places. Irish—that is, the Catholics that came in large numbers before the Civil War—became identified with heavy drinking. The Germans did too, but they evoked less resentment. Nativism did not always go with temperance. Many native (English) workers opposed both foreigners and temperance. Labor newspapers reflected divided opinion as many of them called for restrictions on immigration and "cheap labor" while having no truck whatsoever with any closing of the saloons. Nor do rural-versus-urban resentments explain temperance support. Almost always, Tyrrell finds that wherever the location, the "respectable members" of a community sided with temperance, led its various organizations, and articulated its rationale. Does that fact, then, make the movement "conservative"?[5]

Tyrrell says no. His broad survey found that the movement people did not look back nostalgically or nervously to a former era, they did not exhibit a reactionary temperament, and they did not reflect a restrictive provincialism in their outlooks. Instead, they expressed a confident modernist attitude, at least with respect to their positioning within the changing economic directions of the United States. They also prescribed the social ethic that accompanied the changes. Temperance leaders, Tyrrell writes, "sanctioned the acquisitive and individualistic economic order developing in America, and they optimistically predicted the improvement of the moral state of society on a firm basis of material progress." To that extent as well, business entrepreneurs provided considerable support to the movement. Their modernist instincts led them to link technology to labor, sober and self-disciplined, in a formula for American material progress. They formed a natural alliance with the Protestant religious leadership in a campaign to improve personal virtue and godliness among the national population. They had no doubt that moral improvement underscored material progress. If the movement at times seemed to target immigrants and the foreign born, it did so because therein lay the greatest challenges of a social pathology that threatened American republicanism.[6]

Representing mostly the Whig and later Republican Parties, temperance leaders drew on a political culture that readily appealed to the state to address social evils and promote public morality. Business leaders they may have been, but they did not embrace an ideology of laissez-faire or Social Darwinism. Prohibition, they believed, constituted legitimate state interference. The Maine liquor law of 1851 became the model of this action. Its defenders in the heated

5. Tyrrell, *Sobering Up*, 9, 215–16, 272–73.
6. Tyrrell, *Sobering Up*, 6–7, 78, 273.

debates that occurred along the way to its passage cited the toll of liquor in poverty and broken families.[7]

As far back as the territorial days in Wisconsin, the temperance issue had New York and New England connections. The first white settlers, in the southwest part of the state, came heavily from the upper South. With Democratic Party affiliations as well, temperance claimed no loyalty among them. As the Yankees grew in numbers, however, small temperance societies formed in their parts of the state, with ties to local churches and clerical initiative. New England and New York areas of Wisconsin, like early Milwaukee, Racine, Walworth, Rock, and Waukesha Counties, registered these activities in the 1840s. The Town of Delavan honored the name of a wealthy temperance reformer. Often the societies had but a brief life span. They rose amid religious revivals and waned in their aftermath.[8]

After statehood, however, Wisconsin did little more than pass a bond law, but an unusual piece of legislation it was. Besides requiring liquor sellers to post a heavy $1,000 bond, it had the singular distinction of allowing women to sue for damages against a dealer if she could show the effects of drink on the family; so could a pauper if his condition could be shown to have derived from the sale of alcohol by a particular vendor. "Let those who make drunkards, paupers, widows and orphans pay for it and not tax virtue and sobriety to support such an unholy traffic," said the bill's sponsor. This law of 1849 aroused opposition from the fast-growing population of Germans in the state. They judged the legislation an act of ethnic prejudice by the Yankee citizens, and temperance would ever after in Wisconsin have the appearance of ethnic resentments, Yankees imposing old puritan behaviors on the immigrant settlers.[9] German newspapers like Milwaukee's *Volkfreund* denounced the legislation. The city,

7. Daniel Walker Howe, *The Political Culture of the American Whigs* (Chicago: University of Chicago Press, 1979), 9, 14, 20, 22, 30, 38, 105; Tyrrell, *Sobering Up*, 273.

8. Alice E. Smith, *From Exploration to Statehood*, vol. 1 of *The History of Wisconsin* (Madison: State Historical Society of Wisconsin, 1973), 626–67; Robert C. Nesbit, *Wisconsin: A History* (Madison: University of Wisconsin Press, 1973), 235, 237; Tyrrell, *Sobering Up*, 12–13.

9. Joseph Schafer, "Prohibition in Early Wisconsin," *Wisconsin Magazine of History* 8 (March 1925), 283–86 (quotation, 286); Herman J. Deutsch, "Yankee-Teuton Rivalry in Wisconsin Politics of the Seventies; Section I: Temperance," *Wisconsin Magazine of History* 14 (March 1931), 266.

now heavily German, voted strongly against the temperance referenda, while to the south Yankee residents supported it. Governor William Barstow, Democrat, vetoed the bill of 1855. The Republicans, measuring their loss of support, especially among German Protestants, went easy on temperance for the next several years.[10]

Party politics in Wisconsin reverberated with the temperance issues. Matters came to a boil in the state again just two years before Bascom arrived at Madison. Republicans enacted the Graham Liquor Law of 1872. Introduced by Alexander Graham of Rock County, the bill renewed the license policy with tough enforcement measures provided. The bill specified a large list of grounds for civil suit and heavy penalties for drunkenness. By this time the contested issue had assumed clear ideological divisions, ones that go back to the Jacksonian era of the 1830s. Opponents of temperance embraced the standard of "personal liberty." When the legislation passed, signed by Republican governor Cadwallader Washburn, Milwaukee brewers, including Valentin Blatz and Joseph Schlitz, joined with others around the state to form the Wisconsin Association for the Protection of Personal Liberty. It raised the cry of police state against the Republicans and urged voters to back candidates pledged to undo the law. Also organized in the wake of Graham, and resolved to kill it, came the American Constitutional Union, made up wholly of Germans. Now Wisconsin Germans wrapped themselves in the Declaration of Independence. They gave ringing endorsement to individual liberties and urged that government not infringe on people's "natural freedom."[11] At any rate, Republicans paid heavily for their moral excess and Democrats returned to power in the state with the next elections.[12]

Nationally, the temperance movement was taking a significant turn, and it would have important consequences in Wisconsin, too. Women had always claimed a salience in this cause, as they had in antislavery. Both issues supplied the moral outlets of the Benevolent Empire. In the post–Civil War era two new turns energized the temperance crusade. In December 1874, in Hillsboro, Ohio, a meeting at a local Presbyterian church moved out into the town—to hotels, saloons, anywhere the liquor flowed. The women sang songs as they

10. Richard N. Current, *The Civil War Era, 1848–1873*, vol. 2 of *The History of Wisconsin* (Madison: State Historical Society of Wisconsin, 1976), 142–43, 216–17, 225; Schafer, "Prohibition," 286–87, 290–91, 295.

11. Deutsch, "Yankee-Teuton Rivalry," 267–71, 275–76; Current, *Civil War Era*, 587.

12. Deutsch, "Yankee-Teuton Rivalry," 271, 276, 279, 280; Current, *Civil War Era*, 549–50.

assaulted these places where "respectable" females did not go. This kind of crusading quickly caught on and the country witnessed similar events in other states.[13] The same year—and also in a Presbyterian church—other women, who saw the need for a large organization, held the first convention of the Women's Christian Temperance Union, in Cleveland. The WCTU utilized all the devices of evangelical activity—mass meetings and prayer sessions, large-scale publications widely distributed. And they gained the attention they sought.[14]

Bascom needed little incentive to take up the cause of temperance, but he might have had some prodding along the way. At Williams, Mark Hopkins supported the cause, and at Andover, Moses Stuart extracted from his deep scholarship in ancient Greek and Hebrew his own peculiar defense.[15] Both John and Emma Bascom got involved in the local movement immediately on their arrival to Madison and defended the Graham Law. Emma Bascom worked closely with Lavinia Goodell, who "would become the bane of liquor dealers in courtrooms across Wisconsin," and who led in establishing the Wisconsin Women's Temperance Alliance in 1874. Emma Bascom joined with other Wisconsin women to promote both temperance and women's suffrage. She helped Goodell win a bitter court case that made her the first licensed female attorney in the state. (See next chapter.) In 1879 Bascom won election as president of the Equal Suffrage Association, founded the year before in Madison. The next year, when Frances Willard arrived and helped bring the Wisconsin Women's Temperance Alliance into the WCTU, Emma Bascom became the chapter's corresponding secretary. She later became president of this organization as well. The Bascoms constituted a powerful team for reform in Wisconsin.[16]

Bascom's book *Sociology*, published in 1887, incorporated topics and ideas that he had been presenting at the university over the last fourteen years. Here

13. Tyrrell, *Sobering Up*, 179, 181–82; Ruth Bordin, *Woman and Temperance: The Quest for Power and Liberty, 1873–1900* (Philadelphia: Temple University Press, 1981), 8–9, 18–19. For more details on women in temperance, see Jack S. Blocker Jr., *American Temperance Movements: Cycles of Reform* (Boston: Twayne Publishers, 1989), 61–94. On differences among women on this issue, see also idem, "Separate Paths: Suffragists and the Women's Temperance Crusade," *Signs* 10 (Spring 1985), 460–76.

14. Bordin, *Woman and Temperance*, 22, 36.

15. Tyrrell, *Sobering Up*, 146.

16. Genevieve G. McBride, *On Wisconsin Women: Working for Their Rights from Settlement to Suffrage* (Madison: University of Wisconsin Press, 1993), 6–8, 10–11, 21–27, 41–43, 53, 88, 94.

and in other venues, including pamphlets, talks at local churches, and bacca-laureate sermons, Bascom took up temperance. Like all who used the printed word to support this cause, Bascom measured the social and personal costs of drinking. He, like the others, insisted that temperance never stood alone as an issue; it mattered because it affected so many other human relationships and took a heavy toll on the social organism. If it were only a matter of the indi-vidual drinker, said Bascom, we could pretty much ignore the subject; we would certainly not have recourse to the law to outlaw liquor. So when we deal with temperance, he insisted, we take on also "the extended and inevitable connection of intemperance with crime, insanity, idiocy, the lives of women and children stripped of all safety by it, the great moral perversion and indus-trial weakness that attend upon it." So he wrote in his sociology textbook. In his baccalaureate sermon in 1887 he denounced the liquor trade and its manifest ill effects. "All the forces, divine and human, that struggle to lift society and make it buoyant with a spiritual life, suffer the eternal suffocation of one vile trade that hugs us to its filthy bosom," he said. Everywhere, Bascom went on, drink leaves "poverty and disease and vice." Bascom urged that everyone pays the costs of the inebriate drinker. He made this point in an address to the Congre-gational Church in Madison, his speech published by the National Temperance Society with a ringing endorsement. The drunkard exacts a toll "on the part of us all." We pay for poor houses, prisons, and asylums. The drunkard clogs the wheels of industry, slows the progress of enterprise, and thus he "puts his hand in every man's pocket."[17]

Bascom would make his case against drinking on broad philosophical grounds, but there crept into his language now and then words that suggest personal judgment and esthetic disgust with the habit. The drunkard, Bascom said, has lost all self-control and cannot reform himself. Liquor changes the personality and temperament of its consumer. He becomes mean spirited, selfish; he frequents the saloon and unsavory places. He stands athwart the progress of society in reason and civility. "The debasement and retrogression implied in [drunkenness] are too great." Bascom felt the same way about smoking and smokers. Smoking represented to him every bit a personal and social regres-sion, a downward pull on society's general advancement in refinement and

---

17. John Bascom, *Sociology* (New York: G. P. Putnam's Sons, 1887), 199; idem, *A Christian State* [Baccalaureate Sermon] (Milwaukee: Cramer, Aikens & Cramer, 1887), 18–19; idem, *Prohibition and Common Sense* (New York: National Temperance Society and Publishing House, 1885), 1, 5, 15.

taste. So personal feelings weighed heavily in Bascom's screeds, but he did have a lot more ammunition to wield against drink.[18]

Liquor, Bascom believed, made many innocent victims, but it took its toll directly on the working classes as a group. We hear much talk, he said, about the oppression of labor by capital (and much of that came from Bascom himself), but far less about the oppression from drink. And from that source comes a far heavier toll, he believed. It had to do with money spent, to be sure, and Bascom offered statistics to make the point, but in fact it had a more insidious effect and greater deprivation. Bascom related his discussion of temperance to points made in his earlier sociological essays in *Bibliotheca Sacra*. Drinking and the indulgences that attend it conspire to keep the laboring classes detached from the progressive forces—moral, spiritual—that move the race forward. They deprive them of attachments and interconnections that complete the organic society. The human species advances by integration and inclusiveness, he explained, and all that prevents that vital process of organic formation impairs the whole body, but especially its alienated parts. Bascom wrote: "Not till workingmen seek indulgences more economical, more refreshing, more social, more elevating, will their condition be very much improved." So he spoke too of the "energy of prohibition" as having the quality of fresh air. It would win for workers a more vital engagement with the economic forces that can lift all classes.[19]

Bascom did not want laws to close all the saloons. Such action would smack of invidious class prejudice; nor, he said, did he want to deprive workers of some innocent pleasures. And he recognized that in Wisconsin the subject had a particular sensitivity, given the "beer-drinking customs of our German citizens." But he seemed to suggest that the Germans handled their beer better than the "Americans" did. All that said, Bascom did not know how to get the needed results short of total prohibition. So he endorsed total prohibition. Bascom did not blame immigrants as a group, and he never cited Irish or Germans as corrupting influences in America. He did betray some personal prejudice, however, when he discussed temperance in the framework of history and evolution. He proclaimed that "the Anglo-Saxon race has done more for government

---

18. Bascom, *Prohibition and Common Sense*, 3–4, 6, 9; idem, "Tobacco and Refinement," *Friend, a Religious and Literary Journal* 60 (September 25, 1886), 60; idem, "Why Should I Vote the Prohibition Ticket?," *Christian Union*, September 6, 1888, 246.

19. John Bascom, *The Philosophy of Prohibition* [Pamphlet] (New York: National Temperance Society and Publishing House, 1884), 10–11; idem, *Prohibition and Common Sense*, 6–7 (quotation).

than all other races combined." It has made freedom a stable force in its societies, and its leaders have given a large place to the rule of law. The United States, however, had increasingly in its midst, he warned, many who "belong to nationalities" that have never obtained freedom in their former countries. Now in America these individuals too often embrace a libertarian ethic without respect for the law that keeps freedom in balance. Such is the ethic of the saloon. Bascom feared that excess on one side will yield to excess on the other. Liberty that becomes destructive to the social organism will require an oppression that will resemble the very tyranny the newer groups have left behind.[20]

Intemperance betrayed certain "laws of inheritance" that reflect the appetites, passions, and diseases that have always plagued the human race, Bascom asserted. These effects should by now have become merely atavistic, gradually disappearing with the advance of the race along its evolutionary course. But we have not done enough to combat them. We have allowed them to pass along family lines from one generation to the next. "The blood of the race," Bascom wrote, "has so long been heated and polluted by intemperance" that years of abstinence must now force down its eroding effects. And to "root out" this hardened legacy will require an effort of great moral energy. It will have to rally all the positive, healthy, organic components of the community to heal its degenerative parts. Bascom did not judge the drunkard guilty; he judged him weak. He stood in need of strengthening, restoration, rejuvenation. As society occupied the "seat of sin," more than the individual, it became a matter of creating good conditions and destroying bad ones. So said the Social Gospelers generally. Society, of course, can do only so much, but that it must do. If not, Bascom warned, the drinker will drink and drink even more, "till nature will have no more of him."[21]

All those who defended temperance faced a considerable challenge. Their opponents constantly asked them, by what right does a government assume to tell people what to do or not to do for their enjoyments, their private pleasures, their choice of a lifestyle? From the days of the Jacksonian political quarrels, the Democratic Party and others embraced the mantra of "personal liberty" and cordoned off the reach of government from a large preserve of individual discretion. The liquor issue headed the list of protections. Temperance leaders, who had so many New England connections, there and by their removal to different parts of the country, drew on a rival defense. They invoked a tradition of community that from the time of John Winthrop honored the priority of the

20. Bascom, *Prohibition and Common Sense*, 7, 10–11, 12–13.
21. Bascom, *Prohibition and Common Sense*, 3–5; Tyrrell, *Sobering Up*, 128.

society and its interests, the public weal, against libertarian options. Sumptuary laws of various kinds perpetuated that tradition. Moral philosophers like Mark Hopkins sustained notions of the public ethic.[22]

Nonetheless, the prospect of taking the glass from the tippler's hands, especially the moderate imbiber in polite society, gave a hard burden of argument to the temperance folks, the more so in a country where the language of individual rights had flourished from the time of the national founding. Bascom, though, relished this challenge. Of course he drew on his own New England background, but his defense of temperance came out of a larger arsenal. This issue, as much as any, gave him the opportunity to elaborate his philosophy of state as presented in the materials seen from him previously. The temperance matter shows Bascom's long migration from philosophical idealism into the practical politics of his day.

The philosophy of prohibition, Bascom said, begins with a philosophy of state. He reasserted his conviction that Americans did not have a right philosophy of state, that is, one that sanctioned its positive and legitimate powers. "We are losing the idea of government," he wrote. He found antigovernment prejudices understandable. History chronicled the abuses of state power in plentiful ways. It displayed for all to see its manifold corruptions, its cruel tyrannies. One does not take lightly the heroic achievements of those who fought to liberate humans from these oppressions, Bascom acknowledged. So when he began his pamphlet on "the philosophy of prohibition," Bascom proceeded carefully. He wanted to establish first the grounds on which one could acknowledge legitimate government functions. He had to address those who would confine government to mere protection—the national defense and the public safety. He began with the state's role in fostering economic progress. "Government," he wrote, "is thus always passing beyond the office of protection, [and is] securing the conditions of industry, and laying, in various ways, the foundations of enterprise, intelligence and virtue. This great function of government, by which it combines the power of all, and makes it immediately and universally available, is as natural and spontaneous a function as that of protection, and cannot be dispensed with." Bascom adhered to standard Federalist, Whig, and Republican Party prescriptions, but he wanted to go even further.[23]

We need protection in our moral and mental life, too, Bascom insisted. Human progress moves along many fronts. And whereas Bascom had no doubt that material wealth and virtue went hand in hand, he did not hesitate to say

22. Tyrrell, *Sobering Up*, 227–28.
23. Bascom, *Philosophy of Prohibition*, 3–4.

that prohibition offers the aid we can give to our industrial progress. But Americans, especially in the new age of Darwinian antistatism, gave low priority to the moral business of the state. Our weakened sense of government, Bascom said, has held us hostage to the moral erosion of our community. No better example exists than intemperance, "this unmitigated and malignant evil." We think either that we can do nothing about it or that we should do nothing about it. But society, Bascom lamented, is then left "without defense against physical degeneracy and spiritual debasement." Such intellectual agnosticism, he warned, gives huge advantage to the destructive forces that rend the social fabric. The liquor trade moves on apace. But, Bascom avowed, "we can not let this traffic alone because it will not let us alone."[24]

The organic views of society that Bascom derived from evolution and applied in his social gospel also informed his defense of prohibition. Survival depends for each organism on the healthy functioning, the right coordination and integration of all its parts. So did Bascom see society. Any organization, certainly any state, had within it elements—intellectual, moral, spiritual—that assured its adaptability and progress. Bascom saw these positive aspects in intellectual terms especially, but certainly moral and spiritual, too. In fact, he considered them inseparable. But other elements—erratic, anarchic, cancerous elements— defy integration with the whole and conspire against the social organism. So the social organism must see to its own survival need, and it may have to override individuals' personal choices. Bascom wrote: "Society, as the higher, more inclusive and powerful organism, has a right to life, full life, perfect life, both for its own sake and for the sake of the individual whose fortunes it wraps up in its own fortunes." Putting it more graphically in *Sociology*, he said that the organic movement of society gives society the right to deal with the "dead matter," individuals "morally inorganic and repellent," in its complex. That responsibility necessitates exercising the state's moral muscle; government must "overrule unreason with reason, unrighteousness with righteousness. Government means that or it means nothing."[25]

So stating, Bascom defined the right and proper role of government as defense of the common interest, the public weal, in an expanded idea of what that defense constituted. But that notion also embraced a correct view of what we mean by liberty, Bascom insisted. And for him liberty had a positive, not a

24. Bascom, *Philosophy of Prohibition*, 2; idem, "Why Vote Prohibition?," 246; idem, *A Christian State*, 18; idem, *Prohibition and Common Sense*, 13, 18 (quotation).
25. Bascom, *Prohibition and Common Sense*, 18; idem, *Sociology*, 198.

negative, connotation. It signified empowerment. The crucial questions respecting any actions government takes, Bascom asserted, are, Do they make for the growth of human powers? Do they give life, space, and opportunity to the virtuous qualities that spur evolutionary advance? Bascom wished to stress particularly the role of the state in helping individuals to realize powers they cannot realize on their own. "Individuals combined and consolidated in government, have immense resources which are not to be withheld," he wrote. And he strove mightily to show his conviction that such state power did not compromise its other critical obligation: to protect individual liberty. "The liberty of the individual," he insisted, "is the great trust of the government."[26]

Of course, to be sure, in the narrowest sense, every civil law is a restraint on liberty; it does place some curb on some people's actions. But application only of that narrow view of liberty serves best the interests of the "brutal and lawless" elements in society, Bascom explained. And it fails to examine the destructive toll it takes everywhere. Bascom replied that the state must exercise its right to combat the malevolent forces within it. And what among them more threatens society than the liquor trade? The drunkard, Bascom mourned, "leaves behind him the frayed, weakened, broken ties of society." And does not any society have the right to see to the prevalence of its healthiest qualities against its worst? Are all our good moral instincts to have no leverage in our public exercises? Hence prohibition, Bascom stressed, constitutes above all "a state and civic issue" that brings it right into the business of politics. It has everything to do with creating the Christian state, he insisted. Bascom's liberal theology, with its notions of a progressive redemption, led to this issue especially. "If God's redemption includes the city," he pleaded, "it includes temperance there also."[27]

The kind of thinking Bascom opposed made a sharp but false dualism of individual and government, of private and public. This dualism Bascom never accepted, indeed he could hardly conceive it. He had inherited from evolution a strong sense of integration, in the biological organism as in the social. His social gospel ideas further broke down the dichotomy and resulted in Bascom's asserting that individuals cannot have full and meaningful existence apart from the community. He maintained that conviction also with respect to particular groups—labor, business, women. Liberty then, for Bascom, was not an ideal realized separately, individual by individual. Liberty meant power, personal

26. Bascom, *Philosophy of Prohibition*, 5, 3–4.

27. Bascom, *Philosophy of Prohibition*, 6, 7–8 (first quotation); idem, *Prohibition and Common Sense*, 12–13; idem, "Why Vote Prohibition?," 246 (second quotation); idem, *Sociology*, 198–99.

advancement, enrichment, self-realization. And it derived its gains from sustaining the way each individual relates to the larger whole. Therein only did the critical moral forces that advanced the species become available to the individual. Bascom believed that the temperance question made that point as clear as any. "These men who raise the cry of personal liberty," he wrote, "act in oversight of the fundamental condition of a free government, to wit, that every citizen shall be willing under law to submit his own interest to the interest of the community, both for its sake and his own sake."[28]

The subjects to follow—women, business, and labor—will show that Bascom rarely invoked the language of natural rights. He moved beyond the terminology of the eighteenth century to that of the nineteenth and the more relativist measures influenced by notions of change and adaptation in romanticism and evolutionary thought. That shift led Bascom into judgments that some might fairly deem extreme or excessive, as indeed they often were. Thus, in his sociology book Bascom again answered the questions of temperance critics: What about the rights of the moderate drinker? Have they not a right to purchase intoxicants, and does this right not make the case against prohibition? Bascom answered the question in a dismissive manner: "To answer this question in the affirmative," he said, "is either to give up government by the majority, or to assume that there are certain original rights of so fundamental a character that no government can fittingly violate them, and that among these rights is the free purchase of intoxicating drinks. But there are no such rights." He went on: "All personal rights submit themselves to the public welfare." If we protect individual rights we do so because they protect the public; if they do not protect the public we take them away. Thus prohibition. "To affirm the personal rights of an individual in a case like this," Bascom asserted, "is to enable him to stand across the path of public progress, to check the organic movement of society, and so ultimately to destroy his own well-being as well as that of others."[29] In short, you have no right to be a drunkard.

Of course, all politics are local. Bascom took his literary campaign for temperance to the national media, but he did not hesitate to involve himself in Wisconsin politics, too. The state Prohibition Party had formed in 1867 and in 1881 ran its first candidate for governor. After the debacle of the Graham Law, the Republicans dared not go for prohibition anymore. The new Prohibition Party chose John M. Olin to head the ticket. Olin had but recently come to Wisconsin. He had graduated from Williams College and thus was a student

28. Bascom, *Prohibition and Common Sense*, 11–12.
29. Bascom, *Sociology*, 196–97.

during Bascom's professorship and in the year that Bascom made his unsuccessful bid to succeed Mark Hopkins as president. His connection to Bascom there, however, is not clear. After Olin had a year of law study at Madison, Bascom sought to place him on the university faculty. But the regents had been at war with Bascom over the power to make faculty appointments and in 1875 they had "clipped his wings." Bascom particularly wanted this appointment, though, and apparently even threatened to resign if the regents did not approve Olin. The regents knew Olin's strong prohibitionist commitments. At any rate, the Prohibition Party did poorly in 1881. Olin did not gain a lectureship at the law school until 1885. Even then, regent Elisha Keyes, who hated Bascom and spoke for the liquor interests in Milwaukee, tried to stop the appointment. Two years later, antiprohibitionists on the board fired Olin, to the applause of the good folks who published the *Brewer's Gazette*. Olin later became president of the Wisconsin Bar Association.[30]

Bascom all along was becoming closely tied to the Prohibition Party. He looked to it as the only hope for any effective legislation. Both the Democrats and Republicans had turned away from the subject, though many in Wisconsin, and many women especially, continued to call for prohibition. Mostly, though, the two major parties had given themselves over to "fishes and loaves," as business matters became ascendant in each and moral matters faded from priority. What remained in Wisconsin were the license policies of old, which Bascom considered wholly ineffective, "a feeble compromise with evil." Nor did higher taxes on liquor suffice; they had done nothing to deter consumption, which in fact, he lamented, had increased in Wisconsin in the last ten years. Bascom called Milwaukee an outlaw city, whose political leaders, from police to aldermen to mayor, live in open defiance of even the existing mild regulations. "This city has virtually declared itself independent of the state," he wrote. He took a firmer hand in Madison, where he lived. There Bascom joined the Madison Law and Order League in 1884, formed to enforce Sabbath and liquor regulations. He even chastised the Dane County district attorney, one Robert La Follette, his former student, for lax enforcement of the laws. Bascom endorsed the Maine law as a model for Wisconsin and all states, but ultimately prescribed a national law of outright prohibition.[31]

30. Merle Curti and Vernon Carstensen, *The University of Wisconsin: A History, 1848–1925*, 2 vols. (Madison: University of Wisconsin Press, 1949), 1:250–51, 331; Robert Booth Fowler, *Wisconsin Votes: An Electoral History* (Madison: University of Wisconsin Press, 2008), 48.

31. Bascom, *Prohibition and Common Sense*, 22–23, 8, 20, 21, 23; McBride, *On Wisconsin Women*, 113; Bascom, *Sociology*, 64; idem, "Why Vote Prohibition?," 246.

But at the very local level, the university, matters became intense. In Bascom, the university had a president as outspoken on the issue probably as no other head of a large campus in the United States, and in a state where beer production flourished. As explained by Curti and Carstensen, a confrontation between Bascom and the regents finally occurred in 1885. At its June meeting, the board registered its complaint against Bascom's activities outside the university, in the arena of politics. It did defend the president's entitlement to his opinion on the temperance issue, the right enjoyed by any private citizen. But the board also correctly made the point that a strong partisan commitment to a political party compromised the university's effort as a public institution designed to serve all citizens of the state. Participation in partisan politics, the regents said, injured the university, whatever the political issues themselves and irrespective of their particular merits. George H. Paul for the regents informed Bascom that the board did not at all question his integrity or sincerity and it had no quarrels with his administration of the university. They did have concern about his wisdom in forging "entangling alliances" of a political nature. Matters might become very difficult, the regents implied, between them and the president should he maintain these connections.[32]

This time Bascom himself embraced the standard of personal liberty. He regarded the board's message as an inappropriate interference. He agreed that the president had no right to impose his views on students and asserted that he had never done so. Bascom also insisted that his political commitments and the time given to them should not detract and had not detracted from his official duties as university president. But he did allow that he must not create enemies of the university because of his partisan politics. That point may have led Bascom to back off a bit. While he continued to speak for prohibition he refused to accept an offer of an office in the Prohibition Party. This subject, however, and related personal conflicts and animosities were now beginning to write the script that brought Bascom to resign the presidency just two years later.[33]

So stood Bascom in the dubious and contestable "progressive" movement of temperance. In its larger scope and ambitions, it had great ideals. It wanted earnestly to bring hope of better lives to many and it carried genuine ideas of social justice when it considered who in particular suffered from the abuse of drink—society's least defensible people. Prohibition, though, did not make distinctions. It would punish all who drank, including "safe" drinkers. In that way it so often looked narrow, carping, puritanical. And Bascom himself often

32. Curti and Carstensen, *University of Wisconsin*, 1:262–63.
33. Curti and Carstensen, *University of Wisconsin*, 1:263.

looked like that. But he clung to high idealism in defending his cause. He once said to a younger generation that prohibition would perpetuate the inspiration so recently flourishing in the Civil War. He wanted the fight against liquor to claim the same high moral ground, instill the same moral zeal that the fight against slavery had done. He offered this proposition: "We were one of the latest Christian nations to abolish slavery. We do well to strive to cover up this delinquency by becoming the first of Christian nations to affirm the right, and enforce the duty, of prohibition."[34] Therein Bascom located one of the major progressive causes of the late nineteenth century. The cause of women was another one.

34. Bascom, *Prohibition and Common Sense*, 24.

7

Progressivism 2: Women

Discussions and disputes that surrounded the question of coeducation at Williams found Bascom defending the cause as a professor in the college. The same issue challenged him at the University of Wisconsin, where now he spoke as president of the state institution. But in both locations Bascom brought to bear on the matter a very large perspective. He wrote, as he had long done, as a philosopher, a defender of liberal religion, an evolutionist, a teacher, and a textbook author in the new field of sociology. At Williams Bascom defended coeducation as a subject that addressed not only women's unequal access to higher education in the United States but the whole imbalance of gender relations in America. From the workplace to the dressing room, Bascom had indicated, women suffered a host of disadvantages that demanded attention and corrective action, for the whole matter of human progress and improvement was at stake. In Madison he threw himself into the "woman question" and made the progress of women a major personal commitment.

As did the women who wrote the Declaration of Sentiments at Seneca Falls in 1848, John Bascom believed that custom, ancient habits of thinking, sexual stereotyping, all impeded women's progress, all perpetuated the separate spheres that plagued reform and progress. Bascom's book on sociology opened with a chapter on "Custom." He had much respect for it. But Bascom was also the sociologist informed by the philosopher. The power of intellect, the great outreach of Reason into the sensible world and beyond into spiritual truths, always signified for him the necessary conditions of individual and human progress. On the one hand, he insisted, law and tradition assure stability and growth, and they ought not to yield to any immediate demands for change. Just appreciation of tradition rooted in time and place gives us great statesmen like Edmund Burke, Bascom argued. And certainly one can understand how a thinker like Bascom, who celebrated the organic society, would find value in tradition. But, he warned, many wrongs have come from people's stubborn insistence on things as they always have been. Such an outlook, however, defies human evolution and progress, he asserted. The species must grow in its collective intellect, or it will stagnate. "The root of right is reason," Bascom wrote, "the slow-creeping reason of the aggregate mind." He added: "Customs which are congealed errors must yield to the clear, coherent push of reason proper."[1] Having thus stated the matter, Bascom went on to illustration, and the first application he made of it pertained to women.

Of all the instances wherein custom stood against the right evolutionary path, marriage and sex relations in the modern nations appeared to Bascom as among the most evident. The matter in several ways had worsened over time, and Bascom would point to the stark separation, the separate spheres that now divided males and females. Male superiority as we find it today has its roots in "barbarism," Bascom asserted, but its manifestations now, while milder, remain nonetheless entrenched, he believed. Bascom made no celebration of domesticity, coated it with no gloss of sentiment or idealism. Modern society, he wrote, has assigned women to an "industrial and social sphere" that denies them any meaningful exercise of their human qualities. Bascom laid these errant ways at the feet of custom—custom uninformed by Reason or morality.[2]

Bascom's classroom lectures on sociology and the large book he wrote on the subject asked consideration of the gender issue from many points of view. He pressed the matter with urgent prose.

On women's powers: "It will hardly be denied that women manifestly have the powers that would enable them to enter on a wider activity than now falls to them, and that that activity in turn would rapidly widen the powers which, by their very presence, are leading women to seek a field for their exercise."[3]

On men's power over women: "There is no more fatal concession than that which allows one portion of a community to settle the appropriate aims, ideals, efforts of another portion. It is the right of each class, conscious of its own resources, to define life for itself, under the common limitations of the public welfare."[4]

1. John Bascom, *Sociology* (New York: G. P. Putnam's Sons, 1887), 17.
2. Bascom, *Sociology*, 184, 186–87.
3. Bascom, *Sociology*, 185.
4. Bascom, *Sociology*, 185–86.

And, on sexual equality: "Sex as sex does not modify the fundamental principles governing the rights of men. It is a fact irrelevant to them."[5]

Bascom's writings on this subject reflected two of the intellectual influences we have traced so far in his career. Much in his language incorporated philosophical idealism, as previously employed by transcendentalist Margaret Fuller. For both her and Bascom, women's liberation signified growth in power. It alone could break women from the chains of tradition, exemplified at its worst in marriage and the "brute life" (Bascom) that had described it for centuries. Women had received a training in weakness, Bascom said. Society teaches them docility, attributes to them habits of sentiment and emotion, pretends to favor them for their special kind of religious piety, and celebrates their feminine virtues by bathing them in "the captivating glitter and flattering attentions of social life." Underneath it all Bascom could see only "a profound contempt of women." All the while a popular culture obscures the tyrannies of the domestic prison by displaying in poem and picture "the excellent duties of woman and her holy home functions."[6]

Persons familiar with Margaret Fuller and her celebrated writing on the relations of the sexes in the United States (especially her long essay "The Great Lawsuit" and its extension into her book *Woman in the Nineteenth Century*) might think of her in reading Bascom on this subject. Fuller, a disciple of Emerson and a major thinker among the transcendentalists, also brought the language of philosophical idealism into contemporary American life. Comparisons abound between both writers, but consider just one. Fuller wrote in her book, "What woman needs is not as a woman to act or rule, but as a nature to grow, as an intellect to discern, as a soul to live freely, and unimpeded to unfold such powers as were given her when we left our common home."[7] Fuller urged women to go into the world, break the norms of gender location, become sea captains if so inclined. Bascom, too, related the imperative of intellectual growth in women to enlarged experience everywhere. "It is difficult to believe that the true ideal of womanhood would suffer by more knowledge," he wrote, "wider human interests, broader fields of usefulness, more independent and robust action, physically, intellectually and morally, in shaping the conditions of life."[8]

5. Bascom, *Sociology*, 186.

6. Bascom, *Sociology*, 187–89.

7. Margaret Fuller, *Woman in the Nineteenth Century* (New York: Greeley & McElworth, 1845), 27.

8. Bascom, *Sociology*, 189–90.

An earlier chapter noted the Cult of True Womanhood and the ideal of the "separate spheres" so prominent in the mid-nineteenth century.[9] Bascom urged his readers to rethink the sexual dualism that had created and now perpetuates the separate spheres. Feminist Elizabeth Cady Stanton said that once you concede the innate difference of the sexes you are left with separate spheres. We must reject the rigid differentiation of male and female nature and look for a common nature among humans, said the feminist advocates. Fuller began with the notion of God, whom she described in androgynous terms, a balance of "male" and "female" qualities—the "great radical dualism." Bascom hoped to see a move away from essentialism and prescribed a healthier and more authentic existence for both sexes. It would come when people lived freely, when the soul opened itself to the complementary good effects of both gender types. He specified: "The feminine form should not exclude the essential force of the masculine spirit; if it does, it sinks into weakness. The masculine form should not be wanting in feminine tenderness; if it is, it becomes gross."[10]

Both Fuller and Bascom thus expressed the ideal of harmony. Bascom reinforced this ideal by recourse, as always, to another intellectual source, evolution. Human evolution always referred Bascom to the social organism. His reformist views looked toward the perfection of the whole through the healthy integration of all its parts. That process alone assured progress, compelled the organism into a greater adaptability to its ever shifting and transforming environment. This "movement of enlargement," as Bascom called it, framed his discussion of gender relations in contemporary America. Bascom looked for "new combinations and novel adjustments of living forces." He called for definitions of gender norms that would produce "a higher harmony." The new condition would emerge as "masculine" and "feminine" lost their rigid meanings, as both sexes combined and harmonized the conventional attributes of the other.[11]

Margaret Fuller had said that this new harmonizing could arrive only when both sexes broke from the roles custom had assigned them. They could realize

9. For an effective overview of the historiography of separate spheres, see Linda K. Kerber, "Separate Spheres, Female Worlds, Woman's Place: The Rhetoric of Women's History," in Kerber, *Toward an Intellectual History of Women* (Chapel Hill: University of North Carolina Press, 1997), 159–99.

10. Bascom, *Sociology*, 190. Fuller had written: "Male and female represent the two sides of the great radical dualism. But in fact they are perpetually passing into one another. Fluid hardens to solid, solid rushes to fluid. There is no wholly masculine man, no purely feminine woman." *Woman in the Nineteenth Century*, 103.

11. Bascom, *Sociology*, 186, 190–91.

their own true nature only when they could grow and nurture it through experience of the "real world." Bascom inscribed the same prescription in his own scheme of gender reform. He recognized, however, how entrenched the sexual dualism lay in modern American life and how atavistic it had become. "The two sexes are with us becoming painfully separate in their tastes, habits and conceptions of truth," he lamented. Men in their public location assume a bad distemper wrought from the narrow pursuit of money; women in their private location assume a religious piety and moral virtue that preserves them in purity from the "ugly facts" of the world outside. None in these conditions can assist the other; no higher harmony can ensue. But women suffer the more. Bascom wrote: "When piety is thought especially to become women, piety and womanhood are alike dishonored. When domestic virtues are made pre-eminently and exclusively their virtues, they hang on them like chains and trammel them as uncomfortable garments."[12]

Proposals for reforms for women abounded in the middle decades of the nineteenth century. Some states moved to reduce inequality in the matter of property holding, changing laws that, for example, required a woman to surrender any property she brought into a marriage.[13] Bascom entered the reform discussions on a related issue—divorce. The essay he contributed to the *Independent* in 1882 took up the matter some years after it had become a red-hot topic among feminists. Elizabeth Cady Stanton had addressed it at the Tenth National Woman's Rights Convention in 1860. On the second day the prevailing harmony of the meeting shattered when Stanton proposed that, under certain circumstances, divorce was justifiable. "A long and bitter discussion" followed, there in New York City and then for many days in the nation's newspapers. Stanton made her case by citing individual rights and the principle of happiness, but also by indicting marriage as "legalized prostitution" in the sexual power over women it permitted. She denied to the institution of marriage any moral superiority over the rights of the individuals who entered into it. She struck a nerve.[14]

12. Bascom, *Sociology*, 192–94.

13. New York State led in 1848 and in 1860. Eleanor Flexner, *Century of Struggle: The Woman's Rights Movement in the United States* (New York: Atheneum, 1968), 85–88; Mary P. Ryan, *Womanhood in America: From Colonial Times to the Present* (New York: New Viewpoints, 1975), 103.

14. Ellen Carol DuBois, "Outgrowing the Compact of the Fathers: Equal Rights, Woman Suffrage, and the United States Constitution, 1820–1878," in *Woman Suffrage and Women's Rights* (New York: New York University Press, 1998), 88; *Elizabeth Cady Stanton*, ed. Theodore Stanton and Harriot Stanton Blatch, 2 vols. (1922; New York: Arno & New York Times, 1969), 2:76–77n2.

The divorce proposal made by Stanton met an immediate opposition from some of her feminist allies. Wendell Phillips, partner in the antislavery movement, denounced her position at the convention, though Stanton did receive a majority approval there. Antoinette Brown Blackwell, the first ordained female minister in the United States, also dissented. She maintained that marriage limited the principle of individual rights and imposed "obligations" on a wife to her spouse and children. Liberal divorce laws, she added, will simply make it easier for irresponsible men to forsake their obligations and would place immense economic hardships on women left without support. She spoke for many women who feared that divorce threatened the family. Ernestine L. Rose also supported Stanton, but Lucy Stone, at first enthusiastic, came to have second thoughts.[15]

Bascom tried to do too much in too little space in his essay for the *Independent*. He acknowledged that marriage and the family stood in highest value, and nowhere else would "any loosening of the organic ties be more to be deprecated." The family, he assured, provided the links to all other social connections in the organic whole. But always Bascom emphasized that a true organic whole coexisted with the free and rational life of all its members. It did not establish its legitimacy by coercion or by authority. Often a family presents to the world a coherent unit, a stable piece of the community structure. He warned, however, that unity too often comes by physical domination and the arbitrary power, sustained in law, of the male family head. This exterior unity conceals within the family "a want of interior freedom and interior growth." "The fundamental conditions of a true union of the highest order is that each party shall come to it in the full possession of his and her powers," Bascom wrote. And he insisted that "the highest marriage relation is impossible save on a free spiritual basis." It does not serve the cause of reform to proclaim the divine and holy nature of marriage when that refrain locks in place the long accumulation of abuses from the past. Higher rates of divorce, Bascom believed, may just be the price we have to pay for moral and spiritual progress.[16]

15. Jean V. Matthews, *Women's Struggle for Equality: The First Phase, 1828–1876* (Chicago: Ivan R. Dee, 1997), 112–15; DuBois, "Outgrowing the Compact," 88–89; *Stanton*, 1:184–89.

16. Bascom, "Divorce and the Rights of Women," *Independent*, May 18, 1882, 2. See also another essay Bascom wrote for this publication, "The Freedom of the Family," where he said, "The joy and beauty of the household, its permanent and pervasive organic life, must depend on this condition of freedom, by which every member is allowed . . . the sacred rights of personality and their exercise, without chafing or disturbances." *Independent*, September 18, 1879, 1. Also published with the same title in *Friends' Intelligencer*, September 27, 1879, 502.

From his early years in western New York, and from the examples of his bold sister Mary and of a mother struggling mightily to feed a family of five, Bascom had never found anything relevant in the Cult of True Womanhood. Nor did any of the components of his intellectual training furnish any recommendation of it. Certainly he had no use for it on the subject dearest to his heart, the education of women.

Those who hired John Bascom to head the University of Wisconsin knew well the very public commitment to women's education that he had made at Williams. Yet in 1874 the issue of coeducation at the university still remained unsettled. Back in 1850 the regents had taken some steps by establishing a normal department for the education of "Female Teachers." But in 1858 a bill in the state legislature stipulating that the "University shall be equally open to the admission of pupils of both sexes over the age of sixteen" did not advance. Women would have to wait until 1863.[17] But in January 1874 the regents, perhaps anticipating Bascom's arrival, ended the separate curriculums and put full coeducation in place. Along the way other colleges had taken the leadership in coeducation in the Middle West, led by Oberlin (in the 1830s), Western Reserve, and Baldwin in Ohio; Antioch in Iowa; Washington University in St. Louis; Knox and Northwestern in Illinois. At Carroll College, the state's "pioneer" in Wisconsin higher education, women attended beginning in 1851, and Lawrence Institute in Appleton offered coeducation from its beginnings in 1847.

Women were gaining equal participation in the college curriculum at midwestern state universities. But not easily. The University of Illinois, after its establishment in 1867, admitted women to all courses, although President John Milton Gregory, citing women's distinctive traits, set the institution on a new departure in higher education. He called for a school at the university that would "provide a full course of instruction in the arts of the household, and the sciences relating thereto." The University of Iowa began coeducation at the outset, with four female students in a body of eighty-nine. Indiana University acted in 1867, after decades of debate about coeducation. Even then, when the sole woman to enter that year prepared for graduation, the trustees worried that her walking on stage to receive her diploma would expose the woman's ankles to leering eyes. Nor had the male students treated her, and the twelve additional women who arrived the next year, with gentlemanly decorum. The

17. Merle Curti and Vernon Carstensen, *The University of Wisconsin: A History, 1848–1925*, 2 vols. (Madison: University of Wisconsin Press, 1949), 1:23–24, 101 (quotation), 116–18, 374.

opening at the University of Michigan occurred amid faculty and student hostility that gave a rough reception to the first women to join the student body. Michigan had delayed in part because Henry Tappan, for all his pioneering in American higher education, adamantly opposed coeducation.[18] Women did not necessarily have it easy at Madison either, but male students there seemed more receptive to them.[19]

Coeducation made much slower progress in the eastern region of the country. Andrew Dickson White had clearly egalitarian principles with respect to the education of men and women, and coeducation made substantial gains at Cornell. At times, White moved cautiously, sensitive to public opinion, and to Cornell's already radical reputation, but also owing to reservations from major benefactors.[20] At Harvard, on the other hand, strong opposition came from President Eliot, as it did from the board of overseers. Eliot's inaugural address seemed to anticipate a place for women in the advanced courses at Harvard, but nothing for now. Constant pressure on him, however, kept the coeducation issue alive at Harvard.[21]

In the meantime, obstacles continued at Wisconsin. The regents' effort to find a new president in 1865 had produced two rejections. Its next invitation went to Paul Chadbourne of Williams, who visited the state twice and seemed ready to accept but then declined. The sticking point: coeducation. Chadbourne didn't like it. The board despaired, describing it "difficult, if not impossible" to

18. Winton U. Solberg, *The University of Illinois, 1867–1894: An Intellectual and Cultural History* (Urbana: University of Illinois Press, 1968), 160; Thomas D. Clark, *Indiana University, Midwestern Pioneer*, vol. 1: *The Early Years* (Bloomington: Indiana University Press, 1970), 124–25; Howard H. Peckham, *The Making of the University of Michigan, 1817–1967* (Ann Arbor: University of Michigan Press, 1967), 66. By 1870 eight state universities had opened their doors to women students (in order): Iowa, Wisconsin, Kansas, Indiana, Minnesota, Missouri, Michigan, California. Mabel Newcomer, *A Century of Higher Education for American Women* (New York: Harper & Brothers, 1959), 14. For more details on the patterns of coeducation, see also, Barbara Miller Solomon, *In the Company of Educated Women: A History of Women and Higher Education in America* (New Haven, CT: Yale University Press, 1985), 43–61.

19. Bascom's daughter Florence recalled that male students employed the "opprobrious epithet" "co-eds" in referring to their female colleagues. Florence Bascom, "The University in 1874–1887," *Wisconsin Magazine of History* 8 (March 1925), 303.

20. Glenn C. Altschuler, *Andrew D. White—Educator, Historian, Diplomat* (Ithaca, NY: Cornell University Press, 1979), 69, 99–105.

21. Hugh Hawkins, *Between Harvard and America: The Educational Leadership of Charles W. Eliot* (New York: Oxford University Press, 1972), 194–96.

find a competent leader who did not object to coeducation. It asked the legislature for the necessary authority to establish a separate female department. The university's future lay in jeopardy, the regents said, without such modification of the liberal standards recently secured. In 1867, chapter 117 of the General Laws made a new provision: "The University shall be open to female as well as male students, under such regulations and restrictions as the Board of Regents may deem proper." Thus the Female College came into being, and Chadbourne judged it safe to come to Madison.[22]

One must read the literature of coeducation discussion and debate against a peculiar background. Even champions of women's equality and those concerned with their intellectual progress spoke within the governing ideology of True Womanhood. It made certain assumptions: that women found their fulfillment in the "instinctive arts" of child-rearing, domestic economy, and religion, and that their mental aptitudes did not take them to subjects like mathematics, science, and philosophy. Furthermore, much of the day's medical expostulations severely warned against intellectual activity by women. Such perverse pursuits could have serious physical effects, these experts testified. And no one aroused more reaction, resentment, and criticism than did Edward H. Clarke in 1874. In that year he published his small book titled *Sex in Education*. Clarke did not argue that women had inferior brains, nor that they could not do demanding mental work. He wished mostly to warn that doing this work brought on severe physiological reactions and led to a dangerous impairment of women's health. He focused especially on young women during their years of sexual maturation, the ages fourteen to twenty, and cited the drawing of blood away from the critical organs, causing malnourishment of the ovaries and uterus. Overall, broken health resulted, the consequence of the distorting effects of this mental labor. Clarke furthermore specified the subjects that did the damage: calculus, Latin, Greek, natural science, theology. In effect, he wrote women right out of the prevailing academic curriculums of American colleges and universities. *Sex in Education* had the aura of authority. It had two chapters of case studies. It was "science." And Clarke had served on the faculty of the Harvard Medical College no less.[23]

Clarke's book brought reaction from all over. The protesters included Julia Ward Howe, former abolitionist, currently involved in women's causes, and

22. Reuben Gold Thwaites, *The University of Wisconsin: Its History and Its Alumni* (Madison, WI: J. N. Powell, 1900), 86.

23. Frances B. Cogan, *All-American Girl: The Ideal of Real Womanhood in Mid-Nineteenth-Century America* (Athens: University of Georgia Press, 1989), especially 68–70.

known throughout the country for her inspiring Civil War icon "The Battle Hymn of the Republic." Howe had close connections to the leading American transcendentalists. Immediately on the publication of Clarke's book Howe organized one of her own, an anthology of essays, each one a refutation of *Sex in Education*. In her own lead essay, Howe expressed resentment at Clarke's "intrusion into the sacred domain of womanly privacy." She believed that parents who heeded Clarke's heady counsel respecting their daughters would take them away from a life of high seriousness and into one of triviality, of fashion and social rounds of "flattery and folly," and altogether into a wasted existence. Of the thirteen essayists in Howe's collection, only two were identifiably male. Thomas Wentworth Higginson contributed and so did John Bascom, the new president from way out at the University of Wisconsin.[24]

Bascom's essay took on Clarke in certain particulars. He did not dismiss his book out of hand and judged it "able, candid, and fair." But he also judged it misconstrued, narrow, and prejudicial in its applications, and calling for conclusions that would perpetuate many of the current ills in American higher education. First, Bascom said, whatever disability may owe to women's biology and sexual development, we just have not experimented enough with higher education to draw any conclusions. Nor have we rightly understood these alleged physiological differences, and our ignorance and inattention to them have led many into facile conclusions. Clarke wanted separation of the sexes. But Bascom continued his case for fully integrated college curriculums for men and women, as he had just done in the Williams contest. Separation, he reasserted, is "unfitted for the best development of boys and girls alike." He insisted that "the average girl," even with the weight of possible biological disadvantages, approximated in intelligence the average boy. He had confidence that modern medicine would in time arrive to a better and less hysteric reaction to the female body and would move beyond the myths of intellectual activity's threat to women's health.[25]

Second, Bascom addressed the matter of coeducation as also a curriculum issue. Clarke had argued that were Harvard to admit women it would have to rearrange its course offerings, and at elaborate expense to the institution. But Clarke had it all wrong, Bascom replied. Women and men should have access to an identical curriculum. To be sure, they may choose to pursue different lines of study, but flexibility offered the answer. Bascom even indicated that

24. Introduction to *Sex and Education: A Reply to Dr. E. H. Clarke's "Sex in Education,"* ed. Julia Ward Howe (1874; New York: Arno Press, 1972), 7, 10–11.
25. John Bascom, "Essay X," in Howe, *Sex and Education*, 164–68.

Harvard especially, with its pioneering in the elective system, could lead the way. He feared above all that the maintaining or the creating of separate curriculums for the sexes would have terrible consequences, affirming the worst aspects of the prevailing gender culture, its harsh dualism. A program of study divided into men's and women's tracks, Bascom warned, would result in "a feeble intellectual mood" among women. It would also set women in the direction of making them useful for social intercourse at the expense of intellectual strength. Here he made points similar to Howe's. Dual education as opposed to common education could result only "in strengthening the very evil warred with." A "cast-iron mode" of thinking has too long beset higher education, Bascom concluded. It is time for fresh thinking.[26]

A few years later, Bascom also participated, indirectly, in a symposium on coeducation held at the home of Joseph Cook, a popular lecturer and theological liberal in Boston. Representatives from Boston University and Harvard Divinity School read the major papers and then presented correspondence from others interested in the subject. Historian Francis Parkman said, "I do not believe in co-education, but in the broadest and most complete education for women." Chadbourne, now back at Williams, fought his old battle. He claimed that females' presence on campus distracted male students. He also said that he found it easier "to govern two hundred men" at Williams than he had the mixed student body at Wisconsin. Proponents, however, outnumbered dissenters. The presiders read a letter from Bascom, who cited the record at Wisconsin. Although the women represent only one-fourth of the students at Madison, they win one-half of the academic honors, he reported. Furthermore, they are healthier than the males. He also judged student decorum at Wisconsin superior to that among the eastern colleges, referencing "a decided improvement in manners" in a coeducational arrangement. The faculty at Wisconsin, he added, unanimously approve coeducation. Additional, favorable testimony came from college presidents and faculty at California, Columbia (President Henry Barnard), Michigan (James B. Angell), and from doctors and religious leaders. In a suggestive conclusion, the woman who reported these events for the *Christian Union* summarized the case for coeducation, stating that all the evidence confirmed that coeducation posed no threat to "true women."[27]

26. Bascom, "Essay X," 168–69.

27. Sarah K. Bolton, "Co-Education: A Symposium at Joseph Cook's," *Christian Union*, February 18, 1880, 149. Frances B. Cogan has studied a large body of contemporary literature about American women and locates an alternative ideal to "True Women," one she labels "Real Women." It portrayed women as rational beings, intellectually capable, and physically strong. *All-American Girl*, especially 65, 67, 74–75, 94.

Bascom thought coeducation a settled matter at Wisconsin, but there emerged in 1877 a "last-ditch" and "rear-guard" effort, as the university's historians label it, to derail the egalitarian university. A member of the board took the first step. He wanted the changes of 1874 reversed, with Ladies' Hall turned into a separate female college and having a curriculum appropriate to female idiosyncrasies. A committee appointed by the board would have none of it, asserting that such a step would mark a retroactive and antiprogressive move. Besides, it would cost too much. At the same time, a report from the board of visitors also spoke against open coeducation. The problem, as the visitors saw it, was "the appearance of ill-health" among the female students. Of course, it knew also where to place the blame, for here the shadow of Clarke still hovered over the coeducation debate. Women's monthly changes, the report believed, produced the "condition of bloodlessness," "the sallow features, the pearly whiteness of the eye, the lack of color." These symptoms, it claimed, owed to the strains of mental exertion that these females had to endure as they sought to make up study time lost in the periodic cycle. The visitors conceded the value of education to women, but that value could not override the enduring damage, they insisted. "Better that the future mothers of the state should be robust, hearty, healthy women, than that, by over-study, they entail upon their descendants the germs of disease."[28]

Bascom struggled to contain his anger at this report. He would, alas, have to take on the subject yet again and plead anew the case for integrated coeducation, the common curriculum. He met the visitors on their own grounds and readdressed the health question. Bascom found it appalling that the medical profession today was still invoking "a function familiar from the dawn of human life" and citing it against the progress of women as if the menstrual cycle were a fresh discovery. He had asserted in his earlier reply to Clarke that prudence, and the gains made by modern medicine's understanding of this biological matter, made the recourse to it obsolete. Besides, he added, "it has no more to do with co-education than with separate education." And have we not allowed women to work as operatives, clerks, teachers, housekeepers, and in other activities where hard work prevails? Yet we make no question of the monthly cycle, citing it only against the progress of women in education.[29]

28. Curti and Carstensen, *University of Wisconsin*, 1:376–77.

29. "Report of the President of the University to the Board of Regents," in *Annual Report of the Board of Regents of the University of Wisconsin, for the Fiscal Year Ending September 30, 1877* (Madison: David Atwood, 1877), 38. Coverage of the Wisconsin proceedings from faraway Philadelphia referenced Bascom's "ill-concealed wrath" at the visitors. Editorial, "Co-Education and the Sexes," *Philadelphia Medical Times*, February 2, 1878, 8.

Bascom had resolved also to settle this matter "by facts." He announced to the board of regents that he had personally studied the health matter at the university. Looking at the data of student absences from class for reasons of sickness, he noted 357 on the part of the men and 18 on the part of the women. Were their absences in ratio to the number of males and females in the student body there would have been 155 days of absences on the part of the women, he calculated. And yes, sex differences do have an influence on this pattern, Bascom said. The young men, he insisted, did not take well to confinements, and, "sun-browned and robust," they do not make a good transition to the physical strictures of the classroom. In fact, the president urged, "study is more congenial to the habits of young women, and the visiting committee are certainly mistaken in supposing that they have to work harder in accomplishing their tasks. The reverse is true." Bascom expressed extreme confidence that women students at Wisconsin thrived in better health after their arrival, removed now from the stresses of normal society. His report rendered a forceful conclusion: "The young women do not then seem to deteriorate with us in health, but quite the opposite."[30]

Student opinion on coeducation, at least so far as registered in the *University Press*, strongly supported Bascom. Earlier the student newspaper had reprinted the case he had made for women's education in Howe's anthology. At another point it reprinted the minority report supporting admission of female students that Bascom wrote at Williams, with its strong indictment of gender roles and women's exclusion from the nation's public life. The paper reported positively on student deportment in the mixed classes and later gave a vigorous editorial retort to the visitors' complaints about the women's health. The students regretted that much damage had already come from the visitors' senseless criticism.[31]

Bascom won this battle at Wisconsin, a permanent victory. But for many, and Bascom, too, the cause of women's progress embraced other objectives as well. Little would change, they believed, if women did not have the right to vote, if they did not have the means to effect change in law, if they did not have a more powerful role to play in public life, which voting and political office would gain for them. From today's perspective, such a course seems self-evident. But both among women leaders then and in the historiography of American women's history, suffrage had not always enjoyed high priority.

30. [Bascom], "Report" (1877), 38–39.

31. See the *University Press* for May 1, 1874, October 17, 1874, January 7, 1877, and December 19, 1877.

That situation provides an important measure of Bascom's strong defense of women's suffrage. It shows him positioned on the radical side of the movement, and it also shows him sympathetic to the ardent, emotional pleas some suffragists were making. The literature of the day often reveals how deeply injured some women felt about their exclusion from the most important access to the civic life of the nation—the ballot. Consider these words from 1886, by the three feminist leaders who compiled the records of the women's suffrage movement:

> And here is the secret of the infinite sadness of women of genius; of their dissatisfaction with life, in exact proportion to their development. A woman who occupies the same realm of thought with man, who can explore with him the depths of science, comprehend the steps of progress through the long past and prophesy those of the momentous future, must ever be surprised and aggravated with his assumptions of headship and superiority, a superiority she never concedes, an authority she utterly repudiates. Words can not describe the indignation, the humiliation a proud woman feels for her sex in disenfranchisement.[32]

Until the Nineteenth Amendment wrote women's suffrage into the United States Constitution, the struggle to secure the right proceeded state by state. At the time the Bascoms arrived in Madison in 1874, no state allowed women to vote in a national election. In Wisconsin, where Emma Bascom and her husband joined in the cause, the matter faced a difficult passage. Women in Wisconsin had emerged as an active political presence, even without the right to vote or hold political office, in the fight against slavery. Following the creation of the first national women's organization, the Female Moral Reform Society in 1833, model local societies started in Prairieville (Waukesha) and other Yankee strongholds. Most of the women there had New York State backgrounds. The FMRS concerned itself first with prostitution, but in Wisconsin abolition of slavery soon commanded most attention. Wisconsin women reformers, as seen earlier, also took up temperance. Suffrage in the meantime stood backstage, and "women's rights" had hardly any emphasis before the end of the Civil War. Women's suffrage in Wisconsin rallied the same opposition that antislavery and temperance had provoked. The liquor interest, centered in the Brewers

---

32. *History of Woman's Suffrage*, ed. Elizabeth Cady Stanton, Susan B. Anthony, and Matilda Joslyn Gage, vol. 2, *1861–1876* (1886; New York: Arno & New York Times, 1969), 266–67.

Emma Bascom. (Wisconsin Historical Society, WHi-121042)

Congress, correctly perceived in women's rights the old issues of temperance and Sabbatarianism, which, of course, would mean no beer sales on Sundays and perhaps no other day. The liquor interest also exploited immigrant votes and raised the numbers opposing women's suffrage. Olympia Brown, a national leader in the movement and Universalist minister who had taken a church in Racine in 1878, saw the connection and resented it. She, like Stanton, Howe, and others, considered it "unbearable" that women existed inferior in the United States to "all the riffraff of Europe that is poured upon our shores."[33]

Rages against female equality also came from the Democratic Party kingpin Edward G. Ryan. Now chief justice of the Wisconsin Supreme Court, Ryan made short shrift of any idea that a woman could, for example, be a lawyer. The idea violated "natural law," he said, and explained: "The law of nature destines and qualifies the female sex for the rearing and nurture of the children of our race and for the custody of the homes of the world and their maintenance in love and honor." Thus, women entering the legal profession would constitute "departures from the order of nature." We must be protective of the "peculiar qualities of womanhood": "its gentle graces, its quick susceptibility, its purity, its delicacy, its emotional impulses, its subordination of hard reason to sympathetic feeling." Such was the thinking that any effort for women's equality confronted in Wisconsin.[34]

John and Emma Bascom disdained this mentality and together they joined with others to undo a decision of the state supreme court that Ryan headed. The situation involved the effort of Lavinia Goodell to become the first woman attorney in Wisconsin, pending approval by the state supreme court. Goodell was born in Utica, New York, in the "burned-over district," where her father, William Goodell, had moved the family from New York City in 1836, three years before her birth. William championed abolitionism and other reforms, and his wife, Clarissa, had joined the FMRS. Fugitive slaves passed through the Goodell home. Lavinia aspired to a career in law and answered her sister's

33. Charles Neu, "Olympia Brown and the Woman Suffrage Movement," in *Women's Wisconsin: From Native Matriarchies to the New Millennium*, ed. Genevieve G. McBride (Madison: Wisconsin Historical Society Press, 2005), 232; Matthews, *Women's Struggle*, 124–26; *History of Woman's Suffrage*, 2:335.

34. Genevieve G. McBride, *On Wisconsin Women: Working for Their Rights from Settlement to Suffrage* (Madison: University of Wisconsin Press, 1993), 62, 78, 88; Catherine B. Cleary, "Lavinia Goodell, First Woman Lawyer in Wisconsin," *Wisconsin Magazine of History* 74 (Summer 1991), 260 (quotations).

skepticism by asking, "What is more womanly than the desire to defend and protect the widow and the fatherless and in a field where they have been wronged previously?" After a stay in Brooklyn, Goodell removed with her family to Janesville, Wisconsin. She taught Sunday school and became secretary of the local temperance union. She remained committed to temperance the rest of her life. When she added women's suffrage to her causes, she worked hard for that good, too. These qualities alone would have recommended Goodell to the Bascoms. Goodell gained a law license in Janesville and sought a state license in 1875. Many commented on her personal and intellectual assets in area newspapers. Things looked good until Justice Ryan and the court stopped her.[35]

Emma Bascom took an interest in Goodell's effort. When the young attorney went before the supreme court to outline her case, Bascom urged her to have it printed in the *Wisconsin State Journal*. She had in the meantime invited Goodell to visit her at the president's home in Madison. Goodell wrote to a friend describing Emma Bascom as "an intelligent and cultured lady and in full sympathy with all the advance [*sic*] views of woman's position. . . . She and her husband sympathize warmly with my effort to be admitted." But the court, finding no statutory authority in Wisconsin to support admittance of females to the state bar, ruled against Goodell. That action gave her supporters an opportunity. They now attempted to achieve the desired access by way of the legislature. Their effort received much attention, even outside Wisconsin. Lucy Stone in the *Woman's Journal* gave a lengthy exposure of the court decision and made a renewed appeal for legal equality. Both John and Emma Bascom used their contacts and influence in the state to secure the needed legislation. It came the next year, 1877, when the Wisconsin solons wrote a new statute. It stated that "no person shall be refused admission to the bar of this State on account of sex." The Bascoms had secured a significant change.[36]

Women's suffrage in Wisconsin gained new energy in 1869. Movement leaders Susan B. Anthony and Stanton went to Milwaukee that winter and rallied an enthusiastic audience for the first meeting of the Wisconsin Woman Suffrage Association. When the Bascoms arrived in Madison they became immediately a powerful pair for women's suffrage in the state. But a limited suffrage bill met defeat in 1881. That loss prompted a revival of the WWSA, which convened in 1882, its program headed by Henry Blackwell and his wife,

---

35. Cleary, "Goodell," 243–51.
36. Cleary, "Goodell," 258 (quotation), 261–65; McBride, *On Wisconsin Women*, 88, 93–94.

Lucy Stone. The organization then elected Emma Bascom as a vice president, the same title she had in the state's chapter of the WCTU. Like so many female reformers, Emma Bascom conjoined these two causes. Later on she held the presidency of both organizations. John Bascom presided at the WWSA meeting. And as he had bolted the Republican Party for its lackluster support of temperance, Emma Bascom likewise excoriated the party for its indifference to women's suffrage. She wrote, in a letter to Anthony: "Will [the Republican party], as so repeatedly in the past, turn a deaf ear to reason, and still continue to deny the rights of half the human family? If so . . . it [will] continue deaf, dumb and blind."[37]

That letter also showed the extent of Emma Bascom's full endorsement, with words of appreciation, of the work done by Stanton and her group of feminists. She congratulated them for the gains they were making in advancing human progress by way of sexual equality. "The irrational sentiment," she added, "based upon the methods and customs of barbarous times, is rapidly yielding to reason. The world is learning—women are learning—that character, even womanly character, does not suffer from too much breadth of thought, or from too active a sympathy in human interests and human affairs, but is ever enriched by a larger circle of ideas, larger experience, and more extended activities."[38] In their three-volume history of the women's movement, Stanton, Stone, and Matilda Joslyn Gage heaped much praise on John Bascom. They cited his efforts on behalf of coeducation. To "his wise management" of the effort at Wisconsin they attributed the success it had experienced there. They remarked, too, on "the scholarly address" Bascom gave at an 1882 convention in Madison. He is "always found ready to speak for woman suffrage, both in public and private," Stanton remarked.[39]

Bascom advanced his case for women's rights not only in his sociology, in class and in print, but also in the public arena. He joined the many suffragists who seized the speakers' forums and addressed audiences around the nation. Wisconsin saw them in large numbers. And Bascom had the opportunity in 1882 to offer one of his most important addresses, the one cited by Stanton and her colleagues. He did so at a meeting of the Wisconsin Advocates of the Movement and brought to the subject of woman suffrage a framework that was classic John Bascom.

37. McBride, *On Wisconsin Women*, 46, 59–60, 101, 110, 95 (quotation).
38. McBride, *On Wisconsin Women*, 95.
39. *History of Woman's Suffrage*, 2:647.

Bascom clearly respected his audience because he began with reference to evolution and its complexities. His opening indicates how thoroughly the liberal theologian had appropriated evolution and the organic model as the basis of his views on social reform. Here Bascom's tactics take on special importance. In having recourse to the organic model on which to base women's rights, Bascom placed himself against the rival antifeminists who now rejected individualism and natural rights for the organic model, focusing on the family and insisting that women's rights threatened the social edifice. That emphasis gained currency in the 1870s, the organic ideal as signified by the family above all now given priority over the individual liberties of females who thus threatened the family.[40] Bascom observed how topical evolution had become, even in lay conversation, however much the idea had led to some absurd applications. We must take the widest measure here, Bascom said, and see evolution as the expansion of Reason, opening up the world to new possibilities and human progress. And, of course, he urged a Christian appropriation of evolution. In the new thinking, Bascom instructed, different ideas all come together—evolution, development, growth, the Kingdom of Heaven. Each of them critically underscores what we mean by progress, "from which the resources of reason are springing," Bascom told his listeners.[41]

The topic of woman suffrage, the president urged, owes its substance to these "profound ideas." For what is evolution but the connection of species to species, an endless trajectory of interconnections and interrelationships? Bascom put the organic model right up front. Society, he specified, evolves by "the connection of part with part, and of parts to one whole." So we must consider then how the organic system pertains to this critical question of our day, how society situates men and women. Any measure we take of the subject must answer the overriding consideration of just how society seeks its own good, advances its own progress, indeed anticipates in its actions "the coming of the kingdom of heaven." Bascom never saw the individual as separate from the larger group to which that person belongs, and he affirmed that one cannot prosper, cannot grow, apart from society. Ideally, reciprocity and harmony govern. "The individual should make, and may be called upon to make any needed sacrifice for the community." In turn, the community should exercise its powers on behalf of individuals, all individuals, the inclusive constituent makeup of the social whole. Nothing more properly describes the meaning of growth and progress, he believed.[42]

40. Matthews, *Women's Struggle*, 172. Matthews says that the organic ideal became "the central theme in antifeminist rhetoric."

41. John Bascom, *Woman Suffrage* [Address] (Madison: n.p., [1882]), 1.

42. Bascom, *Woman Suffrage*, 1–2.

With the evolutionary model still in view, Bascom explained that these operations proceed along no prescribed path. They require constant adjustments, shifts, adaptations, as the society works to achieve larger integration of its parts. We know the standard for measuring our progress. "Any movement, therefore," Bascom told his listeners, "which divides society and takes a portion and leaves a portion, is ultimately destructive of society as a complete organization." At each turn, the advancing demands of civilization, virtue, culture, goodwill, and the Kingdom of Heaven will call forth new adjustments.[43]

Thus situating the subject, Bascom, as always, placed society first. Unlike many in the movement, he did not focus on individual rights. He rarely defended women's rights as "natural rights," at least not in the classical Lockean or Jeffersonian sense. That is, he did not appeal to the laws of nature and hold up abstract, universal norms as the intellectual foundation for advancing gender equality. He differed from other strong advocates of woman suffrage to that extent.[44] In this terminology Bascom took careful measures to make distinctions. For although he did maintain that "there are no natural rights in the sense of primary and absolute rights," in an important sense, he affirmed, woman suffrage "is a natural right." One needs to shift the locus of nature from an ideal to a real and practical realm, Bascom believed. He wanted women's equality to have a momentous reference to the historical movement and the point at which society, "civilization," had now arrived. To project equality back onto all history as a point of judgment against it availed nothing, he said. By history Bascom meant evolution. Where stands civilization now on the matter?[45]

Here Bascom's address made a key link. The empowerment of individuals, the essential ingredients of the healthy, adapting social organism, always invokes the activities of the state, he emphasized. The state adjudicates the needs of individuals and the community. Bascom saw the process as an evolutionary norm. Advancing civilization enlarges this role of government, giving expanded strength to the social organism. The state, then, has an obligation to locate and remove restrictions on individuals; these restrictions impede society's progress. That state best fulfills its functions when it both helps to enlarge individual powers and integrates them into the social organism. In other words, the state prepares the way for new rights and provides for their complete exercise when

43. Bascom, *Woman Suffrage*, 2.
44. Elizabeth Cady Stanton insisted that woman suffrage was "based on natural right." *Elizabeth Cady Stanton, Feminist as Thinker: A Reader in Documents and Essays*, ed. Ellen Carol DuBois and Richard Cándida Smith (New York: New York University Press, 2007), 242. Julia Ward Howe referenced "the inalienable right of all men" and women. *History of Woman's Suffrage*, 2:321, 335.
45. Bascom, *Woman Suffrage*, 2–4.

they have accrued. As prime illustration of this point, Bascom cited women's right to the electoral franchise. Women claim that right on "an equality with man," he submitted. The state does not confer these powers, Bascom cautioned, it simply arranges the means to exercise them. By the principles of evolutionary growth, humanity moves into arenas of larger liberty, larger powers. The state acts as an agent of progress when it facilitates the incorporation of new liberty and new power.[46]

In the latter part of his address, Bascom moved from the philosopher's perch to the soapbox. He addressed specifics, and often in anger. But even when he bristled at the status of gender relations in contemporary America, his talk remained thematic. Many impediments to advancement and inclusion in public life beset women today, Bascom lamented. He cited the longstanding and degrading attitudes men have toward women and the construction of female attributes by men. The past weighs heavily and oppressively upon us, he said. We still address women, still define their character, in silly, romantic notions. We pretend to exercise a chivalry that has long since had any good use, if it ever did. "Much of the chivalry of bygone centuries," Bascom avowed, "was thoroughly rotten at heart, and much of the gallantry of the present is only the natural heir of its diseases." Underneath, he insisted, lies a "deep, almost bitter contempt" of women. It makes of them obstacles of show, pageantry, scenic effects. As such it trivializes them. In fact, it does worse. These constructions, Bascom pronounced, deny women intellectual strength; they make women peripheral to the large social interest. In short, in a manner that Bascom habitually marked as the worst of sins, they deprive women of power.[47]

Finally, Bascom wanted to meet the arguments used by opponents of women's suffrage. Some, of course, used the romantic construction of female nature to detach women from the rough unpleasantries of "real" life—in business or in politics. We need to get rid of those notions altogether, as Bascom had said earlier in his address. He did acknowledge that women suffered from certain deficiencies. For instance, they do not have the business sense that men do. They do not exhibit the interpersonal skills and protocol needed for the conduct of affairs. But why should we be surprised? he asked. We raise the two sexes in radically different ways, and train them for dual roles in society. The "deficiency" in industrial virtues, then, has nothing to do with innate sex differences. Women also, Bascom believed, exercise an idealistic and absolutist notion of justice. They sometimes err on the side of excess and lack a rooting in concrete

46. Bascom, *Woman Suffrage*, 3.
47. Bascom, *Woman Suffrage*, 6.

matters. But again, why should we be surprised? Society has denied women that exposure to raw experience and to the range of duties and activities that give our judgments relevance to the circumstances of time and place. These habits, Bascom avowed, represent "the crowning results of the limited circle of action which social customs assign women." They reflect their narrow experience, their social confinements. Women will serve society to the best of their capacities, Bascom asserted, only when they can thrive in the large public domain, where adaptation and resourcefulness grow from the experience therein. Bascom concluded his address: "It is precisely because of our ideal of womanly character, and of the direction in which women are falling off from it, that we are led to think that a larger life would be to them as it is to us all, a nobler and better life—the very life into which God is leading us."[48]

God is leading us." For Bascom the well-being of women had a meaningful and emphatic relation to religion. It provided a cornerstone to his liberal theology and offered a most important illustration of his social gospel. One might assume that Bascom's progressive writings on women came easily to anyone who so embraced liberal theology. But the record shows that there was nothing automatic about it. Women's rights did have male religious advocates. Henry Ward Beecher preached and wrote for the movement and had high offices in the major national women's suffrage groups. Beecher stood with those feminists who made citizenship and the suffrage the foundations of sexual equality. Of all the liberals, Beecher seems most to resemble Bascom on this subject. On the woman question, he judged suffrage a matter of Christian ethics and fairness, but he also welcomed it for its improving effects on the social body: "I say that more and more the great interests of human society in America are such as need the peculiar genius that God has given to women." Beecher had no liking for ideas about "woman's place" and welcomed women to the political arena to wash it clean of its "rotten" male core.[49]

48. Bascom, *Woman Suffrage*, 6–7. University historians Curti and Carstensen relate that four years later, in 1886, Susan B. Anthony gave a public recognition to Bascom. She was speaking at the Women's Rights and Suffrage Convention in Madison and began by turning to Bascom in the audience and stating her appreciation for his good work in the cause. "It was a dramatic moment." Bascom offered some optimistic comments; the cause will inevitably triumph, he assured. Curti and Carstensen, *University of Wisconsin*, 1:291.

49. Gary Dorrien, *The Making of American Liberal Theology: Imagining Progressive Religion, 1805–1900* (Louisville: Westminster John Knox Press, 2001), 214, 228, 231; Henry Ward Beecher, "Woman's Duty to Vote," in *Speeches of George William Curtis [and] Henry Ward*

But from another religious liberal, one of the most influential, women's suffrage received a cold reception. In his later years, after the Civil War, Horace Bushnell wrote the work titled *Women's Suffrage: The Reform against Nature*. Bushnell endorsed the ideal of the organic society as much as Bascom did, and Bascom had found much value in Bushnell's liberal theology. The Hartford minister did believe in a progressive history; he had faith that barriers to equality for all would fade. But as he had little truck for abolitionists, however much he despised slavery, he also did not welcome radical views of gender equality. Females' participation in politics constituted for Bushnell a contradiction of their essential nature. This world, of corruption and vice, he said, threatened the moral purity of women, and they would spoil their good nature by immersion in it, Bushnell warned. He could not square woman suffrage with Christianity, and he certainly gave no credence to any doctrine of natural rights. He even believed that women's suffrage constituted "a challenge of the rights of masculinity." Bushnell remained, as his biographer describes him, a very conservative Yankee Puritan when it came to meaningful social reform.[50]

In the large circle of liberal theology, the Unitarians, of course, had a major place. But a study of the *Christian Examiner*, their intellectual outlet, reveals a host of reservations about women's rights. Its contributors endorsed the prevailing gender dualism and labeled any meddling with it "a violation of the law of Nature," as one of them wrote. Essayists for the *Examiner* did not judge women inferior, only different. Convention generally reigned among the Unitarian contributors. They valued women for their spiritual qualities and saw male pursuits as limited to the material world. The journal perceived nothing wrong with pay inequity. The *Examiner* welcomed women into public life as teachers, or to any role that did not disturb society's natural gender balance. It considered politics as a sphere of action unworthy of women. They would only squander their superior faith and righteousness in that sordid arena. All the *Examiner*'s contributors opposed women's suffrage.[51]

Beecher, ed. Henry Ward Beecher and George William Curtis (New York: National-American Woman Suffrage Association, 1898), 71.

50. Robert Bruce Mullin, *The Puritan as Yankee: A Life of Horace Bushnell* (Grand Rapids, MI: Eerdmans, 2002), 243–46; Matthews, *Women's Struggle*, 171–72. Bushnell did not oppose women having a variety of work activities outside the home. He just did not accept them in locations of authority.

51. Dawson Barrett, "Duties and Rights: Answering 'the Woman Question' in the *Christian Examiner*" (a paper prepared for the author, graduate seminar, Spring 2007), 7, 8, 10, 12–13.

Bascom differed from the generality of liberal religious thinkers on the subject of women in two important regards. First, he avoided essentialism. He rarely talked about the special nature of men and the special nature of women. He did not, like Bushnell, make these distinctions the foundations of God's natural order. He did not cite the "peculiar genius of women," like Beecher, and uphold it as the needed ingredient of a purer world. Second, and more importantly, Bascom foregrounded evolution as the primary consideration in any examination of social roles for the genders. Beecher too subscribed to evolution but on this subject he did not use it as a framework. Bascom conjoined the woman question to his larger social philosophy and to his liberal theology. He allowed a role for the state in bringing a large portion of society into public life through the voting franchise. This action, he emphasized, involved empowerment, a key ingredient of evolutionary progress. Bascom saw human evolution whole. It would be fully human in its best and most improving course when it included humanity whole.[52]

Postscript. In 1912, in a state referendum, Wisconsin (male) voters rejected women's suffrage. In 1919, Wisconsin became the first state to ratify the Nineteenth Amendment.

52. Bascom, as his writings on women and other social issues showed, used evolution in a large schematic framework, one from which he could read and address social issues. Like other religious liberals, he did not make a Darwinian appropriation of evolution. Other champions of feminism did, however. See the illuminating study by Kimberly A. Hamlin, *From Eve to Evolution: Darwin, Science, and Women's Rights in Gilded Age America* (Chicago: University of Chicago Press, 2014).

8

Progressivism 3: Money and Class

Gilded Age America thrives in historical memory with striking signs and symbols: massive private homes, the French "chateaux" on Fifth Avenue New York; summer "retreats" in Newport, Rhode Island; luxuriant travel in private cars in this, the great era of the railroads. Individuals also vie for attention: names like John D. Rockefeller and Standard Oil; Andrew Carnegie and U.S. Steel; J. P. Morgan and "finance capitalism." Money was on the land. The "New South" rose in the post-Reconstruction era. It saw the ravages of raw industrialism and coal mining that stripped the mountains and hills and left the harsh exposure. The Gilded Age South also produced that era's worst record in race relations. Lynching attained record highs in the 1890s; intimidation against blacks made the Ku Klux Klan an odd-looking but frightening force. The end of Reconstruction saw "Jim Crow" segregation, a long-standing fixture of the Southern way of life, sanctioned even by the United States Supreme Court. In the West the age of the cowboy had its brief moment but secured a place in romantic American folklore. As it did so it also obscured the decades of race warfare that destroyed a civilization and removed American Indians from the advancing paths of American life.

And throughout this era, the "labor question." The United States steam-rolled ahead through its "second industrial revolution." Heavy emigration from China and Europe redefined the labor force, visible in its new appearance, from the railroad construction lines in the West, to the mining locations every-where, and in the big cities. The tensions and adjustments posed massive problems, challenging American business management and the labor movement that gained in strength after the Civil War. In this category, too, the Gilded Age made its identity—the most violent era of industrial warfare in American history. To be sure, workers gained materially in this period (approximately 1877 to 1901), improving in wages in years often marked by deflation. But dissatisfaction abounded, and so did strikes and work stoppages. Gilded Age America produced the most dramatic and violent strikes to date: the Great Railway Strike of 1877, the Haymarket Rebellion of 1886, the Homestead Strike in 1892, the Pullman Strike of 1894. In 1881, a prosperous year, 477 work stoppages occurred, involving 130,000 workers, and only once before the end of the century did strikes number fewer than a thousand around the nation.[1]

The Gilded Age has never had a good reputation. The politically liberal perspective of most historians who have written about it places the era between the great, progressive constitutional changes achieved by the Reconstruction program that preceded it and the energetic reforms, at all levels of American government, undertaken in the Progressive Era that followed it. The Gilded Age stands thus as an ugly and unsavory interlude, this age of black and gray, of gaudy taste and conspicuous consumption, this society of unconscionable disparities of wealth and poverty, this culture of violence and race hatred, this political domain of boss rule and the corruption of money and politics. Other historians, like this author, may concede all the moral judgments against this era, the race issue especially, and yet try to see the era on its own terms, indeed even enjoy the whole gaudy show. All should try to see the record whole. And when one views the Gilded Age close up, another fact emerges. This era of American history was alive with new ideas and it produced a reform literature that set the stage for the Progressive movement that applied it. And that's where John Bascom comes in.

Bascom, writing for his former student Washington Gladden's publication *Sunday Afternoon*, stated, "The great social problem of our times is the relation of the working to the wealthier classes."[2] Perhaps no aspect of this era challenged thinkers more than did this "labor question." Here the human dynamics stood out. Beginning in the antebellum decades but now intensifying year after year, a new kind of worker became prevalent—one who owned no property and one who brought no particular skills to his work. The wider use of machinery was diminishing the dominance of the artisan, the skilled worker, the craftsman who made a product from its start to its finish. That kind of worker had long

1. John A. Garraty, *The New Commonwealth, 1877–1900* (New York: Harper & Row, 1968), 128, 135.

2. John Bascom, "A Kind of Co-Operation," *Good Company* (*Sunday Afternoon*) 4 (1879), 294. Bascom contributed five pieces to the journal. See especially "The Kingdom of Heaven," 3 (May 1879), 385–93.

situated itself in the American ideal of republicanism. Thomas Jefferson and others had looked to the yeoman farmer and its type as the model of American citizenry—a small property owner, and an informed participant in the civic life of the local community and the nation at large. The yeoman exemplified the stake-in-society that assured stable democracy. But as Rosanne Currarino writes, "The emergence of a class of permanent wage workers overtly mocked the republican hopes for America." And it did so, too, because the new ranks came so heavily from abroad. The Chinese workers especially confounded long-standing assumptions about work and consumption. They lived by themselves; they were overwhelmingly male and unattached. They worked like machines, but spent hardly a dime, hoarding all their earned income. They defied all the American norms about work, community, citizenship, and government. But did they represent the American future? Did they foretell what now seemed to becoming normative—hordes of hollow men leaving the factories and mines, their faces blank, devoid of spirit? No wonder so much of the reform literature focused on the workers and the lives they led, the quality of their existence in the vast mechanical complex of the industrial age.[3] Bascom, as earlier observed, had already diagnosed the labor question along those lines.

Many critics also saw in the Gilded Age an era of excess and of social disintegration. None felt happy about the obsession with money that seemed now to have overtaken the social imagination and held Americans in its grip. Bascom disliked it, and said as much, on more than one occasion, to commencement audiences at Madison. "Trade," he lamented, "is the fetich [*sic*] of the American people." High finance, "the gambling transactions of Boards of Trade," spread a feverish spirit everywhere. As one who always favored harmony and balance, Bascom condemned this "blind rush of active power," producing a "multiplicity of maladjustments and non-adjustments." Everywhere, he added, we see "a constant tendency to disintegration." Social reconstruction must come from better organization, and none needed it more than American workers, Bascom believed. He would take that perspective into his sustained defense of labor unions. In the popular magazine the *Forum* Bascom wrote, "The tramp is a completely disorganized element," and so too are workers who drift from place to place. So in fact were the mass of laborers generally, whom Bascom saw as an undifferentiated lot with no place in the social structure and thus removed too far from the community's attention. "It is with this unorganized material that society, as an organization, is contending," he wrote. And when labor

3. Rosanne Currarino, *The Labor Question in America: Economic Democracy in the Gilded Age* (Urbana: University of Illinois Press, 2011), 40 (quotation), 43–46.

becomes "alien matter," Bascom warned, it becomes a large social problem. Rending the whole, it throws society into "convulsions." He viewed the social question from the perspective of his evolutionary thinking. The highest direction of the race, he said repeatedly, moves toward moral and spiritual harmony, the dominant direction of history. But the United States today, he had to concede, defies that tendency, and therein lies the challenge.[4]

One fact especially describes this challenge. The struggle of labor against capital, Bascom asserted, does not take place on level ground. All the advantages lie on the side of money, he asserted. Nor did he intend to refrain from judgment on the money classes. He marked the differences between honest wealth and easy wealth, and he reflected—Whig and Republican though his political inclinations—a Jacksonian Democratic bias against speculation and the unproductive wealth it accrued.[5] Bascom highlighted the issue in his sociology book. The prevailing arrangement of economic power, with its array of "industrial usurpations," he believed, makes a mockery of all the claims for the benefits of competition in the marketplace. "The money-power," Bascom wrote, "vigorously asserts itself, and it easily overawes the moral and social forces which should work with it." Bascom also took his case to the pages of the *Independent*. We see one pool of capital formed after another, he wrote for the influential newspaper. "It has no more to do with legitimate commerce than has the quarreling of draymen with each other in a crowded street," he remarked. Bascom decried the illegitimate nature of the new leviathans of corporate America. Even as he addressed the Wisconsin students for the last time in 1887, Bascom warned against "the accumulation of immense wealth in single hands."[6]

While many feared the consequences to republicanism posed by the new working class, Bascom feared much more the damages from large corporations. They are "wholly out of harmony with republican institutions," he said. The threat came in two ways, he explained: directly from tangible corruptions in

4. John Bascom, *A Christian State* [Baccalaureate Sermon] (Milwaukee: Cramer, Aikens & Cramer, 1887), 12; idem, "What Do the Members of a State University Owe to the State?," *University Review* 1 (December 1884), 89; idem, *The Seat of Sin* [Baccalaureate Sermon] (n.p., [1876]), 14; idem, "The Gist of the Labor Question," *Forum* 4 (September 1887), 87–88.

5. John Bascom, *Sociology* (New York: G. P. Putnam's Sons, 1887), 223–25.

6. Bascom, *Sociology*, 211 (first quotation), 252, 220; idem, "Modes of Correction," *Independent*, May 12, 1887, 5 (second quotation); idem, *Christian State*, 19; Sidney Dean Townley, "Diary of a Student of the University of Wisconsin, 1886–1892" (Stanford University, California), 32.

the political process, and indirectly in the spiritual damage to the social body. The large powers in capitalism influence newspapers, legislatures, and even churches, Bascom attested. Railroads give out passes to lawmakers, judges, and stock owners. These "railroad magnates," Bascom pronounced with indignation, give a hundred thousand dollars to a political party to secure favors. They buy college professorships and church pulpits. "Our civil polity is debauched by these methods," he wrote, "and our social fabric shaken." Excessive wealth disrupts "the equilibrium of rights" that democratic society exists to achieve. Bascom did not shy from specifics. He cited the the Standard Oil Trust and the Vanderbilts, condemning the monopolies they had achieved in oil and steamboats and railroads, noting that they have appropriated "millions," gained a quasi-public franchise in the immensity of their holdings, and rendered but a meager social service in return. Why not call it a crime? he asked. "Men appropriate property [by] force and we call it robbery; they appropriate it under . . . free commerce, and we call it enterprise."[7]

Bascom's writings on the social question, however, focused largely on workers. He saw in America a new mass of "unindividualized laborers," whose numbers threatened social "disorganization." He could look back with some appreciation to the old guild system in which, at least, workers, so organized, had a place in the larger society. Bascom also described the degradation of labor. Thousands of individuals sitting before sewing machines and other hallmarks of the new industrial age signified to him the dehumanization of work. The wage system had deprived workers of incentives, Bascom believed. He could sound almost Marxian: "All that the interest of the capitalist requires in reference to workmen," he wrote, "is their bare subsistence." The "absolute dependence" of the worker, he added, "gives the most immediate and complete power to capital." This is no foundation for social progress.[8]

His sympathies notwithstanding, Bascom did bring moral judgments against the workers. He who explained social growth in terms of expanded spiritual enlightenment and gains in awareness, especially in a life that interacted with the world and the social organism in edifying ways, easily saw the discouraging marks of regressive forces in labor's conditions. Modern work had dehumanizing effects, to be sure, and too much of work required only unskilled labor. But Bascom found too many among the laboring classes unequipped for

---

7. Bascom, "Modes of Correction," *Independent*, May 12, 1887, 5; idem, *Christian State*, 17, 10; idem, "What Do the Members?," 95 (on the Vanderbilts).

8. Bascom, "Gist of the Labor Question," 91; idem, *Sociology*, 74, 233–34 (quotation), 255–56.

the growth that skilled labor yielded. "Simple dulness [*sic*]," he complained, "causes labor to gravitate to the most unproductive forms." And labor will not gain advantages or win what it deserves in a race with capital with these low qualities dragging it. Too often Bascom rushed to judgment. He pronounced against raw bad habits he perceived among the working class; it "is so easily, so ignorantly, so fatally, improvident." It gives itself over to gross indulgences—drink and tobacco. Workers succumb to this low behavior because they "are weak and ignorant and vicious." These conditions stack the deck against the cause of labor in the dangerous game it has to play in its contest with powerful capitalists.[9]

Possibly, Bascom's judgments here reflect class and ethnic prejudice, visible among the later Progressives, too. The words above describe only degradation, however much derived from economic oppression, among the working classes. They reflect no appreciation for the vitality of ethnic cultures represented among workers, whether in religious practices, clothing, music, fraternal associations, or other manifestations of social diversity. Bascom did not embrace Anglo-Saxon supremacy. His viewpoints more likely derive from his concern for organic unity and the threats he saw to it in Gilded Age America. On the other hand, he wished to urge on his readers a greater respect for workers and the work they do. He made the point in his made-for-the-classroom moral philosophy text he wrote for his UW students: "Respect is especially due to those who render menial services, as the judgments of men are peculiarly superficial and depressing at this point." Manual work "is wholesome to body and mind" and not to be disparaged.[10]

When Bascom called for Christian attention to the poor and to the labor classes in the 1870s and early 1880s he stood apart from the general opinion in the Protestant churches. Still adhering to economic orthodoxy, the clerical leadership saw little that anybody could do about the situation. In New England, to wit, the *Congregationalist* opined that low wages benefited everybody and spurred the economy. The prevailing view saw labor as merely another commodity, and "like all other commodities," wrote the *Watchman and Reflector*, "its condition is governed by the imperishable laws of demand and supply." One could do no more about the income of workers than one could about the cost of a bar of soap. The two major Protestant newspapers, the *Independent* and the *Christian Union*, accepted these fixtures and added moral judgments against the

9. Bascom, *Sociology*, 64, 73, 147; idem, "Gist of the Labor Question," 90.
10. John Bascom, *Ethics or Science of Duty* (New York: G. P. Putnam's Sons, 1879), 169.

poor, too. The journals associated success with good character and generally saw unredeemable depravity as the causes of the poor's self-inflicted wounds. One can see what labor was up against when noting the summary words of historian Henry May as he described the situation as it existed in 1876: "Buttressed by the nearly unanimous opinion of academic authorities, sustained by the growing wealth and power of the churchgoing middle class, American Protestantism maintained its support of the combined social and religious orthodoxy developed in the prewar period. Christian America was still being guided by the Unseen Hand; church and nation were sound. Greed at the top could be ignored or accepted as a tool of progress. Misery at the bottom could be waved aside as inevitable or, at most, treated by a program of guarded and labeled philanthropy."[11] And, in his effort to overcome this ideology, one can see what obstacles Bascom confronted.

Intellectual shifts in the decades ahead would bring changes of opinion. The new theology gained among major Protestant thinkers and facilitated new thoughts about the social situation and ways by which one could improve it. A new Social Gospel emerged. Bascom began this journey early. But not all who broke from religious orthodoxy embraced progressive reform. No help came from Horace Bushnell, for example, who had so much contributed to theological liberalism. Nor did Henry Ward Beecher, a liberal most of his life, translate new theology into social progressivism. He supported all efforts to give the poor the moral renewal they needed but warned against charity. Alms had wrought terrible damage to English society, he warned. Yes, a few people may suffer poverty as victims of life's circumstances, but, Beecher proclaimed, "no man in this land suffers from poverty unless it be more than his fault—unless it be his *sin*." The *Independent* trumpeted theological liberalism but voiced no more support for labor than it did for women's rights.[12]

Bascom did not find fault with individualism as such or with the free market, and he did insist that the creative entrepreneur deserved a fair return for his work.[13] He did insist, though, that when these forces work at full pace they produce consequences that undo their good. He recognized that free-market ideals had a large appeal to the American imagination. "The sentiment of our time sets strongly in favor of individuation," he wrote. We are loathe to give

11. Henry May, *The Protestant Churches and Industrial America* (New York: Harper and Brothers, 1949), 52–56, 62–63 (quotation).

12. May, *Protestant Churches*, 56, 69 (Beecher).

13. John Bascom, "Labor and Capital," *Independent*, April 28, 1887, 3.

any credit for the good of government and the effective powers of the state. Furthermore, he added, what reforms we do enact serve mostly to protect the powerful interests already in place. "The weak and the poor," Bascom asserted, lack the protection they need. Also, as he told his University of Wisconsin audience, we imagine that we all start the race on equal terms. But we don't. And the more the "natural" system runs its course the more unnatural the effects. That is, there result huge conglomerates of power that squeeze out open competition. History heretofore has given us the overweening power of kings and armies, but now we face a different kind of domination. He wrote: "A community in which wealth has won all its natural advantages, and completed its usurpations, is hardly more bearable than one resting under a military despotism." We know these realities, he stated, but we do not act to undo them. Competition has meaning only in a level playing field, a condition that requires intervention to assure its constancy.[14]

Here the state has a major assignment, Bascom believed. Many people allow its role in protections against the criminals in our midst, he observed. But the legitimate protective role does not end there. It also involves protection of the weak against the strong; the state must see to the equalization of advantages between citizens, "more particularly between the rich and the poor, those who have won the lead and those who have fallen behind." Bascom bristled at those ideologues who dismissed the state as "a blind, hopeless bungler." That prejudice resigns us to only negative ideals of freedom. Positive freedom addresses the concern for real, not hypothetical, opportunity. It legitimizes the positive state.[15]

Laissez-faire ideology, Bascom insisted, knows only theory; it offers models of idealized situations and invokes abstract natural laws, notions that Bascom never warmly embraced. So he, and other reformers, more frequently invoked sociology as supplement to economics and gave it higher priority. Bascom articulated the difference: "The political economist is tempted by his partiality for his science to affirm the complete power of economic laws to order successfully their own result. The student of sociology, with a wider survey of the facts, is inclined to say, that [these laws] . . . do not suffice to order social life, or to carry society . . . steadily forward to its goal." Economics sees individuals, each one pursuing self-interest and personal well-being. Somehow all that individual activity is supposed to produce a harmony that results in maximum good for all. Bascom believed no such process prevailed, and he resented the notion that "society" becomes the accidental, albeit allegedly happy, result of all this

14. Bascom, *Sociology*, 160, 210, 79.
15. Bascom, *Sociology*, 210–11.

John Bascom. (Wisconsin Historical Society, WHi-121048)

self-interest. This fantasy assumes that the public interest will take care of itself thereafter. But sociology knows otherwise, Bascom asserted. It builds from an understanding of evolution and the reality of the social organism to reify society and thus sanction the public interest as in fact superior to individual interest. Economic law does not yield social harmony; it creates discord and destruction.[16] So Bascom, as we observed earlier, made sociology the new star subject in the academic agenda for the new American university.

In Wisconsin, labor had support among some prominent political leaders. Edward G. Ryan reflected Locofoco ideals that had come west from the State of New York and lodged with the Democratic Party here. He had grave suspicions about the state incorporation practices; they served only the interests of capital. Ryan occupied a powerful position among the Democrats. But he and that party also opposed Negro suffrage and women's rights. Wisconsin working-men in general, as historian Richard Current described, showed a hardened hostility toward women in the workplace. They feared the competition of cheaper labor. Nor generally did they take kindly to feminist politics. Milwaukee printers, Germans, refused to print writings by the radical German immigrant Mathilda Franziska Anneke. In Germany she had published the first women's newspaper, the *Frauen Zeitung*, and wanted to renew it in Wisconsin. She championed women's suffrage and female employment in occupations dominated by males. The labor movement in Wisconsin thus had its own trajectory and did not join collateral reform issues. Bascom believed it should.[17]

The UW president centered one point in his case for labor unions on the need for organization. Organization was the way of all flesh in these modern times, he observed, and its ascendancy had served especially to expand the power of corporate business interests. Fairness and equality entered the picture, and Bascom judged it only a matter of right that labor should have the means of organization as much as its corporate oppressors. We need a better balance of power, he urged. Not that many in his circle of intellectuals agreed. Again,

---

16. Bascom, *Sociology*, 74–75; idem, *Christian State*, 17. Bascom wrote a few years earlier: "It is quite without reason to suppose that men collectively will achieve a moral character which does not belong to them separately, and that selfishness by simple extension will take the place of good-will." *The Words of Christ as Principles of Personal and Social Growth* (New York: G. P. Putnam's Sons, 1884), 97.

17. Robert C. Nesbit, *Wisconsin: A History* (Madison: University of Wisconsin Press, 1973), 220; Richard N. Current, *The Civil War Era, 1848–1873*, vol. 2 of *The History of Wisconsin* (Madison: State Historical Society of Wisconsin, 1976), 123.

Henry Ward Beecher, all for liberal theology, women's rights, and temperance, wanted nothing to do with labor unions. The *Christian Advocate*, offering its judgment in 1878, called the labor unions "despotic and revolutionary in tendency" and exhibiting "the worst doctrines of communism." Even Washington Gladden disagreed with Bascom on this subject and did not read it into his first plea for a social gospel when he wrote his *Working People and Their Employers* in 1876. He preached harmony and the Golden Rule as the bridge between the two opposing forces.[18]

Bascom rejected these antiunion prejudices and again reminded his readers of the immense, influential, and corrupting power of the corporations. Whatever faults inhere in labor unions as countervailing objects, Bascom said, they "are one and all insignificant" compared to the progressive role the unions play. He honored them for bringing to the public's attention the needs of labor and the imperative of its becoming integrated into the social fabric. They have their eye on "social evils" and address them before they become irredeemable, Bascom emphasized. Hence "their unspeakable advantage" to the social organism. Labor must have empowerment, the term Bascom used so frequently in defending women's rights. And to that end it must have organization. "When was the liberty of a people ever won without an army?" he asked.[19]

Many opposed labor unions because they feared strikes. The Protestant churches generally did. Again, even the religious liberals expressed these fears. The *Independent* in 1887 wrote: "The most withering and outrageous despotism that has yet shown itself in the world is this of the strike and the boycott."[20] Strong stuff. Strikes suggested radical responses to the social question and had affiliations in people's thinking with socialism and anarchism. During the major strikes of this era public sentiment usually supported the workers. But Bascom's group of people, the Protestant liberal thinkers, came around slowly. Beecher made comments that became notorious during the Great Strike of 1877. Is a dollar a day enough for a man to support a wife and five children? he asked. Well, no, he answered, not if the man smokes and drinks and pursues other irresponsible indulgences. "But is not a dollar a day enough to buy bread

---

18. Bascom, *Sociology*, 234; Gary Dorrien, *The Making of American Liberal Theology: Imagining Progressive Religion, 1805–1900* (Louisville: Westminster John Knox Press, 2001), 247 (on Beecher); Sidney Fine, *Laissez Faire and the General-Welfare State: A Study of Conflict in American Thought, 1865–1901* (Ann Arbor: University of Michigan Press, 1965), 184 (on Gladden); May, *Protestant Churches*, 96. Beecher later became more moderate.

19. Bascom, "Gist of the Labor Question," 93; idem, *Sociology*, 234–37 (quotation).

20. Quoted in May, *Protestant Churches*, 103.

with? Water costs nothing; and a man who cannot live on bread is not fit to live."[21]

Revolution, many believed, lurked just below the surface of this materially comfortable world, and Gilded Age America looked nervously on as violence intensified in this volatile era. Wisconsin went through a round of strikes that grew in number in the 1880s. The most spectacular of them occurred in Bay View (aside Lake Michigan and now a part of Milwaukee) where the unskilled iron workers, mostly Poles, faced a seventy-two-hour workweek, earned a fraction of the wages of the skilled workers, most of British background, and endured the heat and hazards of a tough workplace. (By 1880 immigrants made up almost half of the Milwaukee labor force). The protests followed the May Day events just a few days before in Chicago, the famous Haymarket Rebellion that displayed the violence of anarchism to a frightened and angry nation. On May 5, 1886, in Milwaukee, some fifteen hundred marched from Saint Stanislaus Church to the rolling mills plant. From his location downtown Governor Jeremiah Rusk gave orders to six companies of the state militia to "fight 'em" should the protesters attempt to enter the mills. Two of the companies so placed fired shots, killing five and wounding eight to ten among the assembled mass. Most in the state press applauded the governor's action and had in mind the violence that had torn Chicago within that week.[22] As in other issues, Bascom made his case for labor in public venues. An address he gave in Madison, reported in the eastern press, made a strong plea for labor unions and for strikes as vital for workers' fight against the superior strengths of capital.[23]

Once again Bascom used the pages of the *Independent* to reach to a large reading public. In one instance in this outlet he took on Simon Newcomb, an astronomer and popular lecturer at Harvard, who represented the corps of academics dedicated to laissez-faire economics. In 1886 Newcomb took to the pages of the *Independent* to make his case against labor unions. He purported to judge from the single criterion of the public interest. Unions, he said, have only selfish interests. Because unions strive to have better terms for their workers, such, for example, as working eight hours a day instead of ten, they impair the public interest. The coercive nature of unions, substituting force for voluntary consent, Newcomb labeled "wicked, unjust, and unchristian." He

21. Quoted in May, *Protestant Churches*, 94.

22. Nesbit, *Wisconsin*, 393–94; John Gurda, *The Making of Milwaukee* (Milwaukee: Milwaukee County Historical Society, 1999), 128.

23. "Labor Combinations," *Syracuse Daily Journal*, February 7, 1887 (summary of Bascom's address).

accused unions of having obligations only to themselves and no sense of social responsibility.[24]

Bascom read Newcomb's two short pieces with a sense of outrage. He asked the editor of the *Independent* for the opportunity of a reply. He resented, he said, the "cold and imperious" attitude of Newcomb. Whereas Newcomb saw only self-interest and indifference to a larger good in the labor movement's actions, Bascom saw heroic sacrifice and a motivation derived from a sense of justice, with demands for its realization. And he did not see only material advantage as the good of labor; he saw a growth in manhood, intelligence, and spiritual power. Of course, Bascom acknowledged, self-interest and self-assertion do play a role, but they serve mainly to redress the faults of a system that gives its spoils to capital. Again Bascom called for equity. And to that extent, he wrote, ultimately this subject "is a moral issue." This piece, titled "Labor and Capital," seems to be the last issued from Bascom as president of the University of Wisconsin. Stressing the "moral" center of the labor question, it culminated Bascom's efforts over many years to articulate his versions of the New Theology and indeed a new social gospel.[25]

The Social Gospel envisioned a new role for the churches. Bascom found many faults with the religious institutions of his time. Addressing the matter while at Wisconsin allowed him to reinforce criticism made earlier in his life. The churches, and religion generally, he believed, suffered from frozen dogmas, uncorrected by new understandings from natural science and new learning in the social sciences. The more any church plants itself on dogma, Bascom warned, "the more intractable and more unreliable is it found on progressive, social questions." Instead, he remonstrated, we still heard the evocations about original sin and predestination, "always tending to barrenness," and too little about the dynamic world flourishing outside the parish walls. When it came to social questions, Bascom labeled the churches "blundering neophytes." To that extent, too, Bascom accused, the churches shared blame for the unjust society in their midst. Ninety percent of the churches' money, Bascom told his baccalaureate audience at Madison, goes back into the system of greed in which those churches exist and flourish. No wonder then that socialists and

---

24. Simon Newcomb, "A Plain Man's Talk on the Labor Question: Benefits and Evils of Organized Action," *Independent*, June 3, 1886, 2; idem, "A Plain Man's Talk on the Labor Question: The Moral Side of the Question," *Independent*, September 16, 1886, 3.

25. Bascom, "Labor and Capital," *Independent*, April 28, 1887, 3.

those of unbelief attack the churches for indifference and for collusion, however unknowingly, with the existing power arrangements. They have a point, Bascom conceded. But should the churches speak out politically? They should indeed, Bascom urged.[26]

The Social Gospelers of Bascom's day, and well into the twentieth century, reflected continuity with their evangelical predecessors of the antebellum period. The latter-day voices, too, cited the postmillennial theme of the Kingdom of God, an earthly reality. Bascom usually called it the Kingdom of Heaven. This kingdom has physical and moral and spiritual foundations, they all agreed. Bascom, for one, insisted strongly on these inclusive qualities. The scientist too often sees only the first, a materialist utopia, the religionist only the second, a remote and distant heavenly estate. The philosophical idealist, however, sees things connected, and in earthly settings. And Christianity gives this vision moral substance, Bascom added. We envision the kingdom through Christian faith and philosophical Reason. This Kingdom of Heaven is a moral reality, one in which the whole embraces all its parts, Bascom explained. And here labor demands highest attention. The Christian, the humanitarian, Bascom advocated, looks above all in this wholeness to "the successes of workingmen." "There is hardly the love of humankind in us unless we are earnest as to the condition of this great majority," he wrote in the *Independent*. Bascom addressed the Christian more urgently. "Christianity," he said, "is not merely interested in the progress of laborers; it is identified with it." He looked to the words of Jesus, and wrote: "It is time for the meek to inherit the earth."[27]

Consistent with his course of action on temperance and women's rights Bascom looked to the state for responses to the social question. He brought to this subject some general principles and some specific proposals. He had always held a Whiggish view of the state and its role in promoting a national economy. But Bascom also reinforced in the Whig political party outlook its connection of

26. Bascom, *Sociology*, 174, 239–43; idem, "Moral Questions among Christians," *Independent*, December 18, 1884, 4; idem, *Seat of Sin*, 11–12. See also, Bascom, *Words of Christ*, 56.

27. Bascom, "Labor," *Independent*, February 18, 1875, 5; idem, *Sociology*, 262–63. Charles Hopkins, in his study of the Social Gospel, wrote: "Although definitions of the kingdom were always to lack concreteness, the belief that the ideal preached by Christ was a terrestrial, social kingdom as well as a heavenly or spiritual one was a matter of great importance to a nascent social gospel." Charles Howard Hopkins, *The Rise of the Social Gospel in American Protestantism, 1865–1915* (New Haven, CT: Yale University Press, 1940), 19.

economic behavior and moral programming. And here his views became more egalitarian. A moral society, he believed, will exercise vigilance in assuring a fair distribution of its wealth, the more so as the industrial age created both vast accumulations by some individuals and impoverishment by many. "Large production," Bascom wrote, "must in any long period go hand-in-hand with relatively just and generous distribution." "Relatively just." Bascom did not support socialism, as will be noted. Without the public monitoring, though, economic forces, acting wholly under private control, will create huge disparities of income, even to the point of destroying the very system from which they derive. The state cannot remain indifferent. Furthermore, Bascom believed, the state has full right to decide how much of private wealth it will protect. Assuring "proximate equality," preventing one class from being permanently disabled, restoring those who have fallen—all these imperatives of the ethical state impose on it a "conscientious watchfulness."[28]

This whole discussion, Bascom believed, would gain from severe modification of the public/private dualism that prevailed in the American mind. All modern knowledge conspired against dualistic thinking, he asserted, and nowhere more importantly, he hoped, would it gain than in its social corrections. He made the point clearly in his last address at Madison, the baccalaureate of 1887 that he titled "A Christian State." How often does the "man of enterprise" claim for himself the entire results of his industry? Bascom asked. But the great merchant with connections through the nation and into the world, owes much to the protections provided by his own government, that is, to "the organic state of his fellow citizens." Yet the captain of industry resents any claims made against him by the public, and he demands unlimited utilization of the rewards wrought by his "private powers." Bascom allowed that government has among its most important responsibilities the protection of private property. But, he added, "large accumulations . . . of wealth, which are possible only through the mechanism of society, must submit themselves in justice to the safety of society." Furthermore, he added, the state has an interest in reducing the social toll of private enterprise, as in the damage done by the liquor trade, but in the effects of low wages as well. Again, he raised the public interest to first priority. "Trade that profoundly touches the common weal," he told his students, "must, in justice, be governed by that weal." That idea fit perfectly Bascom's ideal of "the Christian state."[29]

28. John Bascom, *Education and the State* [Baccalaureate Sermon] (n.p., 1877), 6–7; idem, "What Do Members?," 95; idem, *Sociology*, 79, 210; idem, *Words of Christ*, 190, 193.

29. Bascom, *Christian State*, 22–24. Bascom further specified the Christian nature of this sociological prescription in *Words of Christ*, 152, 164.

Those claims of society led directly to taxation, which headed Bascom's list of specific reforms needed to meet the ideals of his sociology. Taxes constitute the fair assessment against those who gain most from the state's services and protections, he argued. Bascom promoted taxation at a time, of course, when that levy had played much less a role in the national economy than it does now, so the very principle needed a defense. Bascom made part of that defense a class issue and again used the baccalaureate address at UW as his forum. "Has the state no right to tax rich citizens for the commonweal," he asked, "and has it the right to marshal its poor citizens into its armies, and bid them lay down their lives for that same commonwealth?"[30] Taxes that do now exist, Bascom also believed, register all the wrong priorities. They fall too heavily on those "low down in the social scale," and the laws allow those who can readily pay to escape them. Too much of personal property escapes taxation altogether, he added. Thus, we miss a major point about taxation: its use in effecting greater social equality, in reducing the disparities of wealth and poverty that plague us now. Bascom preferred a graduated income tax and advocated for it even before it existed in the United States. He considered it "the most just ever imposed" because it levies taxes on whom the imposition belongs. Bascom knew what a tough sell that notion presented. "We prefer to let taxes fall on the simple and the feeble, because this is easy, and sets up no barriers in that rapid and unruffled river of enterprise which constitutes the boast of this great nation, and floats its purple sails." This lament, too, Bascom presented while outlining the parameters of "the Christian State."[31]

Bascom had some other suggestions for securing greater social equality by means of state action. They did not constitute a long list but they did anticipate measures that became common later in the Progressive Era. For one, he called for taxes on inheritance. Accumulation of wealth and its perpetuation over generations Bascom found unjustifiable. Such perpetuation deprives future generations of opportunities, and confounds efforts to preserve a fair race over the long years. Yet we see again the ideal of individual rights skewing the subject in the interest of the powerful, Bascom complained. But he held his ground. "Death must be a final relinquishment of rights," he wrote. Besides, he believed, it's a simple matter: "The world belongs to the living, not to the dead."[32]

30. Bascom, *Education and the State*, 7.

31. Bascom, *Education and the State*, 7; idem, *Sociology*, 214–15; idem, *Christian State*, 10–11 (quotation). Bascom faulted taxes on liquor and tobacco because they fell heavily on the poor. He charged that the state therefore is living off of public immorality. He resolved the dilemma he had created for himself by calling for the outright prohibition of these dangerous products. "Gist of the Labor Question," 94.

32. Bascom, *Sociology*, 226–27.

And for another, Bascom urged the creation of municipal franchises. Some economic functions constitute common social possessions, but we place them in the hands of a few. Bascom had in mind railroads, the telegraph, gas companies, water companies, and some forms of banking. He took a very liberal stance here. He reasoned that these enterprises owed their existence "to a certain stage of social development," the accumulated knowledge achieved by the human race to that point. But they exploited that knowledge to solidify their own operations and control. "These [businesses] are direct outgrowths of the common strength," Bascom stated, "and closely associated with it. If they are allowed to fall unreservedly into the hands of individuals, they confer an advantage oftentimes very great, correspondingly unequal, and so dangerous to progress."[33]

In discussing these changes Bascom, almost habitually, made a clarification: we can pursue these measures without reverting to socialism. The early voices of the Social Gospel had little taste for socialism, and "Christian Socialism" would await the last decade of the century to gain a small representation among its advocates. We need have no disposition "to limit private enterprise," Bascom assured.[34] Bascom saw socialism and communism as the polar opposites of capitalist excess. Both run to extremes and both exist because they yield to our worse tendencies. "Communism is the selfishness of the many striving to extinguish the selfishness of the few." Both also thrive when the creative, spiritual instincts of individuals have succumbed to brute material ones. Bascom had explained earlier that such a regretful transition characterized those who had grown to success and wealth and among whom the social feelings had withered. Socialism, on the other hand, Bascom said, prescribes an equality that would serve no one well, labor included, and he judged socialism the labor movement's least successful strategy. "Socialism takes from labor all enterprise," he wrote. It provides no motive to increase production. Capitalism supplies a better engine for these purposes.[35]

By the time Bascom was completing his years at Madison, his concerns about socialism had intensified considerably. He now saw in it a greater threat to the American situation and to his own social philosophy. As Bascom had

33. Bascom, *Sociology*, 215–16.

34. Bascom, *Sociology*, 227; J. Graham Morgan, "The Development of Sociology and the Social Gospel in America," *Sociological Analysis* 30 (1969), 44.

35. Bascom, *Christian State*, 7 (quotation); idem, "Competition," *Independent*, May 5, 1887, 4; idem, "Freedom in Production," *Independent*, April 22, 1875, 3; *University Press*, June 2, 1875. The UW student newspaper reprinted this essay.

rowed hard for years against the current of American opinion in making his case for the state, socialism threatened that position as much as the capitalist ideology, he now feared. "The serpent's head is above the grass." Socialism, he warned, would make the state "the sole possessor of the means of labor." A state so powerful would overwhelm all else, yielding "the most intolerable tyranny of a class combining in their office both wealth and power." Bascom had no wish to destroy private enterprise, and socialism, he cautioned, would eradicate most of the wealth that capitalism had produced. On this point Bascom stood at one with the Social Darwinist William Graham Sumner. Under socialism, wrote Bascom, "the equality secured would largely be that of poverty." And state power, Bascom reiterated, did not mean state tyranny.[36]

Thus the "social question" stood in Bascom's mind in 1887, his last year in Madison. He now planned to return to Williamstown. But despite the late turmoil in Madison Bascom had reason for satisfaction. He could see many indications of a changed intellectual climate in the United States, marked especially by new, progressive views among different thinkers. If nothing else, a much larger discussion had emerged as conditions in the nation cried out for attention. Some efforts that had begun just after the Civil War now claimed the allegiance of social thinkers who called for positive action. As their voices became louder, defenders of the old orthodoxy dug in their heels and sought all the more to resist the new programs. A brief look at Bascom's place in the discussions follows.

The American Social Science Association formed in 1865 as the Civil War ended. Bascom joined it as a founding member and encouraged its reform aspirations. The new organization drew its participants from public figures— humanitarians, bureaucrats, educators, politicians. Thus it included people like Massachusetts Senator Charles Sumner, William Lloyd Garrison, Henry Villard, Wendell Phillips, and Thomas Wentworth Higginson. It had a few academics, like Bascom, Francis Wayland, and Francis Lieber, and it included the presidents of Harvard and Yale, though the organization had little theoretical bent. The ASSA endured in prominence for twenty years, and Bascom served it as an "energetic" member. He addressed the organization on the subject of law and social reform in 1867. The association spoke the views of those who wanted a larger knowledge base from which to address the social issues of the day and on which to make reform programs. They looked to the social sciences and to the universities for the curricular changes that would give them a larger

36. Bascom, *Sociology*, 51 (first quotation), 245–48 (other quotations).

place in higher education. By the early 1870s one matter stood ascendant among problems before the ASSA: labor, that is, the "social question." The ASSA called for greater attention to the needs of the disadvantaged and for greater compassion among the well-to-do.[37]

The ASSA helped foster a new group of economic thinkers, the "ethical economists." Some of them gained large public prominence. Washington Gladden, Bascom's former student, contrasted the law of supply and demand with the law of love and invoked Christian principles as a restraint on the amoral standards of economic orthodoxy. In turn, Richard T. Ely pressed a new agenda, aggressively, and amid much controversy. Ely will have a formal introduction in the next chapter; he played an important role in Wisconsin's post-Bascom years. Suffice for now to note that Ely, like the other "ethical economists" in the new party—Simon Patten, Edmund Janes James, and Henry Carter Adams—came from a strong evangelical background. This group saw economics as an extension of Christian ethics and that connection meant that laissez-faire thinking must be thoroughly undone. Ely spoke of the "New Economics" and in an 1884 essay in the *Nation* drew clear lines between it and the old economics. Ely pounded the proponents of orthodoxy, charging that they followed brittle, inflexible laws and helped to sustain an ethic of personal selfishness, a gospel of wealth, and an indifference to human misery.[38] When Ely also debated Simon Newcomb in the *Nation* magazine, Bascom sent Ely a letter of support.[39]

The year 1886 produced another source of gratification for Bascom: Washington Gladden published his book *Applied Christianity: Moral Aspects of Social Questions*. Since his graduation from Williams in 1859 Gladden had undertaken several parish ministries before settling in the First Congregational Church in Columbus, Ohio, in 1882. Influenced by Bascom and Horace Bushnell, Gladden embraced liberal Protestantism. "No Protestant minister better epitomized theological change and emerging social conscience than

37. Thomas L. Haskell, *The Emergence of Professional Social Science: The American Social Science Association and the Nineteenth-Century Crisis of Authority* (Urbana: University of Illinois Press, 1977), 97–99, 114; Mary O. Furner, *Advocacy and Objectivity: A Crisis in the Professionalization of American Social Science, 1865–1905* (Lexington: University Press of Kentucky, 1975), 14–15, 18, 22–23.

38. Furner, *Advocacy and Objectivity*, 42–43, 60–62, 87; Hopkins, *Rise of the Social Gospel*, 25–26.

39. Bascom to Ely, December 6, 1886, in the Richard T. Ely Papers, Wisconsin Historical Society.

Washington Gladden," wrote Henry W. Bowden. Gladden opened his book with a chapter titled "Christianity and Wealth" and included other topics, such as "Is Labor a Commodity?," "The Wage Earner and the Churches," and "Christianity and Social Science." This linkage was now moving toward standard prescription among the Protestant liberals, as the ASSA had hoped it would. The modern social sciences, Gladden urged, illuminate scriptural truths. "Anyone can see," Gladden wrote, "that if the human nature with which Social Science deals is the same human nature found in the Bible, then the doctrine of man found in the Bible may, if true, be verified by careful study in the fields of social science." Gladden urged such knowledge on all who engaged in social reform, and he would have it large in the teaching of "every theological seminary."[40]

Two other events of 1886 have to do again with Richard T. Ely. That year he published *The Labor Movement in America*. This book, too, registered both the New Theology and the reform quest of the Social Gospel. Ely believed that Christianity had its primary concern with this world and should strive to bring about "a kingdom of righteousness." In a manner some have found overzealous, Ely joined the cause of labor with the moral course of Christianity. The labor movement represented the expression of the Golden Rule better than any other cause, Ely contended. Like Bascom, Ely supported the right of workers to strike.[41]

All along Ely had been contemplating the creation of a new organization. It would provide a forum for the growing numbers of ethical economists and would take on orthodoxy directly. James and Patten collaborated with Ely for these purposes. The American Economic Association announced its arrival in 1885 by citing the need for more research in economics. But it specified "scientific work," which it would pursue by way of statistical data and historical investigation. It would not fall back on old prescriptions, it stated, and thus it considered advocates of either free trade or protection to fall outside "the realm of science." The platform began with an emphatic statement about government: "We regard the state as an educational and ethical agency whose positive aid is an indispensable condition of human progress." It added: "While we recognize the necessity of individual initiative in industrial life, we hold that the doctrine of *laissez-faire*

40. Henry Warner Bowden, *Dictionary of American Religious Biography* (Westport, CT: Greenwood Press, 1977), 175; Washington Gladden, *Applied Christianity: Moral Aspects of Social Questions* (1886; New York: Arno Press, 1986), 237–38.

41. May, *Protestant Churches*, 140–42; Hopkins, *Rise of the Social Gospel*, 98; Fine, *Laissez Faire*, 236–37.

is unsafe in politics and unsound in morals." The AEA would address the "vast number of social problems" brought on by the conflicts between labor and capital, but the statement also assured that no lasting solutions to them would come "without the united efforts of Church, state, and science." The AEA clearly had a religious bent. The organizational meeting of 1885 had fifty participants, of which more than twenty had connections, past or present, to the ministry. Bascom could see in the AEA's purposes a rendering of his own principles, long since advocated. He does not, however, appear to have been an original member of the association.[42]

Finally, Bascom received much appreciation for his writings, although not the wide influence he would have liked. Henry May summarized: "With his broad learning, his prolific writing, his respectability . . . Bascom remained one of the most influential academic authorities for religious readers, providing successive formulations which were widely imitated."[43] Often critics found Bascom's prose rough-going—abstract and labored. It could be like reading Emerson, finding one's way through uncertain terrain and then coming into an expressive, quotable phrase, a piquant moment amid intellectual travail. A reviewer for the *Independent* called Bascom "a strong writer and essentially a clear thinker" but warned that his readers require a little time and patience "to become used to him." But then the critic went on to quote several passages from Bascom's book, in this case his *Sociology*. He liked, for example, Bascom's expression "The life of society is one of mobile equilibrium." And after quoting another passage he complimented Bascom: "the literary expression is as fine as the thought is strong." A different reviewer, in the *Christian Union*, found that this same book offered "a succession of generalizations." The commentator added: "They are always sensible and often original, but not always sufficiently so to spur the reader on." This review did single out for appreciation Bascom's break from the contract theory of rights—the long, bad legacy of Rousseau, in his judgment—and Bascom's idea of positive freedom, delivered "in a fresh and original way."[44]

42. "Report of the Organization of the American Economic Association," (1886) http://archive.org/stream/jstor-2485628/2485628#page/n1/mode/2up; Furner, *Advocacy and Objectivity*, 75; also, Richard T. Ely, *Ground under Our Feet: An Autobiography* (New York: Macmillan, 1938), 136.

43. May, *Protestant Churches*, 146.

44. Anon., "Bascom's Sociology," *Independent*, August 14, 1887, 9; anon., "Dr. Bascom's Sociology," *Christian Union*, July, 14, 1887, 41.

9

The Wisconsin Idea

Events were going badly for Bascom in Madison. They had been for some time. No state university has immunity from state politics, least of all a university run by officials who had political appointments to their positions. As noted earlier, Bascom, a strong-minded president with strong ideas about higher education, had continuing frustration with a board of regents that refused to grant him the powers he believed he needed for effective leadership. Bascom always acknowledged the legitimate role of the regents; he just believed they had too much control. And anyone might have some sympathy for a university president having to share a role with the regents not only in appointing faculty but even in assigning textbooks. But at Madison, the matter ran even deeper. State politics and board politics blended in a peculiar way. Nor should Bascom have expected this situation not to be so. He had made himself a political figure by his urgent and often strident advocacy for political reform on the hot-button issues previously observed. And at the very least one could expect a university president who rode in the temperance army not to have incurred wrath and resentment from a powerful economic institution in Wisconsin—the brewers.

Bascom's struggles and eventual resignation, or dismissal, have received wide coverage and will not have a large accounting here. Bascom's personal clash with one individual explains much of it, as it brings many of the matters into focus. This story involves one Elisha W. Keyes, as big a personality in state politics as Bascom wanted to be in academics. A brief introduction to "Boss Keyes": His family came from New England, Keyes born in Vermont in 1828 and thus a year younger than Bascom. His parents relocated to Wisconsin in 1837, settling in Jefferson County where the father established a good business with his great mechanical skills. Elisha attended Beloit Seminary but thereafter everything was politics for him. He identified with the Whig Party and then, after the Kansas-Nebraska legislation in 1854, joined with other antislavery

Whigs to launch the Republican Party in Wisconsin. He supported William Seward over Abraham Lincoln for the Republican presidential nomination in 1860. Keyes also practiced law in Dane County. He won election as Madison's mayor in 1865, the first Republican to hold that office. Keyes cultivated his ties with the Grant administration in Washington and gained appointment as the local postmaster. The powerful "ring" that surrounded Keyes helped him earn his very fitting title: "Boss Keyes."[1] The Republican kingpin seems to have abandoned by then any ideological commitments and played the political game for power first and foremost. During Reconstruction, Keyes supported President Andrew Johnson's opposition to the Fourteenth Amendment, by which means he might keep his postmastership. On the other hand, he also supported Republican Senator Matthew Carpenter, a champion of the freedmen.[2] Such a calculating pragmatist as Keyes would find the moral idealism of a John Bascom an irritant.

By the end of the 1870s Keyes had lost power in the state and in his own party. Business interests in Milwaukee had arrayed against the Madison cabal, and Keyes faced a challenge from a rising star among the Republicans, the university's recent graduate and Madison's new district attorney, one Robert M. La Follette. But those circumstances probably made Keyes the more determined to exploit what power he did now have, as a member of the University of Wisconsin Board of Regents. Bascom saw a board dominated by businessmen and pols. "I have got the whole pack of politicians barking at my heels," he wrote to the University of Michigan president. But the "politicians" had a gripe with Bascom, too. The UW president had complained publicly about the drinking problem among students in Madison and had angered Keyes all the more in doing so. Other members of the Board agreed with Keyes that Bascom's politicking hurt the University. And they had a point. Keyes began to make inquiries about a successor to Bascom, this as early as 1884. Bascom threatened to resign.[3]

1. Richard W. Hantke, "Elisha W. Keyes, the Bismarck of Western Politics," *Wisconsin Magazine of History* 31 (September 1947), 30–33, 35–36, 38.

2. Richard W. Hantke, "Elisha W. Keyes and the Radical Republicans," *Wisconsin Magazine of History* 35 (Spring 1952), 205–8.

3. David P. Thelen, "The Boss and the Upstart: Keyes and La Follette, 1880–1884," *Wisconsin Magazine of History* 47 (Winter 1963–64), 103–15. For more details on this controversy, see Merle Curti and Vernon Carstensen, *The University of Wisconsin: A History, 1848–1925*, 2 vols. (Madison: University of Wisconsin Press, 1949), 1:248–74, 261 (quotation).

As this matter became increasingly public, students rallied around Bascom. They held a mass meeting on campus to advertise their support for him and organized a petition for the same purpose. They lauded the president for "his sterling manhood, his independence and the moral enthusiasm he brings to his work." They credited Bascom for the university's intellectual progress and its "increasing prestige among the institutions of the Northwest." To fend off other charges against their president, the students attested that no political partisanship existed in his classroom instruction. The students also knew the realities of the situation and dismissed the move against Bascom as one driven by "personal motives." They also appealed to the alumni to intervene with the board and stop its intrigues against Bascom.[4] A letter from Madison-area alumni followed. In strong terms it denounced Keyes, calling him "one of the most consummate wire-pullers and schemers in the state," who acts solely by personal animus and without regard to the well-being of the state.[5] More distant parties sometimes saw the matter differently. Even when they praised Bascom for the university's great rise in academic stature under his leadership, they nonetheless believed the political situation was damaging the institution and the state and they called for the president to leave.[6]

John Bascom left the University of Wisconsin after the spring commencement exercises in 1887. He returned to Williamstown and for many years more continued to teach at his alma mater. The turmoil in Madison and the relocation to Williamstown had done nothing to moderate his moral commitments, however. He remained a frequent contributor to popular journals that took on the lively political issues of the late Gilded Age, and he took to the stumps for his familiar causes. Within a year of his return to Williamstown, Bascom went to Springfield, Massachusetts, and gave a lecture to the Prohibition Party. He also contributed an essay on prohibitory law and personal freedom to the *North American Review* to make the intellectual defense. Bascom also continued to plead for coeducation, as in his 1891 piece in the *American University Magazine*. And he became more agitated than ever on the subject of money and class.

If anything, his rhetoric even heated up. And on no one did he more apply his wrath than on the easiest target of all, John D. Rockefeller. That one family could amass two hundred million dollars so quickly and bring such distortions

4. *Eau Claire Daily Leader,* June 12, 1885; *Oshkosh Daily Northwestern,* May 5, 1885.

5. *Oshkosh Daily Northwestern,* June 6, 1885.

6. For two examples, see *Janesville Daily Gazette,* June 24, 1885, and *Milwaukee Weekly Messenger,* January 12, 1886.

to the social equilibrium of the nation Bascom found appalling. "He has turned business into unceasing and unflinching warfare," Bascom railed. "He has done this with an open profession of Christian faith. Herein lies the guilt of this man, and of others of the same ilk, and of all who put themselves in fellowship with them, that they confound ethical distinctions and make the world one medley of wrongdoing." Bascom excoriated the University of Chicago for accepting a gift from Rockefeller, a man who made money in violation of the law. The whole matter, Bascom believed, constituted a corruption of higher education. All along, Bascom continued to promote the interests of labor.[7]

The retired president pursued with remarkable energy as well his explorations in intellectual and academic subjects. And by this time Bascom saw himself in a much more comfortable milieu. Many of the ideas he had championed, from his days as instructor at Williams, had gained a larger currency. He was now much less the minority radical. And at Wisconsin, important directions at the university and in the state capital secured his legacy. His intellectual outlines of the Wisconsin Idea acquired new and vital expressions.

Bascom had brought to his presidency an intellectual heritage shaped by his Yorker and Yankee background, but also by major directions in religious and philosophical thinking and in modern science. These commitments he had endeavored to give fruitful application in the arena of social reform, as heretofore detailed. Together, they constituted the beginnings of the Wisconsin Idea. The term has recurring reference down to the present day. One could make an expanded study of it. The Wisconsin Idea became a way of expressing rather formulaically the relations between the university and the state. Wisconsin first drew national attention to this relationship in the Progressive Era, although other universities had their own demonstrations of those relationships. But the period from Bascom's arrival to the beginning of World War I saw the Wisconsin Idea in its most cogent intellectual expression. Wisconsin made its special contribution to American intellectual history in these years when Bascom's ideas saw a manifest realization. This study concludes with that part of the story.

In 1892 Richard T. Ely accepted an appointment at the University of Wisconsin, an offer extended by President Thomas Chamberlin and with the key mediating role played by Frederick Jackson Turner. Turner had studied under Bascom

7. John Bascom, *Sermons and Addresses* (New York: G. P. Putnam's Sons, 1913), 144 (quotation). This anthology, published two years after Bascom's death, does not provide dates for any of the items included. Nor are these pieces included in the bibliography of *Things Learned by Living. Janesville Daily Gazette*, December 30, 1902.

and graduated from the university in 1884. He had gone on to Johns Hopkins University and studied with Ely, returning to teach in Madison. Chamberlin wanted Ely to come to Wisconsin and head its new School of Economics, Political Science, and History, an ambitious program that he hoped would put the university "on the map," he said. Ely matched him in ambition, and he accepted the offer convinced that "I shall be able to establish a school equal to any in the country."[8] Indeed, Ely's agreeing to go "west" was national news. He had become a major figure in intellectual and reform circles and enjoyed wide recognition among the American public. Ely would make a large impact on the University of Wisconsin, in shaping the new school and in influencing the Progressive movement in the state. But he also gave the university a remarkable intellectual continuity. It is hard to imagine how any other individual could have been a more appropriate successor to John Bascom. A striking continuity of ideas and experience relates the two.

Like Bascom, Ely had Yankee and Yorker roots. Born in Lyme, Connecticut, in 1854, Ely descended from early American Puritans. The first of this line had departed England in 1660 when the Restoration renewed problems for Dissenters. The family removed later to Fredonia, New York, where Ely experienced his formative years. The young Ely knew the harsh severities of Calvinism as intensely as Bascom did. He described his father as "an orthodox Puritan." He quit his job a civil engineer because continuing it would require him to break the Sabbath law. The father also disdained celebration of Christmas, pronouncing it a Romish practice, convinced as he was that the papacy represented the "scarlet woman" of scripture. Richard wished to please his father by a like religious dedication, but he did not experience the essential transformation of God's grace. "Try as I might I could not become converted," he later wrote. Nor could he maintain belief in infant damnation of the unbaptized. In turn, he also rejected Calvinist notions of arbitrary grace rather than good works as the path to salvation. Nonetheless, Ely's father made a lasting and favorable impression on his son. Ely described him as a Christian humanitarian. Whatever Calvinism may teach about the future, the father insisted, we all have an obligation to make this world better. That part of his father's religion Richard honored and preserved. But he abandoned Presbyterianism, contemplated at one point becoming a Universalist preacher, and finally opted for the Episcopal denomination.[9]

8. Richard T. Ely, *Ground under Our Feet: An Autobiography* (New York: Macmillan, 1938), 183 (first quotation), 180 (second quotation).

9. Ely, *Ground under Our Feet*, 1, 3, 13, 16, 23.

Ely attended Dartmouth College briefly and then went on to Columbia University. At that time he found his major interest in philosophy. His attraction to philosophical idealism took him to Germany, there hoping to "find the absolute truth." A university fellowship gave him the means. The experience proved to be transforming for Ely, but he did not find the Absolute. Instead he became more interested in economics and came into the tutelage of Karl Knies at Heidelberg. Now Ely joined a group of young American thinkers—Simon Patten, Edmund J. James, John Bates Clark, and others—who drew from the exposure in Germany a different way of looking at their field. Ely explained the difference of the German from the American approach: "Knies conceived of economics as belonging neither to the natural nor to the mental sciences, but to the group of historical disciplines which have for their object the study of man in society in terms of its historical growth." That emphasis broke economics from the realm of natural laws, abstract and mechanical, and placed it into a social milieu. It also opened the subject to moral measures. Knies, Ely emphasized, had a particular sympathy for workers, one that influenced Ely and brought him into his writing on labor, as noted. The historical focus of the German school, Ely believed, made the study of economics more empirical, more "scientific," and a field in which "relativity and evolution played a large role." Ely appropriated all these new readings and brought them into his own Christian framework, making him the leader of the American group of "ethical economists."[10]

So Ely relocated from philosophy to economics, but he carried into economics a philosophical perspective and a Christian ethic. Like Bascom he sided with philosophical idealism, understanding the human mind as a "free creative force." "I have always been an idealist in the philosophical sense," Ely wrote, "firm in my belief that ideas govern the world." Idealism helped Ely to see things whole, inclusively, organically. Idealism broke down the radical dualism that focused our concerns on the spiritual and the afterlife, to the neglect of the worldly and the present. This subject addresses human enrichment and human progress, he asserted. That goal Ely described in idealist terms: "the full and harmonious development in each individual of all human faculties." One cannot view economics narrowly, Ely urged. His words echoed Bascom's precisely:

10. Ely, *Ground under Our Feet*, 45 (quotation), 58 (quotations); Benjamin G. Rader, *The Academic Mind and Reform: The Influence of Richard T. Ely in American Life* (Lexington: University of Kentucky Press, 1966). On the German influence in America broadly considered, see Jurgen Herbst, *The German Historical School in American Scholarship: A Study in the Transfer of Culture* (Ithaca, NY: Cornell University Press, 1965).

"Men's interests are inextricably intertwined, and we shall never become truly prosperous so long as any class of the population is materially and mortally wretched." So Ely, too, employed the organic metaphor and applied it to labor. "As a social body," he wrote, "we can no more be in a sound condition while we have a submerged element, than a man can be whose arms or legs are suffering a foul and corrupting disease."[11]

Ely and the other "rebels" coming back from Germany wanted to reform American economics, to "inject new life" into it. They had a "pugnacious" attitude, Ely admitted, and stood ready "to fight those who we believed stood in the way of intellectual expansion and of social growth." And so they took the lead in forming the American Economic Association in 1885. Three years after the AEA's founding and four years before his arrival to Madison, Ely wrote his major contribution to the Social Gospel, his book *The Social Aspects of Christianity*. Bascom praised Ely's linking ethics and economics in a brief review for the *Dial*. Ely's book illustrates the thinking Ely brought to the University of Wisconsin; the lines of continuity with Bascom appear clearly.

At the outset, Ely's *Social Aspects* showed how his reform program had everything to do with the theological shifts that had occurred in the nineteenth century and the rise of liberal Protestantism, and it reflected of course his own religious history. Ely celebrated the humanitarian character of the Gospels. The longstanding obsession with terror and the fear of punishment that came into Protestantism had obscured that character, he lamented. Ely wanted to recover a gospel of works. That Christian imperative, he believed, superseded everything else: attendance at church, the sacraments, church polity and matters of apostolic succession, personal and private apprehensions of God. The emphasis on love toward others, Ely claimed, distinguishes Christianity from all other religions.[12]

Thus understood, Ely elaborated, the Christian Gospel has two components: theology, which treats of our knowledge of God and of our relation to God, the first biblical Commandment; and sociology, which addresses our dealings with others, the second biblical Commandment. We have long had a preoccupation with the first of these commandments, and at the expense of the second, Ely regretted. But he suggested that the Christian faithful now have the

11. Ely, *Ground under Our Feet*, 95–96 (first quotation), 54–55, 66–67 (second and third quotations); idem, *Social Aspects of Christianity* (New York: T. Y. Crowell, 1889), 62–64.

12. Ely, *Social Aspects*, 3–5; idem, *Ground under Our Feet*, 74–75. For Bascom's comments on Ely, see John Bascom, "Recent Social and Political Discussion," *Dial* 10 (March 1890), 304.

means to amend the failing; they have the modern social sciences to lead in the correction. Sadly, though, the churches have not changed their priorities. Ely severely faulted the church ministers, who, for all their ethical preaching, are "the blind leading the blind" because they themselves have received no instruction in the social sciences. Like Bascom well before him, Ely urged attention to this concern by curricular reform in the theological seminaries. "I should say that half of the time of a theological student should be devoted to social science, and theological seminaries should be the chief intellectual centres for sociology." Increasingly, so now did many more religious leaders. They had better do so, Ely urged, lest the new social sciences yield the ground entirely to Herbert Spencer and William Graham Sumner and render them the intellectual property of an un-Christian Social Darwinism and its brutal effects. Or, as Ely feared, they should do so lest the whole field succumb to a materialist base championed by infidel communism. In 1893 Ely, John R. Commons, and George D. Herron established the American Institute of Christian Sociology, designed to join the work of clergymen and social scientists.[13]

Ely also brought to Madison the strong views he held about government.[14] Like Bascom he championed the usefulness of the state, recognizing the entrenched bias in the American mind against the public sector. But both reformers believed that change could occur. Ely came to this subject from his own experience in Europe and hence brought a language to it different from Bascom's. He chose as one forum for his views the *Christian Union*, also a Bascom outlet, and to which publication Ely committed some thirty-four essays. All modern nations, Ely urged, confront common issues with respect to the administrations of their systems. Less important now than a half century previously, the debate about republics as opposed to monarchies yields to matters with which all states must deal: bad versus good administration. When it comes to taxes, the government of cities, railway management, and control, passing laws does not suffice; what matters is expertise and efficient administration. That necessity demands a new personnel, loyal to the state and professional in everything it does. Ely believed that these factors determined how much of liberty and equality a nation enjoys. His plea expressed his ideas of positive liberty. But if a people does not see the state as a creator of this liberty, if it considers freedom mostly as exemption from government, it will not have a real democracy, Ely insisted. No wonder

13. Ely, *Social Aspects*, 11, 13–15, 17 (quotation), 88; Rader, *Academic Mind*, 133–34.
14. Herbst states that the American reformers coming home from their German training had a worshipful view of the state. He quotes Ely: "It is a grand thing to serve God in the State which he in his beneficent wisdom instituted." *German Historical School*, 67.

then, the situation in the United States. Said Ely: "It is probably not too much to say that we have in America the poorest administration which can be found in any civilized land."[15]

But we do not have to have this problem. Ely elaborated by reference to France and Germany. The former had administrative courts that supplement the work of the civil courts. The latter use administrative officers for a variety of purposes, and they operate in greater detachment from partisan politics than they do here. A transcendent dedication to the ideal of the public good yielded immense benefit, Ely maintained. "The German states," he contended, "have a body of highly trained, incorruptible men, who devote themselves with sincerity to the public service, and are controlled in their acts by a high sense of personal honor and a strong feeling of duty. The German civil service is the admiration of all acquainted with German institutions." Here, too, Ely saw a new charge for American universities. He advocated for greater emphasis on the study of both the theory and practice of administration.[16] These convictions grew in Ely in succeeding years, and when the invitation came from Wisconsin he saw a special opportunity. This university, he testified, had the special advantage provided by its location in the state capital. Ely aspired to make use of the state bureau of labor and other offices for purposes of training students. The courts there offered useful observations for students as well, and the legislature, located down the street, "will give us lessons in practical politics." Here, too, an active university could "exercise a favorable influence."[17]

Frederick Jackson Turner's role in Ely's move provides important links between the major principals here. Turner, product of Portage, Wisconsin, had come to the Madison campus in 1878, entering the preparatory department. He did his most important work with Professor William Francis Allen, a first-rate historian and a scholarly leader among the faculty. Fred Turner had a special interest in journalism at the time and in his senior year became the Madison correspondent for the *Milwaukee Sentinel*. The bitterness between President Bascom and Elijah Keyes had quickened, and Turner wanted to find for the newspaper sources disclosing Keyes's intention to get rid of Bascom. The *Sentinel* gave Turner's report the headline "Keyes After the Scalp of Dr. Bascom of the State University" and furthermore attacked Keyes in heavy editorial rebuke.

15. Richard T. Ely, "Administration," *Christian Union* 34 (December 9, 1886), 9.

16. Richard T. Ely, "Administration," *Christian Union* 34 (December 16, 1886), 10. See also [Ely], "American Colleges and German Universities," *Harper's New Monthly Magazine* (July 1880), 253–60.

17. Ely, *Ground under Our Feet*, 180.

Students rallied in defense of their president, as noted. Bascom, meanwhile, had acted on the request of Professor David Frankenburger for an instructor in rhetoric and oratory. Bascom gave Turner's name to the board of regents. It approved, but Keyes's supporters on the board reduced the salary and Turner took on graduate studies in history before taking a teaching position. The affair left a bitter feeling in Turner and sorrow when Bascom resigned. Turner attended the president's farewell address and wrote to his fiancée, Caroline May Sherwood: "A grand man, and if I ever wept I would feel like doing so at that time."[18]

Turner went on to study at Johns Hopkins University. Working with historian Herbert Baxter Adams, Turner also had courses with Ely. Those studies raised in Turner's estimation the large place of economics in history, one step among many that took the young historian on the road to his famous "Frontier Thesis" in 1893. It also brought Turner into the intellectual pantheon of young academics also influenced by Ely. They included sociologist Albion Small, historians Charles Homer Haskins and Charles M. Andrews, economist John R. Commons, and political scientist Woodrow Wilson. Turner came back to Madison and had talks with President Chamberlin about the new school. When Ely soured on Johns Hopkins after President Daniel Coit Gilman refused him a salary increase (but gave one to young colleague Adams), Turner struck. He urged Ely to accept the appointment at Wisconsin. He knew how to appeal to his former teacher. "Does it not seem to you," he addressed Ely, "that our aim should be to cultivate *Political Science* (broadly interpreted) as a means of good citizenship and preparation for the public service" and for advancing sociological understanding "by the preachers?" Turner added that the academic study of history offers another means of reaching those goals. So Ely signed on enthusiastically. He relocated to Madison for the fall term in 1892. He did not know much about the university he was joining. Bascom, he said, was the only one of its presidents "whom I knew personally," and added that he had had the privilege of editing one of Bascom's books.[19]

18. Allan G. Bogue, *Frederick Jackson Turner: Strange Roads Going Down* (Norman: University of Oklahoma Press, 1998), 29–30, 36 (quotation).

19. Bogue, *Turner*, 46, 69; Ely, *Ground under Our Feet*, 197. When Simon Newcomb attacked Ely in the *Nation* Bascom wrote to Ely and encouraged him to keep up the fight against him. December 6, 1886, in the Richard T. Ely Papers, Wisconsin Historical Society. Bascom also wrote to Ely some years later when Ely had joined the University of Wisconsin faculty: "I am glad you are at the University. It is a good place for influence and I rejoice that that influence is in Your good hands." November 2, 1895, in the Ely Papers.

Ely now seized the day. He celebrated his new undertaking and publicly drew attention to his program and to himself. Five months before his move to Madison Ely used the pages of the *Independent* to reach a large audience. He addressed the topic of "The Proper Aims of Schools of Economics and Politics." These subjects fell under the rubric of "sociology," Ely explained, and they deserve public support. They have three aims. First, they advance "mental culture." Here Ely, like Bascom, brought sociology into the expansive reach of the human mind. "They furnish abundant room for abstract speculation," but always return to matters at hand. Success in sociology advances with gains in philosophy, Ely emphasized. Sociology prevents philosophy from withdrawing from the world and gives it practicality. Second, the new university schools that advance this discipline also combine it with "ethical culture." "No group of studies," Ely wrote, "so draws out and cultivates the altruistic feelings." Social science, he added, gives reasons for our moral codes; it provides them concreteness and makes them appear less arbitrary as they address quotidian realities.[20]

But that was just for starters. Third, Ely outlined for the new academic programs a training and preparation of students for new roles in the modern world. Journalists will need a solid grounding in economics and politics. So will lawyers and so will preachers. Above all Ely located a transcendent purpose for the new academics in the role the universities could play in preparing their graduates for civic functions. Now, on the eve of his move to the University of Wisconsin, Ely assigned the state universities a particularly important role. The state schools, he proclaimed, should form connections to the various rivulets of state governments. He specified: "They should enter into relation with the State bureaus of labor, with the offices of the railway commissioners, insurance commissioners, with boards of control of charitable, penal, and reformatory institutions." These public offices, Ely proposed, should be "laboratories" for these schools. They will all lead toward one high goal: "better government." So much now did Ely look to the state, usefully connected to the university, that he believed the social sciences would in these arrangements "promote most effectively social reform and progress."[21]

The new school enjoyed much success throughout the 1890s. It attracted students from around the world, such wide renown did Ely enjoy. The program had an excellent faculty, "one of the most progressive and influential groupings

20. Richard T. Ely, "The Proper Aims of Schools of Economics and Politics," *Independent*, May 19, 1892, 2.
21. Ely, "Proper Aims," 2.

of social scientists in America."[22] It produced important new scholarship and it constituted a genuine graduate school that yielded new doctorates. Faculty also participated widely in the university extension movement that President Chamberlin initiated in 1891 and the work thus gained wide recognition around the state.[23] Ely himself kept close ties to Hull House in Chicago and to Milwaukee settlement homes. His students did outreach work in midwestern cities. Ely raised money to bring speakers to Madison and the Ely home, a gathering place for the students, welcomed Woodrow Wilson, Jacob Riis, Jane Addams, Theodore Roosevelt, and Alexander Graham Bell as overnight guests. Furthermore, insofar as the products of this program also moved on into positions of importance in Wisconsin's state government, the School of Economics, Political Science, and History fulfilled the ideals of both Bascom and Ely.[24]

For some, however, Ely represented a dangerous radicalism. Many people know that he became involved in one of the most celebrated academic freedom cases in American higher education history. The formal charges involved allegations that he supported labor strikes and was too cozy with the prohibitionists. Others would have implicated him in socialism or simply welcomed the chance to strike at his alleged radicalism. Details of the proceedings received much coverage, even in the eastern press, especially the powerful, conservative *Nation*. But Ely's "trial" ended in a statement of transcendent significance for the University of Wisconsin and beyond. Today one finds the words of the board of regents that vindicated Ely in 1894 inscribed, appropriately, outside Bascom Hall in Madison and on the front entrance to Mitchell Hall at this author's university, the University of Wisconsin–Milwaukee: "Whatever may be the limitations which trammel inquiry elsewhere we believe the great state University of Wisconsin should ever encourage that continual and fearless sifting and winnowing by which alone the truth can be found."[25]

22. Robert M. Crunden, *Ministers of Reform: The Progressives' Achievement in American Civilization, 1889–1920* (New York: Basic Books, 1982), 30.

23. For the role of the Extension movement as a major factor of the Wisconsin Idea, see Vernon Carstensen, "The Origin and Early Development of the Wisconsin Idea," *Wisconsin Magazine of History* 39 (Spring 1956), 181–88.

24. Curti and Carstensen, *University of Wisconsin*, 1:637–38; Rader, *Academic Mind*, 127; J. F. A. Pyre, *Wisconsin* (New York: Oxford University Press, 1920), 294–95.

25. Curti and Carstensen, *University of Wisconsin*, 1:508–27, 525 (quotation). For a large account of this case, see Theron F. Schlabach, "An Aristocrat on Trial: The Case of Richard T. Ely," *Wisconsin Magazine of History* 47 (Winter 1963–64), 146–59.

Other circumstances were laying the foundations of Wisconsin Progressivism and advancing Ely and other social scientists in the years just after the school's establishment. One catalyst was economic depression. It struck the United States with devastating impact in 1893 and lasted into 1898, the worst in American history to date. In Milwaukee, bank failures precipitated the collapse, but the state had no immunity to events occurring across the country. Businesses closed around the state and unemployment skyrocketed.[26] But the crisis induced responses from around the state; indeed, these new activities and formations proved transforming as they virtually redefined Wisconsin politics. David Thelen's valuable study has shown the breadth of new thinking that emerged as citizens gauged the unprecedented circumstances they faced. A politics dominated by class, religion, and ethnic divisions, as noted in an earlier chapter, now created unities across these lines. Ideas became more important than social backgrounds. Everywhere in the state there formed discussion clubs, reform leagues, university extension programs, church groups, and farmer and labor associations. Issues that had registered the separate agendas in the old categories succeeded to expressions of common interests. "The distinguishing social feature of the new mass, progressive politics," writes Thelen, "was its unification of men from all classes as consumers, taxpayers, and citizens. The progressive coalition combined workers and businessmen, foreign-born and native-born, Populists and Republicans, drinkers and abstainers, Catholics and Protestants." Herein "the new citizenship."[27]

John Bascom would have found much that was pleasing and gratifying in the new politics. The crystallizing progressive movement required new strategies and new weaponry. In great numbers, leaders and followers in the new civic organizations turned to the social sciences for illumination. And they knew where to look. Ely's new school at the university had gained wide attention, and Ely even attained, among many, a celebrity status during his academic freedom trial. Thus, "throughout the depression Wisconsin [newspaper] editors fed the interests of their readers by printing speeches and sketches of the new dean of the new economists, Prof. Richard T. Ely." Legions of Ely students were investigating social problems, and demand emerged for social science experts to speak to the myriad clubs and societies interested in advancing

26. John D. Buenker, *The Progressive Era, 1893–1914*, vol. 4 of *The History of Wisconsin* (Madison: State Historical Society of Wisconsin, 1998), 10–12. See the many other parts of this detailed history for more on the depression.

27. David P. Thelen, *The New Citizenship: Origins of Progressivism in Wisconsin, 1885–1900* (Columbia: University of Missouri Press, 1972), 55–56, 288 (quotation).

political reform. In Milwaukee one would now find the Social Science Club, the Social Economics Club, and the Liberal Club. Appleton had the Good Citizenship League, Superior had its Good Government Club, and so on. People asked the university to offer more social science courses, and the institution responded with the hiring of more teachers. Church groups especially looked to Ely and offered invitations for lectures from the Madison professor. Thelen notes that requests for Ely and others came from all social classes and all regions around the state. The Wisconsin Idea was taking new shape amid economic hard times.[28]

The churches in Wisconsin also reflected the shifts in thinking. The Protestant ones had mostly centered their attention on the salvation of individuals, by revivals and moral persuasion, and in their social views they had endorsed the competitive order. Much evidence now showed the gains of the Social Gospel, prominent in religious literature around the country and long an intellectual presence in Bascom's presidency at Wisconsin. Church leaders became more sensitive to the stark class divisions that their institutions reflected and more conscious of the alienation of many more people, especially workers, from their offerings. Here, too, Ely, like Bascom previously, encouraged the churches to reach out, and many did. They showed a greater sympathy to the cause of labor and argued for a "Christian sociology" as the effective means of understanding and addressing the social emergency that the entire state faced. But in Wisconsin politics neither the Democrats nor the Republicans responded to reform ideas. Both parties stood under the control of powerful business interests. Now, however, there began to emerge a new insurgency. It took root among Republicans, and its various proponents came under the leadership of Robert La Follette.[29]

The commonalities between Bascom and La Follette go far back. Both could trace their ancestries to the Huguenots and the harsh treatment they received from French kings. Both married women who had deep backgrounds in New England and who joined them as strong partners in unconventional

28. Thelen, *New Citizenship*, 67–70, 67 (quotation), 75, 144. Then came the Republican Club of Milwaukee, which drew in the reformers in that party. They included future Wisconsin governor Francis McGovern.

29. Buenker, *Progressive Era*, 414–15, 401, 403, 424–26, 418. Prior to La Follette's becoming governor, the Republicans in the state legislature secured some progressive legislation. Measures passed included state regulations in matters of health care, restrictions of railroad mergers, and some higher taxes on utilities. Republicans and Governor Edward Scofield did defeat stronger controls on business and legislation on behalf of labor.

involvement in their political activities. Both lost their fathers at very early ages. Bascom's father died just over a year after the son's birth; Robert La Follette, born June 14, 1855, lost his father, Josiah, only eight months later. Both Bascom and La Follette grew up with females with whom they remained very close (Bob had two sisters and a brother, and like Bascom, was the youngest of four children). Bascom and La Follette also both grew up as farm children (Bob in Primrose township, Wisconsin) and knew the rough, demanding work that farm life entailed. La Follette celebrated it; Bascom did not. Both Bascom and La Follette knew the severities of Calvinism. Bascom saw the toll they took on his mother in her warped religion, and he spent his intellectual life advocating for the theological alternative of liberal Protestantism. La Follette's mother remarried, and John Z. Saxton, age seventy, became the husband to a widow forty-five years old. Saxton adhered to a rigid Calvinism and a moral regime that yielded corporal discipline on the one hand and emotional terror on the other. Saxton once told Bob that his deceased father would roast in hell for his agnosticism. Young La Follette rebelled, in contrast to Bascom, by turning away from religion. But, his biographers tell us, he painfully missed the father he never knew and sought all his early life for a surrogate. Some believe that John Bascom fit the need perfectly. Bob's mother, Mary Fergeson La Follette, always urged him to do something worthy of his deceased father's own admonition "to do right."[30]

Mary La Follette moved the family to Madison in 1873 and Bob entered the university. His mother rented to boarders and Robert did some local teaching to finance his education. He also, in an act of remarkable entrepreneurship, purchased the student newspaper the *University Press*, sold large, new advertising space for it, and made it quite profitable. La Follette also brought to the campus a commitment to the Republican Party that lasted through most of his political career. It derived from his parents' antislavery principles, which they took into abolitionism and their voting for the Free Soil Party. La Follette found heroism aplenty in the Republicans' early commitment to stop slavery. At the university his love for political discussion made him an enthusiast of Bascom's Sunday talks with seniors, where classroom neutrality gave way to a more partisan and polemical atmosphere. Bascom's son and daughter partook of these events as did La Follette's friend and future UW president Charles Van Hise and his future

---

30. David Paul Thelen, *The Early Life of Robert M. La Follette, 1855–1884* (Chicago: Loyola University Press, 1966), 4, 12, 13–14; Nancy C. Unger, *Fighting Bob La Follette: The Righteous Reformer* (Madison: Wisconsin Historical Society Press, 2008), 7, 9, 12, 14–16, 20, 26, 35, 84. Spelling varies on Fergeson; Thelen spells it "Ferguson."

wife, Alice Ring. Likewise, Bob's participation in the Athenaean Literary Society engaged him and Van Hise in a variety of topics and rhetorical warfare with the rival society Hesperian. Oratory was La Follette's passion and he even contemplated a career on the stage. And when the Wisconsin student won a six-state oratory competition it was big news indeed, all around the state. His spirited speech on Iago, whom he described as an intellect diminished by his want of emotion and moral strength, may have reflected Bascom's influence on him. On May 7, 1879, students on the campus held a bonfire celebration when the telegraph wires reported the news of their fellow student's triumph. They greeted him the next day with a brass band at the railway station.[31]

Bob La Follette had other interests at the university. He had no lack of emotion when it came to his attraction to a young woman there, Belle Case. This "bookish" student, dedicated in all her classes before Madison and during, contrasted with Bob at least in the more cavalier approach he took to his studies. He flourished in the social life, even to the point, as Belle related, that he would not let a class obligation keep him from attending a big public event, or a local courtroom trial, or from pursuing his own extracurricular activities, the campus pranks that made him a notoriety among his classmates. Relishing social interactions, La Follette was "chairman of the undergraduate greeters," as a classmate remembered him. In academics, however, he made, in Bascom's case, an exception to his indifference. The president's classes seemed alone to capture his interest and convey importance. Belle La Follette relates: "Here, as in other phases of our university course, my understanding of what President Bascom was trying to implant seems to have been rather vague and general; while to Bob it was concrete truth, the living gospel, whose application was as plain as a pikestaff. In my student days I stood somewhat in awe of Dr. Bascom. Bob loved, honored, and understood him as well then as in later life. He enjoyed and made a good record in the branches which Dr. Bascom taught."[32] But not good enough overall. When it came time for the faculty to approve the senior students for graduation the vote tied on La Follette. Bascom came in

31. Unger, *Fighting Bob*, 10; Thelen, *Early Life*, 18, 30–37; Bernard A. Weisberger, *The La Follettes of Wisconsin: Love and Politics in Progressive America* (Madison: University of Wisconsin Press, 1994), 1, 13, 17. La Follette's speech on Iago has the ring of a moral philosophy class: "The emotions are the native soil of moral life. From the feelings are grown great ethical truths one by one, forming at last the grand body of moral law" (17).

32. Belle Case La Follette and Fola La Follette, *Robert M. La Follette, June 14, 1855–June 18, 1925* (New York: Macmillan, 1953), 1:38.

and cast a deciding vote on his behalf. Well, after all, he did win the oratory contest.[33]

Belle and Bob both made the decision to attend the university "law school."[34] Bascom had inspired in them a zeal for public service, and Bob still aspired to justify himself to his father's memory. Here for him as well came the opportunity for righteous endeavor. Belle became the first woman to earn a law degree in Wisconsin. Upon graduating Bob ran for the office of Dane County district attorney and won, at age twenty-six. How else could he better pursue moral justice and serve the public? But, as biographer Nancy Unger writes, "He wanted also to gain the approval of Bascom by serving the public and doing 'right.'" Bascom would remain in La Follette's imagination as "an approving father figure." La Follette's early involvement in local politics also pitted him against old Boss Keyes, Bascom's inveterate enemy. La Follette brought to his new office a strong, moralistic rhetoric through which less than momentous crimes and injuries rose to infamy and evil most foul in the hyperbolic excoriations of the young D.A.[35]

La Follette also had three terms as congressman in the nation's capital and for the most part produced a record of Republican Party loyalty. The Republicans had a mildly reformist agenda that was anything but radical, and La Follette reflected its rhetorical criticism of big business. He spoke sympathetically for farmers and laborers, but he did little else. After defeat for a fourth term, Bob and Belle returned to Madison and he set his sights on the office of

33. Bascom's role in La Follette's graduation did not become public until 1927. Then Ragmus R. Anderson, the oldest living professor of the university, disclosed the great favor Bascom had done for La Follette in breaking the tie. *Appleton Post-Crescent*, June 20, 1927. Belle La Follette had much admiration for Bascom and cited aspects of his teaching: his accommodating science and religion; his connecting the spiritual life to the "everyday world"; his advanced views on the day's social problems; his urging of students their loyalty to the state; and his encouraging students to think and reason for themselves. Nancy C. Unger, *Belle La Follette: Progressive Era Reformer* (New York: Routledge, 2016), 25. Belle La Follette deserves inclusion as among the most remarkable of Bascom's students.

34. Started under Bascom, the school consisted of local attorneys teaching on campus and the students receiving additional training in a Madison attorney's office.

35. Unger, *Fighting Bob*, 33, 35, 72 (quotation), 74; Weisberger, *La Follettes*, 9, 10; David P. Thelen, "The Boss and the Upstart: Keyes and La Follette, 1880–1884," *Wisconsin Magazine of History* 47 (Winter 1963–64), 103–115. See Thelen, *Early Life*, for examples of La Follette's prosecutory verbiage (75).

governor. Here he had some titanic fights, mostly within his own Republican Party. And here he moved, very slowly indeed, toward a reformist program. He failed twice to win the nomination, the party "machine" of Stalwarts standing by their old favorites. But then he got religion, of a very secular kind. He claimed it came when powerful Republican senator Philetus Sawyer tried to bribe him. La Follette reacted in moral outrage. He crusaded against the powerful corporations, which he now linked to the corruption in state politics, and he put together an agenda that included tax reform, utility and railroad regulation, banking legislation, workers' protection, and—his favorite—direct primaries.[36]

His campaign drew an assemblage of enthusiasts from the ranks of the University of Wisconsin alumni who had great personal loyalty to La Follette but who also saw new opportunities for themselves outside the privileged apparatus of the party establishment. Many of these alumni came from the Bascom years and shared their former teacher's "Christian-based, socially involved philosophy," John Buenker reports. These new enthusiasts and UW faculty as well gave La Follette their support and efforts. In Chicago, in 1897, La Follette delivered an address he titled "The Menace of the Machine." He had found his calling. Back in his home state he sought out the county fair audiences and championed the direct primary as the cure-all for political corruption. But he did more, for here was a man of no mean political skills. La Follette proved himself a veritable genius at traditional politics and coalition building. He crafted from an assortment of political outsiders the most efficient and effective electoral apparatus in the state's history. La Follette won the governorship in 1900 and took office in January 1901, the first Wisconsin-born governor and the first graduate of the state university to hold that office.[37]

So what is one to make of La Follette and the connection to John Bascom? La Follette claims to have been a reformer from the beginning, citing in his autobiography his early reading of Henry George.[38] But biographers find this claim not quite right. And it leaves the question where La Follette got his ideas and fashioned his reform programs. He could have drawn from a bountiful political and social literature by the end of the decade when his own reformist agenda crystallized. La Follette, though, did not read widely in these materials (Henry Demarest Lloyd, Ida Tarbell, Edward Bellamy, Jacob Riis, John

36. Unger, *Fighting Bob*, 87, 117; Thelen, *New Citizenship*, 299–300.

37. Buenker, *Progressive Era*, 439, 445; John D. Buenker, "Robert M. La Follette's Progressive Odyssey," *Wisconsin Magazine of History* 82 (Autumn 1998), 11.

38. Robert M. La Follette, *La Follette's Autobiography: A Personal Narrative of Political Experiences* (1911; Madison: University of Wisconsin Press, 1960), 10.

Dewey, Lester Frank Ward, the Social Gospel advocates, the socialists). Neither, though, can one argue that La Follette emerged from Bascom's classes armed with a social philosophy through which he aspired to define his political career. But that influence is large and visible nonetheless, evident in two important ways, and in delayed reaction.

La Follette, just six months into his first term as governor, welcomed Bascom on a return visit to the campus. And he addressed his guest: "Believe me, sir, this welcome is deeply sincere and heartfelt." The governor commented on all the changes in the state and in the university since Bascom's departure fourteen years previously. He recited the great debt the state and the institution owed to Bascom and the faith in both that Bascom had maintained amid the trials and discouragements he had endured during his administration. La Follette went on about the university in warm praise of its former leader. "For thirteen years—the most precious years of its life—this state had a great thinker, philosopher and teacher at the head of its highest educational institution." Probably what Bascom most cherished from La Follette's welcome came in the governor's citing the moral tone Bascom had inscribed on the campus, "underlying all work, and all life in the institution, pervading its whole atmosphere entering into the daily thought and being of each student." It "admit[ted] of no compromise with error and evil" but still respected the individuality of all students, helping to make "well-rounded, full-orbed men and women" with a leavening influence in the Wisconsin citizenry. La Follette also made a special point of recognizing one of Bascom's cardinal ideals: service to the state. "No student ever left this university while you were its president, whose college education was not thoroughly seasoned with this sense of higher moral obligation to serve the state."[39]

The most oft-cited statement by La Follette concerning Bascom comes from the autobiography. Reviewing his years at the university, La Follette wrote: "The guiding spirit of my time, and the man to whom Wisconsin owes a greater debt than it can ever pay, was its President, John Bascom." La Follette likened Bascom to Ralph Waldo Emerson. Bascom, he added, "was the embodiment of moral force and moral enthusiasm; and he was in advance of his time in feeling the new social forces and in emphasizing the new social responsibilities." The former student cited Bascom's Sunday afternoon sessions with the seniors and his classroom, too, as "among the most important influences in my early life." Bascom, La Follette remembered, constantly held before the

39. *The Political Philosophy of Robert M. La Follette, as Revealed in His Speeches and Writings*, comp. Ellen Torelle (Madison: Robert M. La Follette Co., 1920), 302–5.

students their debt to the state. "He was forever telling us what the state was doing for us and urging our return obligation not to use our education wholly for our own selfish benefit, but to return some service to the state." For all of these ideals, La Follette believed, Bascom "may be said to have originated the Wisconsin idea in education."[40]

But for greater substance in seeking Bascom's influence one should look to La Follette's own political speeches and addresses. Like Bascom, La Follette in his writings cited just distribution of power as the critical measure of the healthy society. Bascom inveighed against the distortions and dysfunctions that come when one or several powerful sectors dominate the social organism. La Follette put the same notions in more starkly political terms. On the matter of powerful business corporations, he wrote, "The supreme issue . . . is the encroachment of the powerful few upon the rights of the many. This mighty power has come between the people and their government." No progress in social justice, said La Follette, can come without a resolve to undo these usurpations of power. "It is against the system built up by privilege, which has taken possession of government and legislation, that we must make unceasing warfare," he urged.[41]

On occasion La Follette gave his political points some sociological and historical framework. When he did, his words came right out of Bascom's Sunday sessions or his sociology text or his public speeches. Bascom often warned that rich capitalists would never yield to labor out of good will. La Follette made the same point with more drama in a special message to the Wisconsin legislature in 1903: "No man, no body of men, wrongfully amassing riches out of the toil and savings of others, ever willingly relinquished such tribute, no matter how unjustly levied."[42] As he continued, La Follette showed that he remembered Bascom well and rendered his teaching to his own advantage. "Throughout history," the governor instructed the solons, "the struggle has continued between the few, vigilant, aggressive, persistent, well organized, rich, and powerful, and the many, unorganized, though strong in individual numbers, and irresistible in concerted and continuous effort."[43]

But redress of these imbalances and these inequities, La Follette believed, also required some rethinking, some better priorities than those now prevailing. La Follette time and time again referred to the "will of the people" in making his case against powerful and privileged interests. In that way he sounded more

40. La Follette, *Autobiography*, 12–13.
41. *Political Philosophy*, 20–21.
42. "Capital will never give of its own generosity," Bascom had said in his Syracuse address in 1887.
43. *Political Philosophy*, 90.

populist than Bascom. And he gave that will, somewhat naively, a monolithic form, as if it were one voice, one mind, arrayed against everything else. La Follette, though, was giving emphasis to a new norm embraced by all the Progressives and certainly one urged by Bascom for years at the University of Wisconsin. For all shared the conviction that American thinking must give greater place to the "public interest." That ideal would provide the reformers' program the leverage they needed to undo the ideology of individualism and the free market that sheltered big corporations from any legislative interference. La Follette made that point, among many instances, to the state legislature in 1904. Railroads, he said, are entitled to fair profits from their investments and expenses and may turn to the law to secure them. La Follette hastened to add, though, that "the public, each community, and every individual, has rights equally precious." Those rights, as La Follette stated in other pieces on railway regulation, have no meaning apart from the role of the state to give them force. The people know, the governor proclaimed, that only "an enlightened public policy that employs all the power lodged in state and federal government" can address and resolve "the industrial question."[44]

A festive event occurred in Madison, Wisconsin, on June 5, 1904. The university was celebrating its fiftieth anniversary. Representatives from many universities around the country attended the ceremonies. John Bascom prepared the baccalaureate address, but illness prevented his traveling to Madison. John Olin read it. Then his former student, now governor, Robert La Follette addressed the audience. La Follette was making the university an integral part of his Progressive agenda. He did so the more readily as he adapted directly from Bascom his ideals of service to the state and the responsibility to it that graduates inherited as a debt. He had made the point earlier when he addressed an alumni meeting in 1901. However the matter of student obligation to the state may exist now at the university, said La Follette, "I well remember when it found expression in every convocation and was heard from time to time in every classroom." The university, the governor emphasized, must deliver to the state above all else a new influx of good citizens. And of a particular kind: "Men and women who will fight the battles of the state, against all the combination of evil." They will instill "into the mind of every citizen and tax payer" a new appreciation for the university's good work. La Follette envisioned the university and its graduates as that force to which the awakened citizens looked for protection of their rights and for advocacy of "clean and honest service" at all levels of

44. *Political Philosophy*, 87–89.

state government. La Follette would often speak also of the material advantages to the state that the university rendered—in agriculture, mining, manufacturing, and commerce. "On this material basis alone," he assured, "the university is paying back to the state an hundred fold every dollar appropriated to its support."[45]

The fiftieth anniversary event also coincided with the inauguration of a new university president. Many members of the class of 1879 attended because they were celebrating their twenty-fifth anniversary and were to witness the installation of one of their own, Charles Van Hise, as the new president. For the first time a graduate of the University of Wisconsin assumed office as its president. Governor La Follette had all the more reason to rejoice as now his classmate and longstanding friend received this honor, and indeed because his daughter Fola also received her degree at the event.[46]

Charles Richard Van Hise surpassed Bascom by one year in having the longest tenure of UW presidents. How had he arrived to this position? Both of Van Hise's parents had joined the pioneering throng that brought easterners to Wisconsin in the middle nineteenth century, his mother, Mary, from Maine and his father, William Henry, from New Jersey. Born May 29, 1857, Charles grew up in several Wisconsin small towns as his father relocated the family with his changing business adventures. As a student at the university, Van Hise found a new love for science and came under the long influence of Professor Roland Irving, the geologist. Van Hise did not have the worshipful feelings for John Bascom that his friend Robert La Follette had; only later did he appreciate and emulate his former teacher. As student, Charles did not project a sophisticated persona. A bit clumsy and socially awkward, he struck people like Belle La Follette as "a rather countrified-looking student." But he excelled brilliantly in his academics. Belle attended classes with Charles and remembered him as "the outstanding genius of our class of 1879." He could solve problems that not even the instructor could, she reported. In 1903 many at the university did not share the enthusiasm of Frederick Jackson Turner, who wanted Van Hise named university president. (The Turners and Van Hises lived across the street from each other.) Critics believed he would not look presidential. Along the way, Belle and Bob formed friendships with Charles and with classmate Alice Ring, later Charles's wife. The two couples remained socially close, and Belle recalled Sunday dinners together where Bob and Alice, with their "spontaneous wit, repartee, and storytelling," had the whole group in laughter "until one

45. *Political Philosophy*, 293–94.
46. *Political Philosophy*, 293–94.

would think the glass of scuppernong wine had gone to our heads." Belle also remembered Charles as studious and serious but fun-loving, too. He joined at times in Bob's campus pranks, on one occasion stealing apples from the university orchard.[47]

Charles Van Hise gave new dimensions to the Wisconsin Idea, but his intellectual perspective derived from science, not religion, as in the cases of Bascom, Ely, and Commons. To be sure, Van Hise entered the university fully charged by the "simple and fundamentalist faith" he brought from his family and small-town background. But that faith began to wane, and certainly his increasing involvement in scientific studies spurred his transition away from religion. Van Hise seems to have found some persuasion, too, in the writings of a famous atheist, Robert Ingersoll. Ultimately, Van Hise located himself in the intellectual circles of modern thinkers like sociologist Lester Frank Ward, scientist/theist/evolutionist Joseph Le Conte, and geologist John Wesley Powell. Personal anguish often attended the intellectual adjustments Van Hise felt compelled to make. In his senior year, he wrote to Alice Ring: "The more I study, the more I doubt . . . and the more dissatisfied I am that I cannot believe." But he emerged eventually thoroughly comfortable in the rational and empirical mind of modern science, and a self-described "universal skeptic."[48]

Van Hise pursued his studies in geology with a team headed by the man who succeeded Bascom as university president, Thomas Chrowder Chamberlin. The group did pioneering work in micropetrology, and its four-volume *Geology of Wisconsin* appeared in the years 1877 to 1883. Van Hise earned his master of science degree in 1882 and then became the first person to receive the doctoral degree from the University. He joined as a full-time faculty member shortly thereafter. In the year of his graduation he wrote to Alice: "It would be fine if I could become professor in my own Alma Mater! This is a dream so deep down that it would never be expressed to anyone but you, and will probably never become anything more than a dream." Now, after twenty-eight years at the university as student and professor, Van Hise became its president.[49]

Van Hise offered in his inaugural address a learned disquisition on American higher education, its history, and the UW's strategical situation with respect to them. He began with a half-century glance back at the university's progress to

47. Maurice M. Vance, *Charles Richard Van Hise: Scientist, Progressive* (Madison: State Historical Society of Wisconsin, 1960), 8–9, 14, 20, 36, 72; La Follette and La Follette, *Robert M. La Follette*, 161–62.

48. Vance, *Van Hise*, 28–29 (quotation), 43; Curti and Carstensen, *University of Wisconsin*, 2:13.

49. Vance, *Van Hise*, 21 (quotation), 26–27.

date, focusing on its previous presidents. We who graduated in the Bascom years, he said, will hold as "above price" the intellectual attainments that carried us successfully into the world. Van Hise referenced a particular quality about Bascom and here he sounded very much like his friend and classmate. "The most treasured remembrance, the most potent influence which [the graduates] carried away from the university, was the pervasive, mastering, moral power of John Bascom, whose personality wrought itself during his presidency into every graduate." We share in those high ideals, Van Hise assured, "and have been led to stand steadily for the right."[50]

Van Hise became with La Follette a major voice of the Wisconsin Idea, and the new president's inaugural address anticipated some of its dimensions. In reviewing the historical developments that shaped the American university, the new president focused on England on the one hand and Germany on the other. The German model, which he celebrated, gave new directions to American higher education, he observed, as he drew attention to Johns Hopkins University and its founding in 1876. The University of Wisconsin had already found its way among the new developments and would stake out its own position, he assured. It would blend and adapt as needed. Van Hise accentuated the importance of all fields of learning, from pure sciences to the humanities and social sciences. An enthusiast for democracy, Van Hise also assured that the university would always be open to both sexes and to children of artisans and laborers for whom access had not come easily heretofore. He promised that the university would repay its debt to the state, in two ways. He stressed that already graduates from the School of Economics, Political Science, and History had achieved results in reforming state law and in influencing "a healthy and powerful public sentiment" in the state. "Soon such men," he added, "will be found in every city and hamlet, leading the fight against corruption and misrule."[51]

Second, Van Hise envisioned a vital role for the UW faculty. He believed that advancement in scholarship would have good practical effects. In words that augured a major evolution in Wisconsin politics and academics, Van Hise pointed out that "in Germany the university scholar is a man of affairs." He explained that every prominent German and Austrian professor serves as an official adviser to the government. He wished the same good arrangement in the United States. "Already, in America," he indicated, "we see the beginning of this movement. University professors are asked to serve on tax commissions,

50. Charles Van Hise, "Inaugural Address of Charles Richard Van Hise," *Science*, n.s., 20 (August 12, 1904), 195.

51. Van Hise, "Inaugural Address," 196–98, 201 (quotation).

in the valuation of railroads and in various other capacities. Within the next half century the number of such men in these and similar positions will increase many fold. The college-trained man, and especially the university trained man, is, directly or indirectly, to control the destinies of the nation."[52]

In 1913 Van Hise addressed an audience of no less than one hundred people from Philadelphia who were visiting the university. After first citing his "amazement" at so large an entourage, Van Hise proceeded to honor the visitors' request for information about the operations of the Wisconsin Idea. Obliging, he offered many details about academic programs and extension activities. But he began with a philosophical statement. He might have gained inspiration for it from many sources, but it clearly shows how much this former student of John Bascom shared his teacher's vision on a critical point. (University historians Curti and Carstensen judged this statement of such significance that they printed it in full at the end of their two-volume study.)

The university, Van Hise told the visitors, has the duty to seek truth and to advance knowledge. But it can realistically do so only on the principle "that knowledge is nowhere fixed, that all things are fluid. The ideas which we hold today will not be held tomorrow in precisely the same form." This fact of knowledge's fluid character, Van Hise insisted, pertains to all categories, as much to religion and morals as to politics and sociology. The university, however, is not an iconoclast, he insisted. Its purpose is not to destroy traditions and customs. But it must make all things the subjects of sober inquiry and exploration. "Nowhere," said President Van Hise, "is there fixity or completeness in regard to human relations any more than with regard to physical or chemical relations." He added: "Just as the spirit of authority represses or destroys universities, so the spirit of freedom creates and inspires them."[53]

Van Hise's inauguration events at Madison occurred just as the political situation in the state took a dramatic turn. La Follette legislation had met effective resistance from the Stalwart Republicans in the legislature. The North Western and the Milwaukee Road railways spent more than $50,000 to defeat La Follette in 1904. Furthermore, influence was coming from outside the state to stop La Follette. James J. Hill, the "empire builder" of the Great Northern Railway, is said to have sent sixty men to the state to fight La Follette.[54] Nonetheless, in 1905 the dam broke. The Progressives triumphed with passage of major reforms: a now permanent tax commission with expanded powers;

52. Van Hise, "Inaugural Address," 202–3.
53. Curti and Carstensen, *University of Wisconsin*, 2:606, 608.
54. Buenker, *Progressive Era*, 477.

enabling legislation for a state income tax; a comprehensive civil service law; recodification of the state bank examination system; a strong antilobbying law; establishment of a state department of forestry, a response to La Follette's interest in conservation; and others. The civil service reform had the important input of Charles McCarthy and John R. Commons. In 1901 the legislature had created what became the famous Legislative Reference Library. It served as a key organizational locus of the Wisconsin Idea because it enabled the political leaders at the other end of State Street to draw on information, as provided by faculty research, useful in crafting new bills. In 1909, under Governor Francis McGovern, work began in the legislature on a workers' compensation bill, already achieved in other states. It headed a short list of other important legislation on behalf of workers. Here again Commons and McCarthy, and other UW faculty, too, played key roles. The law passed in 1911. Opponents of the reform did not like the roles played by the many university faculty in this progressive legislation.[55]

La Follette and Van Hise intended to defend the university, and they had inherited from John Bascom a set of ideals by which to do so. La Follette wrote that he had specific intentions: "to build up and encourage the spirit which John Bascom in his time had expressed." His appointment of alumni to the regents gave him one means. Close consultation with Van Hise and Professors Ely and Commons gave him other means. They further assisted the governor in the difficult political challenges of his administration. All wanted the university to act energetically in all of the state's business, in its economic improvement, and in its legislative reforms. They viewed the service function of the university comprehensively and took inspiration from Bascom's urgent call for a symbiosis of state and university. Fola La Follette had observed the La Follette–Van Hise collaboration closely. She wrote: "Two students of the class of 1879, Bob La Follette and Charles Van Hise, profoundly influenced in youth by a great teacher, were now, as mature men, collaborating to sustain former President Bascom's ideal of the relation of a state university to the State."[56]

55. Robert S. Maxwell, *La Follette and the Rise of the Progressives in Wisconsin* (Madison: State Historical Society of Wisconsin, 1956), 153–64. McGovern boasted that the 1911 Wisconsin state legislature "did more for the cause of workingmen than has ever been done before in any American state at a single legislative session" (164). Also, Buenker, *Progressive Era*, 488–89, 493, 509–10. Charles McCarthy details the political activities in this Progressive Era in his book *The Wisconsin Idea* (New York: Macmillan, 1912).

56. La Follette and La Follette, *Robert M. La Follette*, 307. Belle wrote the early chapters of their biography and Fola the later, a work she took on when Belle died in 1931.

Van Hise's presidential administration and the ideals by which he defined it show a strong Bascom influence in the way he expanded on the relations of state and university. Even more than Bascom did, Van Hise called on the university faculty to commit its time and hard work to research. No professor, he insisted, could neglect the obligation to advance scholarship. He showed little sympathy with professors who complained that their teaching consumed their university work, and some did complain. The state university, Van Hise believed, had a special obligation in this matter because the state itself gained hugely by faculty research, even "pure research." Van Hise became a missionary for the cause. If the public but knew the great gains to be had, it would gladly provide the funds to support this work, he avowed. The president took to the crossroads to broadcast far and wide this wonderful reciprocity of gain for state and university. But others heard, too. The university in the Van Hise years attracted new faculty who wanted to advance knowledge. Its reputation expanded nationally and around the world.[57]

Bascom called on graduates to go out and serve the state. Van Hise called on the university itself to go out and serve the state. A slow convert to the extension program, Van Hise moved to expand it. He furthermore urged faculty to take roles on the state commissions, key vehicles of the Progressive political program.[58] Van Hise became the ardent spokesman for this new and important dimension of the Wisconsin Idea: the faculty as experts in state government. No state surpassed Wisconsin in the large place it gave to these connections. Van Hise himself exemplified the practice. He served on several state boards and commissions, most of them dealing with conservation, in which he became an advance figure in another major reform program in Wisconsin. His early research had alerted Van Hise to the alarming destruction of forests in the Lake Superior region and elsewhere in Wisconsin. Scientists, he urged, had an obligation to transform their learning into public policy by disseminating their knowledge when opportunity allowed. Van Hise did so for conservation—by speeches to public audiences around the state and even by a lecture course he gave for the public in Madison. When the 1911 legislature created the commission on conservation Van Hise headed it. He also sought national legislation. He faulted Americans for their dangerous habits: "more profligate in the destruction of the soil than any other people at any other time." In 1910 he published his book *The Conservation of Natural Resources in the United States.*[59]

57. Vance, *Van Hise*, 106–8.

58. Wisconsin established commissions for railroads, conservation, taxes, and insurance.

59. Vance, *Van Hise*, 151–52, 160; Curti and Carstensen, *University of Wisconsin*, 2:88; Buenker, *Progressive Era*, 555.

Richard T. Ely had such a national reputation that he had connections everywhere, and they included his own students from his Johns Hopkins years. He brought two of them to Wisconsin and each played significant roles in the Progressive movement. John Rogers Commons and Edward A. Ross became the best known of them. Commons especially contributed an important dimension to the evolving Wisconsin Idea.[60] Ely asked Commons to join the School of Economics, Political Science, and History in 1904. The young economist arrived just in time to hear Van Hise deliver his inspiring inaugural address. Ely wanted Commons to write a history of American labor. He had found the graduate student at Hopkins very impressive and made him an assistant in writing Ely's very popular book *Outlines of Economics*.

Commons was born in Hollansburg, Ohio, in 1862. His parents came from two different parts of the country. His mother's side registered the familiar migratory pattern out of New England, Vermont in her case, into the Western Reserve, a location of antislavery feelings and temperance promotion. His father came from the South, fleeing North Carolina to escape the slaveocracy. He was a Quaker. Mother Clara. a graduate of Oberlin College (a pioneer in coeducation and locus of the student antislavery movement) had the stronger influence on John. The son endured with unease her strict Calvinist orthodoxy; he remembered *Foxe's Book of Martyrs* as early reading favored by both parents. His mother took her religion right into the women's crusade against the saloon. Young John embraced the cause. He helped his mother with an "anti-saloon" publication in Oberlin, one that Commons believed led to the formation of the Anti-Saloon League in Ohio in 1893. He cast his first vote for president in 1884, supporting the same person for whom John Bascom that year was campaigning in Madison—John St. John of the Prohibition Party.[61]

Commons had grown up in small-town Indiana, where his family had relocated, attended schools there, and then enrolled in his mother's alma mater. He and other students at Oberlin, Commons reported, formed a Henry George Club, the first sign of Commons's emerging reform bent. Then he went to Johns Hopkins. Commons related that he pursued that opportunity because

60. Ross, a sociologist, came to Madison in 1906 at Ely's behest. His many publications constitute another intellectual contribution to Progressivism. Ross would make for an interesting dimension to this study but he did not articulate, as did the others here, any particular aspect of the Wisconsin Idea.

61. John R. Commons, *Myself: The Autobiography of John R. Commons* (1934; Madison: University of Wisconsin Press, 1964), 7–9, 21; Lafayette G. Harter Jr., *John R. Commons: His Assault on Laissez-Faire* (Corvallis: Oregon State University Press, 1962), 12.

of Ely, having read about his future mentor in Simon Newcomb's attack on Ely and his book on the labor movement. Commons quickly became an enthusiast for Ely's "new economics" and grew in commitment to social reform along the lines of the Christian faith. Commons hoped as well that his work in that cause would appease his mother, who wished mightily that her son would enter the ministry. Along the way from Johns Hopkins to Ely's bringing him to Madison, Commons taught at Indiana University and at Syracuse University, and did work for the National Civic Federation.[62]

Commons brought to the University of Wisconsin a published record that reflected his wholesale commitment to liberal religion and the Social Gospel. Ely found that record just as important as the new project in labor history that both now envisioned. Commons scholars pay scant attention to this critical background. However, it provided the framework for his scholarship at the University of Wisconsin. His publications in economics and history there moved him away from Christian sociology as such, but they did not alter his objectives. Commons gave a new expression to the Wisconsin Idea because he provided it a new methodology, a different approach to progressive reform. And by these means he hoped to realize the ideals marked out so clearly in his Social Gospel phase.

Many issues troubled Commons as he looked at the United States of the early 1890s. Here stood a Christian nation in the midst of manifest social problems but apparently lacking the will to confront them. Christians have wealth and power, and if they had the will they could remove the glaring contrasts among the social classes and rid the avenues and byways of paupers and tramps, Commons believed. The churches must lead because they hold human beings to be children of God, made in his image. Commons found it "scandalous" to see God-like people crushed by poverty, crime, and intemperance. But the churches do not act, and Commons believed he knew why. They labor yet under an archaic, "medieval" theology, he said, a stark dualism of body and soul, spirit and matter. "To-day," Commons wrote, "this doctrine leads the Christian Church to preach salvation only for a future life — salvation for the soul apart from the body. Oppressive and unjust conditions in this life are looked upon as ordained means of grace to discipline the soul and turn its longings towards the hereafter." Thus, too, Commons believed, the church attacks only the symptoms of the disease and not the root causes. It chooses simply to close the saloons, pass Sunday labor laws, and bewail the corruptions of the city machines. Commons continued to speak for temperance

62. Commons, *Myself*, 8, 39, 40, 43, 50; Harter, *Commons*, 13–17.

laws but now saw the evil of drink as rooted in the social conditions of a changing America.[63]

Commons prescribed a cure for the faltering churches: they must embrace sociology. He became a major advocate of a modern Christianity fortified by sociological scholarship, a critical idea, as we have seen in Bascom and others, of liberal Protestantism's outreach to the world. At Indiana, Commons had joined with Ely to organize the American Institute of Christian Sociology, and he served on the editorial board of the *Kingdom*, its publication. Bascom and Gladden joined, too. Commons also put together "A Popular Bibliography of Sociology" to make available to general readers and "especially the Christian minister" the important works on social problems. "People," said Commons, "need not only the heart of love, but also the knowledge widely to guide their love."[64] Commons had great hopes for this partnership. "Sociology," he explained, "has rightly been said to be one half of religion; theology is the other half." "Religion is love to God, and sociology love to man, and on these two hang all the law and all preaching." Thus, he urged, the minister "should begin with the organic nature of society, showing that it is based properly on Christian ethics." Commons's writing reverberated with couplets in sentences like this: "Love and knowledge, Christianity and science, theology and sociology, must unite to save the world." Commons called the Bible an inspiration for the sociological minister. "What a wealth of social philosophy you can get from that book!" he proclaimed.[65]

Christianity and sociology have a key, common understanding: the organic nature of society. Man, said Commons, is a social animal and part of a growing organism. No man or woman is self-derived, he emphasized. Social environment plays a crucial role, a point that led Commons immediately to cite the wretched conditions that preclude legions of children from any hope of healthy integration into the larger society. Today, Commons narrated, we find men doomed to long hours of labor, seven days a week, with no holiday. How, he asked, can a healthy Christian ever emerge from such alienating circumstances? Like Bascom in the later 1860s and long after, Commons looked at the laborer and "the pitiful qualities of his soul." And typically, like Bascom, Commons painted a picture

63. John R. Commons, "The Christian Minister and Sociology," in Commons, *Social Reform and the Church* (New York: Thomas Y. Crowell, 1894), 14–15; idem, "The Church and the Problem of Poverty," in *Social Reform*, 30–31 (quotation); idem, "Temperance Reform," in *Social Reform*, 107–14. Ely wrote the introduction for this collection of essays.

64. Charles Hopkins, *The Rise of the Social Gospel in American Protestantism, 1865–1915* (New Haven, CT: Yale University Press, 1940), 194, 166, 162.

65. Commons, "Christian Minister," 19–21, 26; idem, "The Church and Political Reform," in *Social Reform*, 75.

of contrast, with the wealthy as much detached as the poor: "The exclusiveness, luxury, ostentation, of the upper four hundred are but the glossy side of the shield to the herding, deprivation, and ignominy of the four hundred thousand who support them." We have but one alternative, Commons asserted: "to reform society from top to bottom."[66]

Recourse to environment also carried with it in Commons's thinking the fact of evolution. He accepted it as scientific truth and as religion's opportunity. Christians should understand the human soul not as an autotelic entity but as an admixture of its large milieu. Biology informs sociology, wrote Commons, and sociology helps us create the sustaining, Christian environment. He believed that evolution prescribed the path of human progress. Here Commons presented his own version of "Reform Darwinism." We have arranged a social situation, he explained, that does not permit a natural selection of the best. Tenements, factories, and saloons suppress all the personal factors that would make for growth and achievement. And these conditions, Commons added, persist unchanged because our laws, written by the powerful, perpetuate them. Commons called for "a higher natural selection" whereby survival derives not from force and cunning; instead, "freedom, security, and equal opportunity" lay the grounds of a healthier competition.[67]

Such was the logic of Protestant Liberalism and the Social Gospel in Commons's early writings.[68] He needed but one ingredient more, which Commons joined others in prescribing: the active role of the state. Government, Commons advised, can alone effect real reform. Collective intelligence best achieves comprehensive reform. The state, said Commons, does the work of the church. It seeks the larger presence of moral power in the world and has the means to put it in place. "Ethics cannot work without coercion," Commons contended. But from local levels of government to the national, Commons saw enclaves of personal and corporate power that both appropriated state power

66. Commons, "Christian Minister," 11, 18, 21–22, 107–14; idem, "Church and Poverty," 34–35; idem, "Church and Political Reform," 74–75.

67. Commons, "Christian Minister," 6–7; idem, "Natural Selection, Social Selection, and Heredity," *Arena*, July 1897, 91–93, 96–97. To make his case against laissez-faire and the "natural course of things," Commons pointed to the sorry results of this regime. He cited tenement conditions, drinking, crime levels, family disruption, and poverty. "We cannot placidly rely on any abstraction of natural selection to wipe out crime and intemperance and to preserve the family. Rather do these evils multiply. Evolution is not always development upwards." "Christian Minister," 6–7; idem, "Social Economics and City Evangelization," *Christian Laity*, December 1898, 767–68.

68. See also, R. A. Gonce, "The Social Gospel, Ely, and Commons's Initial Stage of Thought," *Journal of Economic Issues* 30 (September 1996), 641–65.

and prevented the popular will from affecting government for the advantage of the whole. The real lawmakers, Commons chided, lie outside the state. They are unknown to the U.S. Constitution. They work through lobbies and political machines. Commons castigated the "self-appointed, private organizations" that have amassed so much power in the recent decades. He supported the initiative and the referendum and proportional representation in the states, the programs of the Populists and, soon, the Progressives. But already, in the early 1890s, Commons was talking about economic reforms, too: monetary changes, income taxes, public control of utilities, inheritance reform. His appointment to the University of Wisconsin gave Commons the opportunity to pursue these objectives by new, expanded means.[69]

The years after 1904 mark a momentous period in Wisconsin history, and in fact they have won it a place of significance in the national record. The state became the "laboratory of democracy." Visitors came from around the country and beyond to observe the legislation of reform, carried out energetically under La Follette's governorship. The reform continued with moderation under his Republican successor, James O. Davidson, and then moved to triumphant record under Republican governor Francis McGovern.[70] He in fact proved to be the most extensive reformer of the three.[71]

The record of Wisconsin Progressivism has received much scholarly attention, and this study does not review all of it. This concluding chapter has focused on the place of the university in that history and the intellectual origins of the

69. Commons, "Church and Political Reform," 76–77, 81, 83, 93–94; idem, "Proportional Representation," in *Church and Social Reform*, 173–74; idem, "Political Economy and the Law," *Kingdom* 24 (January 24, 1895), 254; idem, "Progressive Individualism," *American Magazine of Civics*, June 1895, 568–70.

70. For examples of the wide attention Wisconsin received in these years see Vance, *Van Hise*, 112, and Buenker, *Progressive Era*, 567–68 n93. The most famous reports came from Lincoln Steffens, pioneer of the new investigative journalism, or muckraking. Steffens championed the Wisconsin reforms of the La Follette era and gave attention to the university, too. See his "Sending a State to College: What the University of Wisconsin Is Doing for Its People," in *Portraits of the American University, 1890–910*, ed. James C. Stone and Donald P. DeNevi (San Francisco: Josey-Bass, 1971), 118–33. The piece first appeared in *American Magazine*, February 1909.

71. Reforms under McGovern included the first successful state income tax law, creation of a highway commission, a water conservation law, creation of a state insurance fund, and a workman's compensation act (designed by Commons). Robert C. Nesbit, *Wisconsin: A History* (Madison: University of Wisconsin Press, 1973), 422–26, 429–31.

Wisconsin Idea in John Bascom, and the extensions and refinements, briefly considered, of his successors at the UW. Through all of the Wisconsin reform governors' administrations, Charles Van Hise served as UW president. His biographer, in explaining the character and purposes of Van Hise's academic leadership in that office, gives a large place to John Bascom. "His influence on the University which was to emerge under Van Hise's administration was not exceeded by that of any other man." Maurice Vance so writes because he saw but "a short step" from Bascom's ideas about the state and the university to Van Hise's practice of appointing university professors to the various state boards and commissions where they could apply their expertise. So also with the UW-Extension programs, Vance believes. Van Hise made them logical extensions of Bascom's university ideals. Coming into influence at the university in the years after Bascom's presidency, "it remained for Bascom's successors to see and take these steps, but when this was done, his contribution to the principles underlying the Wisconsin Idea was clear."[72] At the top of Bascom Hill today, near the plaque given by the class of 1910 citing the words of the 1894 statement on academic freedom, stands another plaque. It has the words of Charles Van Hise: "I shall never be content until the beneficent influence of the University reaches every home in the state."

Ely, La Follette, Commons, and Van Hise give us a group portrait of the Wisconsin Idea at work, broad reformist ideals finding their way into practical legislation in the state. In his autobiography La Follette described with evident pride how he effected this arrangement. "While I was governor," he related, "I sought the constant advice and service of the trained men of the institution in meeting the difficult problems which confronted the state. Many times when harassed by the conditions which confronted me, I have called in for conference President Van Hise, Dr. Ely, Professor Commons, Dr. [Paul] Reinsch and others." La Follette referenced the Saturday lunch club established for these purposes and believed that the discussions with these participants and several others worked in the cause of "intelligent democratic government."[73] And thus did the Wisconsin Idea crystallize out of its mixed and various ingredients. La Follette stood at both ends of an intellectual progression: as Bascom's student, and thus present at the creation, and as the governor of Wisconsin who brought intellectual ferment into state politics.

72. Vance, *Van Hise*, 79–81, 111.
73. La Follette, *Autobiography*, 14, 15. Ely said that he was never "a close advisor" of La Follette, but acknowledged that the two did see each other "frequently" and were often guests at each other's homes. *Ground under Our Feet*, 216.

Postscript

John Bascom died on October 2, 1911, in Williamstown. Emma Bascom survived him another five years and they lie today with their children in the cemetery on the college grounds.

At his former university, the Wisconsin Idea, whose intellectual foundations Bascom had laid, was soon to undergo a severe test, a test the university failed. The issue was World War I, which the United States entered in 1917. United States senator Robert La Follette had long and loudly opposed American involvement in the war and spoke against the preparedness campaign led by President Woodrow Wilson. La Follette saw the war as one of commercial greed. He warned that the war would cost the government money and thus induce tax increases. Ordinary citizens would suffer most. They would pay for a war that gave them nothing in return while business would pay nothing and alone would profit from it. La Follette also feared that the war obsession would create a "dreadful diversion" from the progressive political program at home. When the president announced his intention to arm American ships, the Wisconsin senator led a filibuster to prevent that action. He fought to the last. And when Congress approved Wilson's request for a declaration of war against Germany in April 1917, La Follette spoke for four hours on the Senate floor against it. He reaped a harvest of outrage and abuse. The former president Teddy Roosevelt called La Follette a "shadow Hun" and urged his expulsion from the Senate. So did others.[1]

1. Nancy C. Unger, *Fighting Bob La Follette: The Righteous Reformer* (Madison: Wisconsin Historical Society Press, 2008), 239–58. On La Follette's path of rethinking his way to anti-imperialism, see Richard Drake, *The Education of an Anti-Imperialist: Robert La Follette and U.S. Expansion* (Madison: University of Wisconsin Press, 2013).

All around the United States progressive thinkers flocked to the colors. While fighting to extend democracy at home they joined in President Wilson's call now to make the whole world safe for it. The matter became a test of the Wisconsin Idea. Would the university act to defend the rights of the dissenting senator to speak as he did against the rush into war? Would it become a forum for open discussion of the war, or would an intolerant patriotism impose a total intellectual conformity? Or, would the occasion of war call for a new way of exercising the "service" ideal of the American universities? In Wisconsin, many opposed American intervention, many Germans, of course. But the professorial response at UW showed how much the institution still remained a "Yankee" one. The UW reflected the pattern everywhere. American universities turned their campuses into armed camps to make soldiers out of students. They reconfigured their curricula across the board and even contrived courses on "war aims." Academic freedom took a beating.[2] The war's few opponents on the campuses met strong retaliation. The University of Wisconsin followed this course despite the fact that critics faulted it for insufficient patriotism.

The Wisconsin intellectuals supported the war, to a man, without qualifications. Richard T. Ely volunteered to work for the National Board of Historical Service, formed by J. Franklin Jameson, a stalwart in the American Historical Association. Jameson convened a meeting of seventeen historians "to consider the problem of what they and their fellows can do for the country in time of war." Ely wanted no tolerance for dissenting professors. Other Wisconsin academics joined Ely in working for the board. Ely also requested the assistance of the board in getting evidence of the damage La Follette was doing to the war cause. When the Madison chapter of the Wisconsin Loyalty Legion formed in January 1918, Ely became its president.[3]

The University of Wisconsin faculty also moved against La Follette. That campaign began in late 1917 under the initiative of Ely, John R. Commons, and historian Carl Fish. They sought "to purge the state politically . . . [to] put La Follette and all his supporters out of business." Commons, after an acrimonious meeting with La Follette in Washington, DC, returned to Wisconsin determined to help elect opponents of La Follette. The faculty resolution against the senator passed by near unanimous vote. It advanced the charge that La Follette's actions and speeches "have given aid and comfort to Germany and her allies in the

2. See Carol S. Gruber, *Mars and Minerva: World War I and the Uses of the Higher Learning in America* (Baton Rouge: Louisiana State University Press, 1975).

3. Gruber, *Mars and Minerva*, 120, 208.

present war."[4] President Van Hise, under much pressure to demonstrate the loyalty of a "German" state to the American cause, presided at the faculty meeting. Van Hise turned on the senator. "I strongly believe," he said, "the policies of Senator La Follette in relation to the war are dangerous to the country." And of all the condemnations of him, this one La Follette experienced as the most personally painful and most difficult to comprehend. As daughter Fola put it: "One signature [in the faculty resolution] which Bob found it especially hard to believe could have been placed beneath a statement accusing him of disloyalty to his country was that of his intimate friend Charles R. Van Hise, the classmate who had shared with him the teaching and ideals of John Bascom, former president of the university."[5]

Outside the political domain, the Wisconsin Idea was undergoing a significant transformation, one wrought by the changing realities and character of academic life in the United States. In the Wisconsin Idea's intellectual history Bascom played two major roles at the UW. Academically, he continued the work that had dominated his career to that point, his explorations in philosophy and theology and their extensions into social subjects and reform issues. He also, as university president, pursued the course in academic programming by which he hoped to place his institution in march step with the best directions of American higher education in his time. But at least in one key way these two efforts stood at cross-purposes to each other.

4. Merle Curti and Vernon Carstensen, *The University of Wisconsin: A History, 1848–1925*, 2 vols. (Madison: University of Wisconsin Press, 1949), 2:111–22; Gruber, *Mars and Minerva*, 207–10; Lafayette G. Harter Jr., *John R. Commons: His Assault on Laissez-Faire* (Corvallis: Oregon State University Press, 1962), 64–65; Paul W. Glad, *War, a New Era, and Depression, 1914–1940*, vol. 5 of *The History of Wisconsin* (Madison: State Historical Society of Wisconsin, 1990), 9, 33–40.

5. Belle Case La Follette and Fola La Follette, *Robert M. La Follette, June 14, 1855–June 18, 1925* (New York: Macmillan, 1953), 2:842–44, 849–50 (quotation). When Van Hise died unexpectedly in 1918, La Follette thought of writing to his widow. He expressed his feelings about so doing in a letter to Belle: "I would like to write to Alice, but I don't know as I can put together such a letter as I would really be glad to send. He of all men in Madison was the last who ought to have been willing or could have been forced against his will to join a mob and murder the reputation of a life time friend who had pushed him into the position which had given him the very power which he used to destroy that friends [*sic*] reputation and standing before the Country" (2:909). Ely later recanted his action regarding La Follette.

Bascom, as noted in his annual reports to the board of regents, emphasized that the UW must move in the direction of research, the pursuit of new knowledge. Faculty will best utilize their talents if their scholarly investigations find their way into the classrooms and laboratories of the university, he believed. "Thorough scholarship" will thus yield a "subdivision" of the existing curriculum; academic specialization constitutes the new path of the higher learning, as the best universities in the nation now exemplify, Bascom stated in his reports to the board.[6] But Bascom still saw the world through his philosophical eyes. Knowledge must build from insights of the immediate into visions of a large and spiritual reality. To that great ambition he continued to dedicate his own writings, such that his *Sociology* book had a governing religious and metaphysical framework. His last report to the regents in 1887, in fact, stated that "the center of university instruction is philosophy," to be supported by social subjects.[7] Many students long remembered that Bascom gave just that imprint to the intellectual atmosphere at Madison.

But academic life was breaking down, from the large synthesis of the college era to the array of new academic disciplines in the university era. Creation of the American Economic Association in 1885, led by Ely, exemplified the new directions. Other professional organizations emerged. The Modern Language Association had begun in 1883 and the American Historical Association in 1885. The American Sociological Society formed in 1902 and the American Political Science Association in 1903. When the American Council of Learned Societies was created in 1919 it had the membership of thirteen different scholarly organizations. By this time, too, the AEA had shifted significantly. The original zeal for an ethical economics and a Social Gospel that had inspired the creation of the AEA soon had the great majority of its members engaged in narrowly focused, empirical research.

At Wisconsin the School of Economics, Political Science, and History soon split into separate departments for each of its subject components. And even within the newly formed academic disciplines differentiation intensified. Ely himself observed these changes, recognized their necessity as new knowledge proliferated, but lamented a certain loss that accompanied the transition into modern scholarship. Years before, Ely had gone to study in Germany in pursuit

---

6. John Bascom, "Report of the President of the University to the Board of Regents," in *Annual Report of the Board of Regents of the University of Wisconsin, for the Fiscal Year Ending September 30, 1878* (Madison, 1878), 27–28. Hereafter cited as "President's Report," with the appropriate year.

7. "President's Report, 1887," 36.

of philosophical idealism. He returned an economist. In reflections from late in his life he recalled the time when "economics was an integrated whole." Soon, however, the process of specialization set in, and "not with happy results," he believed. "Since the early days at Wisconsin," Ely wrote, "the process of differentiation has gone a long way. In my opinion it has gone too far. Economics has been cut up into so many particular fields that an ever increasing number of economists know more and more of less and less." Economists now, Ely lamented, can barely speak to each other beyond the boundaries of their narrow scholarly preoccupations.[8]

The career of John R. Commons best illustrates these academic shifts. In his years before Wisconsin his writings reflected the Social Gospel ideals of his mother, and he addressed subjects ranging from prohibition to the social roles of the churches in the city, as earlier detailed. Sociology meant the application of religious principles to political reform. Little of that framework continued in his work at the UW. Commons's scholarship had progressive and reformist purposes, to be sure, but Commons employed a thoroughly naturalist and empirical perspective. And to make the hard data of the social sciences serve the purposes of reform Commons had to enter a different intellectual universe. Now Commons was addressing all the complexities of statutory law, garnered from the large collections that Charles McCarthy had assembled for the Legislative Reference Library. His work with the new state commissions started by the Progressives found Commons and the members with whom he worked immersed in a "mass of statistics on railways," as Commons put it, and on other subjects of reform legislation. This work required processing hundreds of pages of code, prepared for the Industrial Commission. Commons described how the shift in focus had him training his students "to see that details and their meanings are science." Sometimes, he said, he and his students puzzled over a new detail for an entire class. Even his broad field of labor history now moved into new course subjects—labor legislation, labor management, labor unions, immigration. One by one Commons turned over instruction in these subjects to his former graduate students. Moral inspiration may yet have given Commons the drive he brought to this part of his career, but the intellectual business of it had placed him in far remove from the gospel imperatives that had launched his earlier career.[9] So the new directions that American higher education took in these years do point to some tensions in Bascom's academic ideals. But

8. Richard T. Ely, *Ground under Our Feet: An Autobiography* (New York: Macmillan, 1938), 189–90, 192.

9. Harter, *Commons*, 204; John R. Commons, *Myself: The Autobiography of John R. Commons* (1934; Madison: University of Wisconsin Press, 1963), 108, 126–27, 159, 130–31.

Bascom was a thinker who inscribed change as an ontological reality of his intellectual universe. He always called for creative responses to change. He would ask only that one bring to any issue as large and expansive a vision as possible. As such, the Wisconsin Idea could never become merely a service ideal. Nor would it lead the education of students into a merely utilitarian training and its allegedly practical enhancements.

Thus, while we have seen continuity of thinking from John Bascom to the later Wisconsin intellectuals who gave shape to the Wisconsin Idea, we do not see always an exact fit. But intellectual history is rarely a matter of direct influence, one thinker to another, rarely a straight trajectory. It has been observed that Wisconsin progressivism had something of an accidental character about it, that it could in fact have occurred in any number of states.[10] But by the series of combinations, connections, and events that we have observed, Wisconsin, in its university and in its state capital, did bring together some like-minded but quite different personalities. Intellect and politics intersected and wrote a significant chapter of Wisconsin's history and of the United States's record in the Progressive Era. And that combination also yielded the Wisconsin Idea.

In 1876 President Bascom arranged to have a statement from him placed in the student newspaper, the *University Press* (Robert M. La Follette, owner and publisher). Bascom wanted the students as well as the faculty to read the piece he called "The Spirit of the University." That spirit, he wrote, is something that transcends the classroom and the formalities of the campus life; instead, he said, it is "an inspiration, a growing estimate of truth, an appetite for excellence . . . The central quality of our spirit as a University," Bascom avowed, "should be a large-minded love of knowledge, a thorough disposition candidly and completely to know the truth." He urged that the University of Wisconsin "escape the spirit that dare not inquire lest it should break in on beliefs already entertained."[11] In 1973 the Wisconsin state legislature inscribed in the state statutes a statement about the University of Wisconsin. It referenced in now familiar language the charge to the university system to extend knowledge and its applications "beyond the boundaries of its campuses" and to do so through the vehicle of all its areas of learning: humanistic, scientific, professional, and technical instruction and research. And it emphasized: "Basic to every purpose of the system is the search for truth."[12] Here certainly are marks of continuity, for John Bascom gave these high ideals of the Wisconsin Idea their first formulation.

10. See John Milton Cooper Jr., "Why Wisconsin? The Badger State in the Progressive Era," *Wisconsin Magazine of History* 87 (Spring 2004), 14.

11. John Bascom, "The Spirit of the University," *University Press*, March 10, 1877, 2.

12. *Wisconsin Statutes and Annotations*, chapter 36:01(2).

A Bascom Bibliography

This listing builds on the "Partial List" of addresses and writings by John Bascom in his autobiographical reflections *Things Learned by Living*, published in 1913, two years after Bascom's death. It is supplemented by the "Bibliography of Wisconsin Authors" prepared by the Wisconsin Historical Society. I have not located all of the items in these lists but cite them here as Bascom presented them. I have added several items to the original lists and made several corrections therein.

Books

Political Economy. Andover, MA: Warren F. Draper, 1859.

Political Economy: Designed as a Text-Book for Colleges. Andover, MA: Warren F. Draper, 1860.

Æsthetics, or The Science of Beauty. New York: G. P. Putnam's Sons, 1862; Revised, Boston: Potter and Ainsworth, 1871.

Philosophy of Rhetoric. New York: G. P. Putnam's Sons, 1865.

The Principles of Psychology. New York: G. P. Putnam's Sons, 1869.

Science, Philosophy and Religion. New York: G. P. Putnam's Sons, 1871.

Philosophy of English Literature. New York: G. P. Putnam's Sons, 1874.

A Philosophy of Religion, or The Rational Grounds of Religious Belief. New York: G. P. Putnam's Sons, 1876.

Comparative Psychology, or The Growth and Grades of Intelligence. New York: G. P. Putnam's Sons, 1878.

Growth and Grades of Intelligence. New York: G. P. Putnam's Sons, 1878.

Ethics or Science of Duty. New York: G. P. Putnam's Sons, 1879.

Natural Theology. New York: G. P. Putnam's Sons, 1880.

The Science of Mind. New York: G. P. Putnam's Sons, 1881.
The Words of Christ as Principles of Personal and Social Growth. New York: G. P. Putnam's Sons, 1884.
Problems in Philosophy. New York: G. P. Putnam's Sons, 1885.
Sociology. New York: G. P. Putnam's Sons, 1887.
The New Theology. New York: G. P. Putnam's Sons, 1891.
An Historical Interpretation of Philosophy. New York: G. P. Putnam's Sons, 1893.
Social Theory. New York: Thomas Y. Crowell & Company, 1895.
Evolution and Religion, or Faith as a Part of a Complete Cosmic System. New York: G. P. Putnam's Sons, 1897.
Growth of Nationality in the United States. New York: G. P. Putnam's Sons, 1899.
The Goodness of God. New York: G. P. Putnam's Sons, 1901.
Sermons and Addresses. New York: G. P. Putnam's Sons, 1913.
Things Learned by Living. New York: G. P. Putnam's Sons, 1913.

Pamphlets, Essays, Addresses, Sermons

"Mental Vigor: Its Component Parts." [Address] Dialexian Society, New York Central College, 1852.
"Modes of Mental Action." [A. M. Oration] *Williams College Magazine*, 1853.
"Nature as Emotional Expression." [Address] North Adams, MA: Greylock Sentinel Press, 1853.
[Anon.] "Empirical Psychology, or The Human Mind as Given in Consciousness, by Laurens P. Hickok. . . ." *North American Review* 84 (April 1857), 364–79.
Belief and Action. [Baccalaureate Sermon] Williams College. Boston: T. R. Marvin and Son, 1861.
"Buckle's History of Civilization." *New Englander* 21 (April 1862), 173–93.
"The Laws of Political Economy in Their Moral Relations." *New Englander* 21 (October 1862), 649–68.
[Anon.] "The Morality of Political Economy." *National Review* 15 (April 1862), 404–34.
"National Repentance." *Independent*, February 27, 1862, 2.
"On Temperance." [Address] Williams College, 1863.
"Our Duty to the Community." [Sermon] North Powell, VT, 1863.
"Political Economy of Agriculture." [Address] *Massachusetts Agricultural Reports*, 1865.
[Address] Agricultural Society, Pittsfield, MA. *Transactions of the Berkshire Agricultural Society for the Year 1865*, 3–12.
"Fairs and Their Purposes, Part 1." [Address] Massachusetts State Board of Agriculture, 1866.
"Intuitive Ideas and Their Relation to Knowledge." *Bibliotheca Sacra* 23 (January 1866), 1–49.
"The Relation of Intuitions to Thought and Theology." *American Presbyterian and Theological Review* 4 (April 1866), 272–91.
"Utilitarianism." *Bibliotheca Sacra* 23 (July 1866), 435–52.

[Address] Agricultural Society, Greenfield, MA. *Massachusetts Agricultural Reports*, 1867.

"Cause and Effect." *Bibliotheca Sacra* 24 (April 1867), 296–317.

"Conscience, Its Relations and Office." *Bibliotheca Sacra* 24 (January 1867), 150–75.

"The Natural Theology of Social Science." *Bibliotheca Sacra* 24 (October 1867), 722–44.

"Temperance." [Sermon] Great Barrington, MA, 1867.

"The Natural Theology of Social Science, No. II." *Bibliotheca Sacra* 25 (January 1868), 1–23.

"The Natural Theology of Social Science, No. III: Value and Natural Agents." *Bibliotheca Sacra* 25 (April 1868), 270–315.

"The Natural Theology of Social Science, No. IV: Labor and Capital." *Bibliotheca Sacra* 25 (October 1868), 645–86.

Secret Societies in College. [Sermon] Pittsfield, MA: Berkshire County Eagle, 1868.

"Agricultural Fairs and Their Purposes." *Annual Report of the Secretary of the State Board of Agriculture* (1869), 55–62.

"Consciousness: What Is It?" *American Presbyterian Review*, n.s., 1 (July 1869), 478–91.

"Fairs and Their Purposes, Part 2." [Address] Massachusetts State Board of Agriculture, 1869.

"The Foci of the Social Ellipse." *Putnam's Magazine* 14 (December 1869), 713–25.

"The Natural Theology of Social Science, No. V: Exchange and Currency." *Bibliotheca Sacra* 26 (January 1869), 120–62.

"The Natural Theology of Social Science, No. VI: Credit and Consumption." *Bibliotheca Sacra* 26 (July 1869), 401–42.

"The Natural Theology of Social Science, No. VII: Man's Intellectual Constitution, and the Growth of Society." *Bibliotheca Sacra* 26 (October 1869), 609–46.

"The Human Intellect." *Bibliotheca Sacra* 27 (January 1870), 68–90.

"Inspiration and the Historic Element in the Scriptures." *American Presbyterian Review*, n.s., 2 (January 1870), 90–105.

[Address] North Adams, MA. 1871.

"Darwin's Theory of the Origin of Species." *American Presbyterian Review*, n.s., 3 (July 1871), 349–79.

"Good Will." *Independent*, September 14, 1871, 1.

"Good Will." *Friends' Intelligencer*, October 7, 1871, 501.

"Grounds of Fellowship." *Independent*, December 28, 1871, 1.

"Instinct." *Bibliotheca Sacra* 28 (October 1871), 654–85.

"The Losses of Bigotry." *Independent*, October 19, 1871, 2.

"New Bottles for New Wine." *Independent*, November 16, 1871, 1.

"A Prayer for Rest." *Independent*, August 3, 1871, 4.

"The Sphere of Civil Law in Social Reform." *American Presbyterian Review*, n.s., 3 (January 1871), 40–51.

"Wrinkles." *Independent*, December 7, 1871, 9.

"College Organization." *Independent*, September 5, 1872, 2–3.

"Evolution, as Advocated by Herbert Spencer." *Presbyterian Quarterly and Princeton Review* 3 (July 1872), 496–515.

"Government of Colleges." *Independent,* July 4, 1872, 2.

"Inauguration of Dr. Chadbourne." [Address] Williams College, 1872.

"The Influence of the Press." *Bibliotheca Sacra* 29 (July 1872), 401–18.

"The Influence of the Pulpit." *Bibliotheca Sacra* 29 (October 1872), 698–719.

"Led of the Spirit." *Independent,* February 1, 1872, 2.

"The Majority Report." *Williams Vidette* 6 (July 6, 1872), 1–2.

"The Minority Report." *Williams Vidette* 6 (July 6, 1872), 4–11.

"Reaction of the Ideal." *Independent,* October 3, 1872, 2.

"Reciprosity." *Independent,* December 12, 1872.

The Threefold Kingdom. [Address] Albany: Weed, Parsons and Company, 1872.

"The Nation." *Bibliotheca Sacra* 30 (December 1873), 465–81.

"Respect for Man." *Independent,* July 31, 1873, 953.

"Smith College." *Williams Review* 4 (October 18, 1873), 13–14.

"The Supernatural in Religion." *Independent,* February 13, 1873, 196.

"Taine's *English Literature.*" *Bibliotheca Sacra* 30 (October 1873), 628–47.

"Essay X." In *Sex and Education: A Reply to Dr. E. H. Clarke's "Sex in Education,"* edited by
Julia Ward Howe, 164–69. 1874. Reprint, New York: Arno Press, 1972.

The Freedom of Faith. [Baccalaureate Sermon] Madison: Atwood & Culver, 1874.

"Growth." *Independent,* July 23, 1874, 4.

"Honor." *Independent,* January 1, 1874, 1635.

"Dress." *Transactions of the Wisconsin Agricultural Society* 13 (1874–75), 434–52.

"Economy in Farming." *Transactions of the Wisconsin Agricultural Society* 13 (1874–75), 148–60.

"Consciousness." *Bibliotheca Sacra* 32 (October 1875), 676–702.

"Development of Public Instruction." *Independent,* October 7, 1875, 1.

Faith and Reason. [Baccalaureate Sermon] 1875.

"Freedom in Production." *Independent,* April 22, 1875, 2–3.

"Labor." *Independent,* February 18, 1875, 5.

"Professor Albert Hopkins." *Bibliotheca Sacra and Theological Eclectic* 32 (April 1875), 350–61.

"The State University." *Independent,* July 22, 1875, 2.

"The State University." *Independent,* August 26, 1875, 7.

"Fealty to the State." *Independent,* January 6, 1876, 3–4.

"God's Poor." *Independent,* September 21, 1876, 1.

The Seat of Sin. [Baccalaureate Sermon] Madison, 1876.

"The Synthetic or Cosmic Philosophy." *Bibliotheca Sacra* 33 (October 1876), 618–55.

"Condition of Progress in the Agricultural Classes." *Transactions of the Wisconsin Agricultural
Society* 14 (1877), 110–20.

Education and the State. [Baccalaureate Sermon] Madison: Democrat Co., 1877.

"An Honest and So a Sound Ballot." *Independent,* August 30, 1877, 2.

"University Colleges." *Transactions of the Wisconsin Agricultural Society* 16 (1877–78), 251–56.

"Coeducation." *Independent,* January 17, 1878, 1.

The Common School. [Baccalaureate Sermon] Madison: David Atwood, 1878.

"Conventional Conscience." *Sunday Afternoon,* February 1879, 108–10.

"The Freedom of the Family." *Independent,* September 18, 1879, 1.

"The Freedom of the Family." *Friends' Intelligencer,* September 27, 1879, 502.

Government by Growth. [Baccalaureate Sermon] Milwaukee: Cramer, Aikens & Cramer, 1879.

"A Kind of Cooperation." *Good Company (Sunday Afternoon)* 4 (1879), 294–99.

"The Kingdom of Heaven." *Sunday Afternoon* 3 (May 1879), 385–93.

"The Destruction of the Poor." *Good Company (Sunday Afternoon)* 5 (1880), 489–92.

"Examinations." *Western* 6 (1880), 497–99.

"Names." *Good Company (Sunday Afternoon)* 5 (1880), 238–40.

"A Search for the Supernatural." *Independent,* September 9, 1880, 2.

Tests of a School-system. [Baccalaureate Sermon] Milwaukee: Cramer, Aikens & Cramer, 1880.

"Atheism in Colleges." *North American Review* 132 (January 1881), 32–40.

"The Degeneracy of Empirical Philosophy." *Unitarian Review and Religious Magazine* 15 (April 1881), 342–50.

"Improvements in Language." *Western* 7 (1881), 492–509.

"Logic for Life." *Western* 7 (1881), 270–73.

"Philosophical Results of a Denial of Miracles." *Princeton Review,* n.s., 8 (July–December 1881), 85–95.

"The State Universities of the North-Western States." *Western* 7 (1881), 134–45, 229–38.

Truth and Truthfulness. [Baccalaureate Sermon] Milwaukee: Cramer, Aikens & Cramer, 1881.

"The University and the High Schools." *Western Journal of Education* 11 (1881), 155–59.

"What Is the Trouble with Religion?" *Independent,* June 16, 1881, 3.

"Freedom of Will Empirically Considered." *Transactions of the Wisconsin Academy of Sciences, Arts, and Letters* 6 (1881–83), 2–20.

"Divorce and the Rights of Women." *Independent,* May 18, 1882, 2.

"The Gains and Losses of Faith from Science." *Christian Philosophy Quarterly* 1 (July 1882), 1–16.

"The Heroic in Faith." *Friends' Intelligencer,* May 13, 1882, 196–97.

"Instruction in Philosophy in Colleges and Universities." *Education* 2 (May 1882), 437–45.

The Lawyer and the Lawyer's Questions. [Baccalaureate Discourse] Milwaukee: Cramer, Aikens & Cramer, 1882.

"Woman Suffrage." [Address] Madison, 1882.

"Dynamic Sociology." [Review] *Dial* 4 (July 1883), 59–61.

"Freedom of Will, Empirically Considered." In *Christian Thought: Lectures on Philosophy, Christian Evidence, Biblical Elucidation,* edited by Charles F. Deems, 49–64. New York: Wilbur R. Ketcham, 1883.

"Mind and Matter: Their Immediate Relation." *Journal of Christian Philosophy* 2 (January 1883), 195.

"Mind and Matter: Their Ultimate References." *Journal of Christian Philosophy* 2 (July 1883), 456.

The Natural and the Supernatural. [Baccalaureate Sermon] Milwaukee: Cramer, Aikens & Cramer, 1883.

"Seeds of Growth in the Soil of the South." *Independent,* June 28, 1883, 4.

"The University of Virginia." *Independent,* December 6, 1883, 7.

"First Principles." *Transactions of the Wisconsin Agricultural Society* 22 (1883–84), 226–36.

"Public Press and Personal Rights." *Education* 4 (September 1883 to July 1884), 604–11.

"The Historic Sense." [Address] Annual Convention of the Beta Theta Pi. Chicago, 1884.

"Moral Questions among Christians." *Independent,* December 18, 1884, 4.

The New Theology. [Baccalaureate Sermon] *Christian Union* 30 (July 10, 1884), 36–38.

"The Part Which the Study of Language Plays in a Liberal Education." *Addresses and Proceedings, National Education Association of the United States* (1884), part 2, 22–23.

The Philosophy of Prohibition. [Pamphlet] New York: National Temperance Society and Publishing House, 1884.

"Theories of Will and of Morals." *Dial* 4 (January 1884), 226–28.

"The University and the State." [Address] *University Review.* Kansas, 1884.

"The University of Wisconsin." *Descriptive America* 1 (1884), 121–22.

"What Do the Members of a State University Owe to the State?" *University Review* 1 (December 1884), 89–91.

Hero Worship. [Baccalaureate Sermon] University of Wisconsin, 1885.

"Inspiration." *New Englander* 44 (January 1885), 89–103.

Prohibition and Common Sense. [Pamphlet] New York: National Temperance Society and Publication House, 1885.

Common Sense and Spiritual Insight. [Baccalaureate Sermon] Milwaukee: Cramer, Aikens & Cramer, 1886.

"Herbert Spencer on Ecclesiastical Institutions." *Dial* 6 (February 1886), 272–73.

"Practical Benevolence and Length of Pastorate." *Pulpit Treasury* 3 (March 1886), 694–97.

"The Pulpit and Practical Benevolence." *Pulpit Treasury* 3 (January 1886), 567–69.

"Tobacco and Refinement." *Friend, a Religious and Literary Journal* 60 (September 25, 1886), 60.

"Books That Have Helped Me." *Forum* 3 (May 1887), 263–72.

A Christian State. [Baccalaureate Sermon] Milwaukee: Cramer, Aikens & Cramer, 1887.

"Competition." *Independent,* May 5, 1887, 4.

"The Gist of the Labor Question." *Forum* 4 (September 1887), 87–95.

"Labor and Capital." *Independent,* April 28, 1887, 3.

"Modes of Correction." *Independent,* May 12, 1887, 5–6.

"The Prayerful Spirit." *Sunday School Times* 29 (February 1887), 84–85.

"Scientific Theism." *New Englander and Yale Review,* April 1887, 346–57.

"Books on Evolution and Life." *Dial* 9 (July 1888), 59–61.

"Economic Harmony." *Independent,* March 22, 1888, 1–2.

"Moral Harmony." *Independent,* March 29, 1888, 2.

"Social Harmony." *Independent,* April 5, 1888, 3–4.

"Prohibitory Law and Personal Liberty." *North American Review* 147 (August 1888), 135–40.

"Why Should I Vote the Prohibition Ticket?" *Christian Union,* September 6, 1888, 246.

"Competition." *Independent,* January 17, 1889, 2, 3A–3B.

"The Functions of the State." *Independent,* January 31, 1889, 3.

"The Ideal Element in the Good Teacher." [Address] Semi-Centennial, Westfield Normal School, MA, 1889.

"Moral Force of Law." *Independent,* February 28, 1889, 3.

"The Wrong Mark." *Independent,* October 31, 1889, 3.

"Complexity of Social Facts." *Independent,* January 30, 1890, 4–5.

"A Day to Discuss Public Questions." *Independent,* July 3, 1890, 9.

The Growth of Civic Society. [Baccalaureate Sermon] Law Class, University of Wisconsin, 1890.

"Joseph White." [Memorial] Williamstown, MA, 1890.

"The Liberty of Our Schools." *Independent,* November 13, 1890, 6–7.

"Methods of Social Control." *Independent,* February 27, 1890, 6.

"Notable Discussions of Religion and Philosophy." *Dial* 11 (November 1890), 182–85.

"Recent Social and Political Discussion." *Dial* 10 (March 1890), 303–6.

"The Unity of Social Facts." *Independent,* February 13, 1890, 5.

"Æsthetics." In *Encyclopædia Britannica, American Supplement,* 50–52. 1891.

"The Bennett Law." *Educational Review* 1 (January–May 1891), 48–52.

"General Principles of Prohibition." In *Cyclopædia of Temperance and Prohibition,* 496–99. New York: Funk & Wagnalls, 1891.

"Herbert Spencer on the Principles of Justice." *Dial* 12 (October 1891), 0–002.

"Liquor Logic." In *Cyclopædia of Temperance and Prohibition,* 401–3. New York: Funk & Wagnalls, 1891.

"A New Policy for the Public Schools." *Forum* 40 (March 1891), 59–66.

"To the Young Men's Christian Association." [Address] Massachusetts Agricultural College, 1891.

"Catholics and Our Common Schools." *Independent,* August 4, 1892, 6–7.

"Civil Law and Social Progress." *Independent,* September 15, 1892, 3–5.

"Two Notable Books on Ethics." *Dial* 13 (November 16, 1892), 307–9.

"Jonathan Edwards." *Berkshire Historical and Scientific Society* 11 (1893), 3–25.

"The Largeness of the Man." *Congregationalist,* October 5, 1893, 454.

"Office of a Christian College in Connection with Social Duties." [Address] Williams College Centennial, 1893.

"The Reconciliation of History and Religion in Criticism." *Dial* 15 (September 16, 1893), 146–49.

"Coeducation." *American University Magazine* 2 (May 1895), 314.

"Inspiration and Interpretation." *Dial* 14 (October 16, 1895), 213–15.

"The Philosophical Basis of the Supernatural." *New World* 4 (June 1895), 279–87.

"A Standard of Values." *Quarterly Journal of Economics* 10 (October 1895), 54–66.

"The Grievances of the Working Classes." *Independent,* December 10, 1896, 9.

"Professor [Cyrus Morris] Dodd." [Memorial] 1896.

"Religious Literature, Theoretical and Practical." *Dial* 20 (May 1, 1896), 278–80.

"Faith Instinctive." *Dial* 23 (September 16, 1897), 148–49.

"Changes in the Spirit and Form of Prayer." *Independent,* July 21, 1898, 160–62.

"Introduction to the Study of Sociology." *Expositor*, 1898.

"Philosophy or Religion?" *Dial* 24 (January 16, 1898), 46–47.

"Faith and Fantasy." *Dial* 26 (March 16, 1899), 198–200.

"A Minimum Wage." *Independent*, January 5, 1899, 9–11.

"The Alleged Failure of Democracy." *Yale Review* 9 (November 1900), 253–64.

"Competition, Actual and Theoretical." *Quarterly Journal of Economics* 14 (August 1900), 537–42.

"The Complexity of Religious Beliefs." *Dial* 28 (January 1, 1900), 18–20.

"Mark Hopkins." *Historical Collections of the Berkshire Historical and Scientific Society*, Vol. 3, 1900.

"Faith as a Theory and as an Experience." *Dial* 30 (May 1, 1901), 305–6.

"Phi Beta Kappa Address." University of Wisconsin, 1901.

"Books for Adults: Social Studies." *Congregationalist and Christian World*, November 22, 1902, 749.

"Constitutional Interpretation." *Yale Review* 10 (February 1902), 350.

"The Literature of the Day: Criminals and Delinquents." *Congregationalist and Christian World*, February 22, 1902, 276.

"The Literature of the Day: Reconstruction and the Constitution." *Congregationalist and Christian World*, May 24, 1902, 752.

"The Scope of Faith." *Dial* 32 (February 16, 1902), 126–27.

"The Sources of Authority in Teaching." [Address] *Proceedings of the Fiftieth Annual Session of the Wisconsin Teachers' Association*, 1902, 104–15.

"The Supernatural." *Bibliotheca Sacra* 59 (April 1902), 238–53.

"Changes in College Life." *Atlantic* 91 (1902–3), 749–58.

"Correspondence: The Gifts of Millionaires." *Outlook*, January 31, 1903, 269–71.

"Immoral Money." *Independent*, February 26, 1903, 489–90.

"Is the World Spiritual?" *Bibliotheca Sacra* 60 (April 1903), 223–43.

"The Literature of the Day: Heredity and Social Progress." *Congregationalist and Christian World*, May 30, 1903, 770.

"The Literature of the Day: The Rise of Political Parties." *Congregationalist and Christian World*, February 14, 1903, 243.

"The Literature of the Day: The Social Unrest." *Congregationalist and Christian World*, February 21, 1903, 280.

"The Use of Wealth." *Independent*, January 29, 1903, 248–50.

"The Addenda of Psychology." *Bibliotheca Sacra* 61 (April 1904), 209–31.

"The Literature of the Day." *Congregationalist and Christian World*, February 27, 1904, 302.

"The Right to Labor." *Quarterly Journal of Economics* 18 (August 1904), 492–512.

"Wisdom by Growth and Growth in Wisdom." [Baccalaureate Sermon] In *The Jubilee of the University of Wisconsin*, 33–51. Madison: Jubilee Committee, 1904.

[Untitled Baccalaureate Sermon] University of Wisconsin, 1905.

"Economics and Ethics." *Bibliotheca Sacra* 62 (April 1905), 211–28.

"Has the Christian Ministry a Permanent Social Basis?" *Homiletic Review* 49 (June 1905), 418–21.

"An Open versus a Closed Shop." *North American Review* 180 (June 1905), 912–17.

"Railroad Rates." *Yale Review* 14 (November 1905), 237–59.

"Social Forecast." *Independent*, March 30, 1905, 695.

"Causes and Reasons." *Bibliotheca Sacra* 63 (January 1906), 125–49.

"Debate on the Railroad Bill." *Moody's Magazine* 2 (July 1906), 166–71.

"Greylock Reservation." *Berkshire Historical and Scientific Society*, 1906.

"Industrial Corporations and Commercial Obligations." *Moody's Magazine* 1 (March 1906), 401–7.

"Professor [Arthur Latham] Perry." *Berkshire Historical and Scientific Society*, 1906.

"Reconciliations of Instruction." [Address] Normal School, North Adams, MA, 1906.

"The Three Amendments." *Annals of the American Academy of Political and Social Science* 27 (May 1906), 135–47.

"The Unemployed in London." *Bibliotheca Sacra* 63 (April 1906), 335–51.

"Whose Business Is It?" *Independent*, September 13, 1906, 614.

"Æsthetics and Ethics." *Bibliotheca Sacra* 64 (January 1907), 33–50.

"American Higher Education." *Educational Review* 34 (September 1907), 130–43.

College Tax Exemption. [Pamphlet] 1907.

"Divine Giving." [Sermon] Williamstown, MA, 1907.

"Is Language a Living Thing?" *Pedagogical Seminary* 14 (1907), 117–20.

"Watered Stock, Unjustifiable." *Moody's Magazine* 3 (June 1907), 161–64.

"Coeducation in College Training." *Educational Review* 36 (December 1908), 442–51.

"Laurens Perseus Hickok." *American Journal of Psychology* 19 (July 1, 1908), 359–73.

"Social Democracy." *Independent*, December 3, 1908, 1297.

"Surveys of American Philosophy." *Dial* 44 (March 16, 1908), 176–77.

"The College Library." *Educational Review* 38 (September 1909), 139–49.

"Immortality." *Bibliotheca Sacra* 66 (January 1909), 1–14.

"The Unemployed." La Salle Extension University, 1909.

"College Optimism." *Williams Alumni Review* 1 (1909–10), 6–10.

"Athletics." *Williams Alumni Review* 2, no. 4 (1910), 6–14.

"The College Library." *Williams Alumni Review* 2, no. 2 (1910), 7–15.

"Difficulties of Faith." *Bibliotheca Sacra* 67 (January 1910), 1–19.

"Reason and Religion." [Address] Coffee Club Papers, 1910.

"Stocks, Their Origins, Functions, and Dangers." *Moody's Magazine* 9 (April 1910), 256–60.

"As One Whole." *Bibliotheca Sacra* 68 (October 1911), 627–40.

"Basis of Theism." *Bibliotheca Sacra* 68 (January 1911), 132–53.

"The Case of Mary Wollstonecraft." *The Dial* 51 (August 1, 1911), 76–78.

Index

Abbott, Lyman, 86
abolitionism and antislavery, 9–10, 60, 114, 125,
  139, 148, 171, 198
academic freedom, 205; Bascom on, 67, 89–90,
  107, 209; Ely and, 182, 183; Van Hise on,
  195
Adams, Henry Carter, 168
Adams, Herbert Baxter, 180
Addams, Jane, 182
Agassiz, Louis, 30
Ahlstrom, Sydney, 85
Alison, Francis, 13
Allen, William Francis, 179
American Council of Learned Societies, 207
American Economic Association, 169–70, 177,
  207
American Free Trade Association, 94
American Historical Association, 205, 207
American Home Missionary Society, 59
American Institute of Christian Sociology, 178,
  200
American Political Science Association, 207
American Social Science Association, 168–69
American Sociological Association, 207
American Temperance Society, 111
American transcendentalists. *See individual names*
anarchism, 161
Anderson, Ragmus R., 187n33

Andover Theological Seminary, 5, 8, 18, 76;
  Bascom as student at, 18–19
Andrews, Charles M., 180
Angell, James B., 76, 136
Anglo-Saxons: Bascom on, 117–18
Anneke, Mathilda Franziska, 159
Anthony, Susan B., 142, 147n48
Antioch College, 44n26, 132
Anti-Saloon League, 198
Appleton, Wisconsin, 60, 184
Auburn Theological Seminary, 5, 15–18, 20, 78;
  Bascom as student at, 16–18

Bacon, Francis, 77
Baldwin College, 132
Banner, Lois, 46n30
Baptists, 59
Barnard, Henry, 63–64, 136
Barnes, Albert, 98
Barstow, William A., 114
Bascom, Abbie Burt (first wife), 18
Bascom, Cornelia (sister), 8, 10, 11, 51
Bascom, Emma (daughter), 65
Bascom, Emma Curtiss (second wife), 65, 69,
  204; and temperance movement, 115; and
  women's suffrage, 139–43, 204
Bascom, Florence (daughter), 65, 69, 133n19
Bascom, George (son), 65

221